# COLD
# MOUNTAIN
# PATH

# COLD
# MOUNTAIN
# PATH

## THE GHOST TOWN DECADES OF
## McCARTHY-KENNECOTT, ALASKA
## 1938—1983

# TOM KIZZIA

## PORPHYRY
### PRESS

#### McCARTHY, ALASKA

Photo credits appear on p. 329.

Design by Katrina Noble
Composed in NCT Granite, typeface designed by Nathan Zimet
Map by Kristin Link

Printed and bound in Canada on 100% post-consumer recycled paper.

PORPHYRY PRESS
https://porphyry.press/

LIBRARY OF CONGRESS CATALOGING-IN-PUBLICATION DATA ON FILE

LIBRARY OF CONGRESS CONTROL NUMBER: 2021942097

ISBN 978-1-7367558-0-8 (hardcover)
ISBN 978-1-7367558-1-5 (paperback)

COVER PHOTO: Abandoned Copper River & Northwestern track near Strelna, 1960
FRONTISPIECE: Bradford Washburn photo of McCarthy, 1938

*Clambering up the Cold Mountain path,*
*The Cold Mountain trail goes on and on:*
*The long gorge choked with scree and boulders,*
*The wide creek, the mist-blurred grass.*
*The moss is slippery, though there's been no rain.*
*The pine sings, but there's no wind.*
*Who can leap the world's ties*
*And sit with me among the white clouds?*

GARY SNYDER, COLD MOUNTAIN POEMS

TRANSLATED FROM THE WORK OF HAN SHAN,
CLASSICAL CHINESE POET OF THE TANG DYNASTY

IN MEMORY OF

*Jim Edwards 1931–2016*
*and Howard Knutson 1930–2021*

# CONTENTS

# INTRODUCTION

## THE LOST DECADES

This is the story of a town that disappeared in the snows of Alaska's Wrangell Mountains.

A great deal was going on in Alaska during the decades this story took place, with the war against Japan and the drive for statehood and the discovery of oil. But the remote mountain town of McCarthy slipped outside history. The community's life drained in 1938 when the Kennecott copper mines closed and the last train left. For half a century, McCarthy was a ghost town, home to just a few hold-outs, joined over time by various prospectors, dreamers, back-to-the-landers, chiselers, escape artists, hippies, speculators, preachers, and outlaws. An old and makeshift way of life persisted against the quiet undertow of the past, that ebbing toward the nature that was here before.

After a while, though, the town that disappeared was found again, because to live in the presence of so much nothing had become rare in the modern world. Thus the future found its way in—a road, a bridge, a national park. A mass shooting that left six dead. The world moved on.

We all have ghost towns, impermanent places we dream of returning to. Here was Alaska's.

Several years ago, I wrote a nonfiction book about certain contemporary events in the town of McCarthy. The ghost town decades were long past. The Kennecott mines was a national historic landmark, and the mountain range was a national park. My book was about a large clan known as the Pilgrim family, whose charismatic patriarch, Papa Pilgrim, showed up in the valley peddling his own version of American history, ordained by his own version of the Bible. I sketched out a few chapters of local history from before Wrangell-St. Elias National Park was established but set those chapters aside rather than distract from the book's headlong subject, which was the desperate escape of Papa Pilgrim's fifteen children from his own version of fatherhood.

In that book, I wrote about my own cabin in the valley near McCarthy. My connection to the community was how I first met Papa Pilgrim. When *Pilgrim's Wilderness* was published, I was invited to talk at the Kennecott Recreation Hall, a wooden-floor gymnasium from mining days owned by the National Park Service and restored through a public-private partnership.

My neighbors, it turned out, were curious about the deleted chapters. They wanted to hear stories from the lost decades, when this familiar landscape of ruins supported an odd, weirdly vibrant community of scavengers and schemers—a town half dead, alders clawing at its foundations, but half brimming with the kind of entrepreneurial brio that Mark Twain wrote about on an earlier western mining frontier. This human persistence in the ruins often confounded visitors who arrived with preconceived notions of ghost towns, as Chris Richards, the self-proclaimed mayor of Kennecott, complained whenever he found tourists trying to lift tools and other relics off his porch.

Frontier moments never last. The national park brought rules, settlement, jobs, even a few businesses. Memories from the earlier time, when the whole valley seemed up for grabs, were fading. Old-timers—including the ghost town's few children, now grown—were finally ready to loosen their grip on accounts of those days, worried that key events would be forgotten, or that some other guy's version would be remembered as accepted truth. People were even willing to break long habits of local reticence and talk to me about the mail day murders, describing what led up to that morning in 1983 when the lost decades ended and my own story here began.

The McCarthy-Kennicott Historical Museum asked for copies of the lost chapters. I volunteered to expand them, in part as a fund-raiser, and this book is the result.

Local histories encourage a digressive kind of storytelling and incline a writer to a generous spirit of inclusion. I have tried to rein in that generosity. It would challenge any reader's patience to keep track of every character and crackpot feud, even in a ghost town. Passed-over pioneers may, indeed, feel lucky once they see how history—this history, anyway—has treated a few of their neighbors.

Even so, the story braids as it moves along, like those rocky glacial outwash rivers in the Wrangells, continually changing course because they are so overloaded with material.

During a lifetime in the area, the homesteader Jim Edwards was renowned as an inventive recycler of Kennecott's past. His pile of scavenged steel and iron—"Kennecrap," in the local lingo—was second to none. "I know I'm only ever going to use 10 percent of all this," he once said. "The problem is, I don't know which 10 percent."

In that spirit, I dedicate this local history to him.

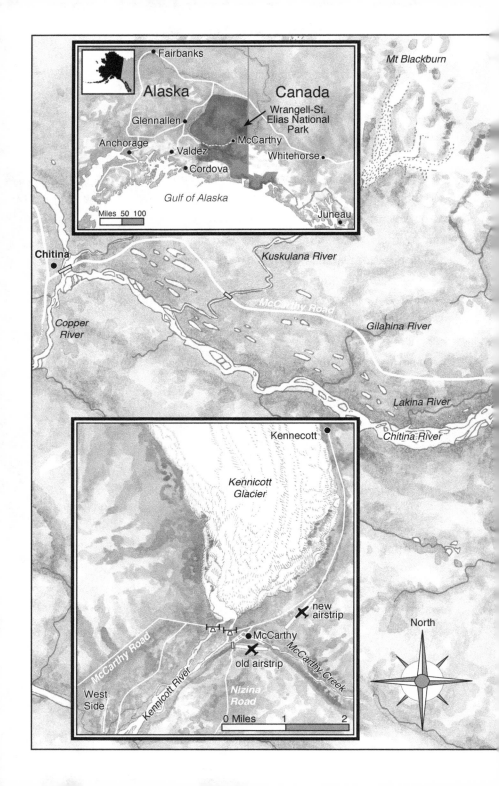

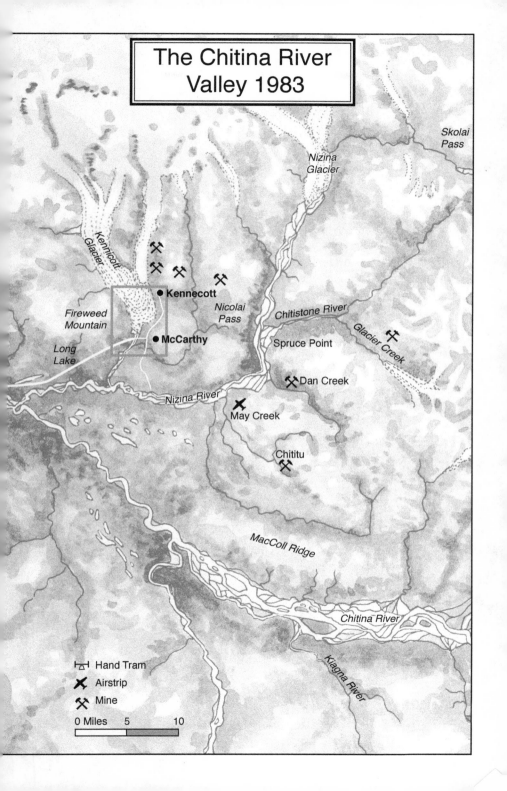

# PROLOGUE

## THE HERMIT KINGDOM

On my first trip to McCarthy, I sat in the noisy fuselage of a small Cessna while dawn filled the white mountains below. We landed on a remote airstrip, silent and eye-rinsingly bright under a sun with no warmth. Snow boots squeaked in single-digit cold. A shoveled path led toward a house of plywood and Visqueen plastic, where locals gathered once a week to wait for the mail plane. The path was blocked by police tape. I held my *Anchorage Daily News* reporter's pad in my ski glove, but there seemed to be no locals to interview. The wounded had been flown out. I stood on the runway talking to an Alaska state trooper and a national park ranger. Authorities had not yet released the names of the dead. Laid out carefully in the snow were three heavy vinyl black bags.

The pea-coated ranger, a big man with a mustache, had landed in his own plane to assist. Like the national park that employed him, he was new to the area, but he knew the town a little, he told me, knew who was wintering over, and he had come to help search for possible additional victims.

An older bush rat in a duct-taped down jacket shuffled across the airstrip. I watched the ranger extend a beefy palm. "I'm sorry for your loss," he said. The bush rat kept his hands in his pockets and scowled. "This is not the time for that," he said, as if the government man were exploiting the tragedy to ingratiate himself.

I was a young newspaper reporter covering the police beat that winter in Anchorage. We got a news bulletin from the state troopers on the night of March 1, 1983: six dead in a ghost town. The next morning I found myself flying into Alaska's past.

Like most people who had lived in the north for any amount of time, I'd heard of McCarthy. It was a boomtown back in a picture book era of copper mines and ore trains, abandoned now—but not entirely. After the Great Depression, after the Kennecott Copper Corporation left and the rails were torn out, a small, isolated community had carried on, into the modern pipeline era, as a kind of rumor. In the geography of Alaskan romance, McCarthy had a reputation as a hermit kingdom, contrary and self-reliant, where settlers tougher than the rest of us were salvaging, in postapocalyptic fashion, the rusted relics of a profligate past.

I looked around. This cold periphery of the modern world seemed utterly cut off—no stores, no phones, no law enforcement. Yet the encounter I'd just witnessed between bush rat and park ranger was a reminder that even this part of the north was changing. Two years earlier Congress had established new national parks across Alaska, a sweeping gesture in defense of "unspoiled" nature at a time when Big Oil was transforming so much of the forty-ninth state. Tiny, backward McCarthy, accessible by small plane or a rough summer road, was now the only human settlement inside a protected mountain wilderness much bigger than Switzerland. The feeling of solitude could not last.

Standing alone on the snowy airstrip that morning while the state troopers went about their work, it was hard to feel regret about the passing of pioneer days. All this isolation seemed dangerous, crazy-making.

A trooper pointed into the woods. I walked twenty minutes along the crusted ribbon of a snowmachine track until I found a few false-front buildings. Barking dogs drew me to Bonnie Morris's small log cabin, snowbound in a grove of bare poplars. Furs hung from pegs by the door.

Bonnie Morris was furious about the loss of her friends and neighbors, longtime residents who showed young people like her how to live and take care of the land. "These are the people who inspired the rest of us when we came here to build a sane and healthy life," she said. "A nobody came in here and wiped out the pillars of one of the few self-sufficient communities in Alaska."

There weren't two dozen people living in the whole valley that winter, Bonnie said. She told me about two young newlyweds up toward the Kennecott mining camp, just home from their honeymoon. Bonnie had brought them a mincemeat pie with a heart carved on top. There was an older couple who opened their home as a community center on mail day every week. And Maxine Edwards, who lived across the river. She taught Bonnie how to turn deprivation into an elegant dinner party. Maxine caught a ride to mail that day on Bonnie's dog sled. Bonnie's lead dog was in heat, so she handed off her outgoing envelopes and turned homeward. Maxine promised to stop by for cookies later on.

Bonnie and her boyfriend, Malcolm, never heard the mail plane buzz the town. That was unusual. Maxine never stopped by. Eventually, Bonnie and Malcolm went up the creek to cut cabin logs and smelled smoke, and that was unusual, too, so far from town. They heard a few gunshots, but those were not unusual sounds in the woods around McCarthy.

After dark, making dinner by kerosene lamp, they tuned in the Christian station in Glennallen—the only radio signal they could get—and learned that six people had been killed in McCarthy. No names. They counted through their neighbors.

"About that time the helicopter came circling overhead, shining its beam down into the woods," Bonnie said. "We thought there was somebody still out there. We were huddled under the bed. Finally the troopers found us. We were the only light, the only surviving couple in town."

When I got back to the airstrip, a local man, middle-aged and gentle-voiced, stood beside the propeller of the chartered Cessna, speaking with the troopers. He looked perfectly comfortable on that bright, cold afternoon in a navy watch cap, a heavy quilted jacket and overpants, and sunglasses—prescription glasses, I would learn, years later, their smoky plastic frames selected for the essential homesteading quality of durability.

Jim Edwards had lived in McCarthy longer than anyone alive. He had flown out here as a young man, not so many years after the last train left the country, and the old-timers he met then, the ones who stayed when everybody left, now lay in the local cemetery. He helped bury them.

Then he raised a family of his own, at a homestead just across the river. When his son and daughter grew up and moved away, he and his wife opened their home to the young people who started moving into the valley. He had seen plenty of con men during his years in the Wrangells and for the most part had been pleased by this new generation. Nothing's simple here, he said, so the simplicity-in-nature crowd never stuck around long. But good people had made this their home.

This was always a special valley, Jim Edwards told me, with a gleam of unextinguished pioneer hope. He was the ghost in Alaska's rearview mirror. McCarthy could get through this, he said.

The city beckoned. Jim Edwards's story would have to wait. I had to fly back over the mountains, sketching out in the noisy little plane a tale about a lone gunman and a heart carved in a mincemeat pie. I could already picture my dramatic arrival in the newsroom just before deadline.

Jim Edwards asked for a favor. His voice trembled. Would I track down his son, who worked in a hangar at Merrill Field? He wrote a note on my reporter's pad and tore off the page and folded it.

Flying above the summits in the sinking light, I was buffeted, more torn by conflicting emotions than I had ever been on a newspaper assignment. Thrilled, with the impervious zeal of a cop reporter, to be bringing my editors a story from a lost world. And terrified to be carrying the news to Jim Edwards's son that his mother was dead.

# PART ONE

... *Does it care?*
*Not faintly. It has all time. It knows the people are a tide*
*That swells and in time will ebb, and all*
*Their works dissolve.*

ROBINSON JEFFERS, "CARMEL POINT"

# 1

# The Last Train

AT DUSK ON November 10, 1938, in heavy snowfall, the last train to leave the Wrangell Mountains approached the Copper River. The steam locomotive pulled two combine cars with people and baggage and a string of flatcars bearing salvageable hoists and compressors and machine-shop tools. The train hauled no ore. Hand brakes were applied as the train descended the Kotsina bluff, the steepest grade on the entire railroad to the coast. Across the river waited the little town of Chitina, where crews usually switched out and where the last train planned to stop for the night. The locomotive slowed to ten miles per hour as it crept onto the river bars atop a wooden trestle.

The train had departed that morning from the Kennecott Copper Corporation mining camp and proceeded in stately fashion down the Chitina River valley, stopping at every station or section house to drain waterpipes and pick up stragglers. The next morning the train would continue south, via the trestles in the Copper River canyon, to the steamship docks at Cordova.

Families at Kennecott had only one day to pack. The snowstorm had forced the company's hand. The small depot by the concentration mill was disappearing under white as the passengers assembled. The giant rotary plow needed to battle the deep drifts and slides of the Wrangells had already been shipped out. Winter had always been the railroad's great adversary and cost driver, forcing the deployment of maintenance crews in isolated section houses and line shacks. During the 1930s, with copper production declining, the railroad halted winter operations altogether and the mine stockpiled ore. The snows of 1938 would close the curtain forever.

Nell McCann, traveling with her husband and newborn, would miss her small red-with-white-trim millworker's cottage perched above the glacier's lateral moraine. She had been an office secretary at Kennecott for a decade and spent most of that time in the women's dorm, but after two years of married life in a house of her own, the mountain camp had come to feel like home. Nell also fretted about the suitcases-only rule. She had been forced to leave behind her hand-crank Victrola record player and a Maytag washer.

Her friend, Ethel LeCount, a nurse, ran to the depot to wave goodbye and slipped in the snow—"I fall kerflop," Ethel wrote in her journal. She was part of the skeleton crew staying behind. Another month and Ethel, too, would be gone—along with hospital care for anyone who remained in that little saloon town at the toe of the glacier.

Like Nell, Ethel LeCount would recall her time in Kennecott fondly, writing in a letter: "I liked the sound of the humming trams that brought the copper ore down from the mines and the rumble of the machinery in the big red mill that crouched like a great watchful lion on the hills above the camp."

From Kennecott, the last train descended five miles to McCarthy. The town had grown up on the glacier's cobbly outwash plain to provide civil society and adult recreation, two things the corporation-run camp could not. Station agent William Hermann was given ninety minutes to collect his papers and belongings. What about the safe, he asked his boss. "The hell with the safe, everything stays behind," was the official reply.

Everyone knew a day like this was coming. Up in the mines, high atop Bonanza Ridge, the company had been knocking out tunnel supports to get the last valuable ore—"pillar retreat," in the mining vernacular. Roast turkey and dismissal bonuses had been served up at farewell banquets, one down at the recreation hall and another at the last mine bunkhouse still in use. The big diesel-electric generators in the powerhouse had been dismantled and shipped out, and 194 tons of ammonia solution, used to leach copper out of limestone, too corrosive to leave in tanks and uneconomical to ship south, was "syphoned to waste" onto the glacier.

The company had been letting maintenance slide at the mill and on the railroad. In the mines, workers finally unionized, and the Kennecott bosses, rather than import a trainload of strikebreakers as they had in 1917, went along—another form of deferred maintenance. It was never more clear that this remarkable outpost, however impressive its central steam heat and electricity, was no bridgehead of civilization.

Indeed, the frailties of the wooden trestle that carried the last train across the Copper River had long foretold this day. In a ritual every spring, rails and ties would be pulled off the trestle and temporarily stacked. Ore from the trams would pile up in Kennecott. When the frozen Copper River shuddered and let go of winter, crushing heaps of ice would tear away the wooden pilings. River clear again, they would rebuild the entire 950-foot trestle bridge with the help of a motor-driven tram suspended across the river from a cable. The Alaska Syndicate, the private New York partnership financing the entire project, had calculated it would be cheaper to drive timber pilings annually for the life of the Kennecott copper deposit than to erect a permanent steel span.

One year a locomotive and a tender full of bunker oil plunged into the river when the trestle, weakened by late November ice, collapsed under their weight. The engineer swam free that day, but the fireman drowned. Workers managed to hoist out the locomotive, flush the glacial silt, and put it back in service. Locomotive number 74, the Mikado engine in that accident, was now pulling the last train. Another accident killed five men when the bridge collapsed in the midst of repairs, according to a short history of the railroad written by a rail buff who visited Chitina in the late 1930s, just as the line was shutting down. At least fifteen men were killed overall on those disposable wooden trestles, he was told.

Business boosters in the towns of Cordova and Chitina had hoped for more from their Wall Street champions. The railroad promoters had come north at the century's beginning with plans for an elevated ten-span steel bridge across the Copper, just upriver from the confluence of its biggest tributary, the Chitina River. A lawyer for the Alaska Syndicate told Congress they envisioned new mineral discoveries in the McCarthy region and a future of agriculture, with crops exported by rail. A second line would strike north from Chitina, linking up with steamboats on the Yukon River—a solid, permanent route to the Interior through the glaciers and peaks of the coastal range. Politicians described the Copper River canyon as the gateway to Alaska's future.

Such golden gateways, no less illusory, have figured prominently in Alaska's politics ever since.

The abandonment of McCarthy and Kennecott was set in motion, historian Melody Webb Grauman wrote in "Big Business in Alaska," her classic account of the mines, when old and new models of frontier capitalism collided at the start of the twentieth century—when the last of the muscular Gilded Age buccaneers ran up against the country's new anti-monopoly and public-resource Progressives.

Rails had opened the West in the decades after the Civil War. Generous land grants and congressional subsidies enriched the private promoters of railroads as they marched and stumbled across the continent, leading the way for permanent non-Native-American settlement. This same vision of the frontier pushed north after the "discovery" of copper in the Wrangell Mountains: the bold financiers of industrial capitalism would be the true Daniel Boones of territorial expansion.

First, rights to the minerals had to be obtained under federal law. Copper, a soft metal, had long been a source of wealth for the region's Indigenous people, the Ahtna, a branch of the Athabaskans. They fought skirmishes with other tribal groups to protect their trade monopoly in these mountains. A Russian expedition sent up the Copper River in 1848 to find the source of the metal never returned, and after that the Russians left the river alone.

Yet when American prospectors arrived in the spring of 1899, the popular story went, Ahtna chief Nicolai gave away the copper cheaply—"traded a multimillion-dollar copper mine for a cache of food," as local historian Lone Janson put it in her sweeping narrative of the railroad, *The Copper Spike*. Nicolai's people were "in the grip of one of their interminable bouts of famine," Janson wrote. It was left to a later historian of the Ahtna to note that while there

An Ahtna family at Taral on the Copper River, 1898.

had been spring famines before that forced children to eat tree bark, things were far worse by 1899 with white newcomers hunting out the game, burning forests to keep down the mosquitoes, and intercepting salmon in commercial nets.

The copper was not found along the mainstem Copper River but far up its biggest tributary, the Chitina, the Ahtna word for "copper river" (the Ahtna called the Copper River the "beyond river"). To Chief Nicolai, it may not have seemed that he gave up much to get the food cache. The Ahtna picked their copper out of creeks in native nuggets of the pure element, and they gave it trade value with the time and labor they took to fashion tools. The mountainside streak of ore to which a Native guide led the outsiders needed to be smelted and purified. Nor was that particular bornite deposit of use to the prospectors, it turned out—the astonishingly rich Bonanza lode would be found the next year, fifteen miles away. Yet development of the mines would soon drive the original inhabitants out of the valley.

The failure of the denae, or local head men, to file their own mining claims and reap profits for their people was a matter not only of cultural difference but of law: Alaska Natives could not legally stake mining claims at that time, as their citizenship would not be recognized until 1924. "Overriding the argument of whether Nicolai was duped or not," wrote Alaska anthropologist and Ahtna historian William Simeone, in a study of the region's subsistence patterns for the Alaska Department of Fish and Game, "is the fact that the Ahtna were never compensated by the mining industry for the use of Ahtna lands or the minerals extracted from those lands."

The great Kennecott claims were staked in 1900 by the prospectors Clarence Warner and Tarantula Jack Smith, part of a team staked by investors to explore the Wrangell Mountains. The mining properties were soon re-sold and sewn up by a well-connected adventurer from the East, a young mining engineer named Stephen Birch. In 1906 he returned to New York and persuaded J. P. Morgan and the Guggenheims, with their western silver and lead monopolies, to capitalize development of a mine in Alaska with a railroad to the sea. America had turned to electricity, and demand for copper wire was high. Some of America's leading capitalists set out to extract one of the most densely valuable copper deposits ever found, a mythical plug of high-grade ore running hundreds of feet through Bonanza Ridge, bringing new enterprise in their wake.

"To the true pioneer belong the first-fruits of conquest in a new and forbidding land," Stephen Birch wrote in a magazine article, "and if he have faith to stick he reaps again when capital follows and makes possible a hundred profitable activities that before were not possible."

It was still the age of the swashbuckling plutocrat. With their steel-age brawn, the Alaska Syndicate's owners brought six thousand workers into the country to build the 196-mile Copper River & Northwestern Railway, dismissed by naysayers as the "Can't Run & Never Will." Engineers built 30 miles of bridges and trestles, snaking past glaciers and over moraine-topped ice. The titans of Wall Street gathered up other mines, coal leases, steamship lines, and salmon processors and made plans for a smelter in Prince William Sound. They were willing to spend a private fortune to open up Alaska—provided they got to help themselves once it opened.

"We want to go into the territory and build railroads and smelters and mining towns and bring men there and populate the country where it is habitable, and do for it what the earlier figures in American railroad building did for sections of the great West," Daniel Guggenheim told the *New York Times*.

But political sentiments in the nation were shifting. Resistance had stiffened to the monopolies, trusts, and railroad robber barons whose greed and haste had for decades crashed the nation's banks and stolen the savings of families. New voices spoke up for conservation and public use of resources and for the workingmen who built the trestles. Reformers shone a spotlight on inside deals and political giveaways. President Theodore Roosevelt, a Republican, set aside national forests for lease only and closed Alaska to new coal claims, pending reform legislation from Congress.

Efforts by the Alaska Syndicate to tie up preexisting leases to the Bering River coalfield near Cordova, as portrayed by muckraking journalists in magazines such as *McClure's* and *Collier's*, turned Alaska's golden gateway into a spectacle of scandal. A five-year battle over the Alaska coalfields even helped tip the 1912 presidential election, when the Republican incumbent, William Taft, sided with the syndicate and Wall Street. Roosevelt, indignant over this and other offenses against his record by the man who succeeded him, barged into the race with his "Bull Moose" Progressive Party, splitting the

Republican vote and allowing the victory of Democrat Woodrow Wilson.

Anti-monopoly battles were no less fierce in Alaska. A Home Rule movement led by such figures as James Wickersham, the federal judge who cleaned up Nome, portrayed the syndicate as a powerful financial octopus that suppressed unions, fired strikers, jacked up freight rates, and resisted Alaskan "home rule" because it would mean taxes and services for the people. The western monopoly boss was a bad guy familiar to popular culture of that day. Syndicate leaders were accused of rigging elections and the courts. They were caught tampering with a jury in the murder trial of a Valdez deputy, who fired into an unarmed mob protesting the syndicate's right-of-way. The company official accused of approving the jury-tampering payoffs shot himself.

The syndicate had many backers in Alaska, of course, grateful for its investment and jobs. They joined the corporation in lamenting meddlesome government reformers, asking who exactly these resources were being conserved for? Protesters shoveled Canadian coal into the water at the Cordova docks in 1911, and newspapers all over the country did not miss the comparison to the Boston Tea Party.

But the temper of the times was antitrust and the fervor to protect Alaska practically biblical. With hearings underway in Congress over Alaska's coal, the *Seattle Post-Intelligencer* reached for a phrase from Psalms in an editorial comparing monopoly to theft and plague and "the destruction that wasteth at noonday."

Driven by such sentiments, Alaska's voters sent Wickersham repeatedly to Washington, DC, as the region's non-voting delegate in Congress. He pushed for the government to reject the syndicate's offer and build its own railroad in Alaska, as the government was then building its own canal in Panama.

The Copper River trestle had to be rebuilt every year after breakup, until the railroad was abandoned in 1938.

Congress finally sorted out a coal-leasing program for Alaska in 1914. By that time, no one wanted Alaska's coal. The railroad had already turned to oil-fired locomotives to haul copper ore. The syndicate dropped plans for a coal-fired smelter in Prince William Sound. Then the U.S. Navy tested the Bering River coal and found it crumbled too easily, falling through their grates.

President Wilson rejected the notion of buying out the Guggenheim railroad, and in 1915 the federal government committed to a public utility railroad over a different route, from Seward to Fairbanks. Abandoning dreams of empire, the syndicate's financiers converted their holdings into stock corporations. The Copper River & Northwestern became a model of the new twentieth-century capitalism, Melody Webb Grauman wrote, a means to remove a resource, operating at a loss as a business expense. The museums and opera halls of New York City thrived, but there were no more promises of farms and towns, or tracks to the Yukon, or a steel bridge at Chitina. No more addresses to Congress about industry and progress populating the valleys. And in 1938, with most of the high-grade ore gone and the huge profits reinvested in copper deposits in Utah and Chile, Kennecott left Alaska.

◄——►

Long before the last train pulled out, there had been a best-selling novel, *The Iron Trail* by Rex Beach, published in 1913 and based on the building of the railroad ("I saw the unpeopled north grow into a land of homes, of farms, of mining-camps, where people lived and bred children. I heard the mountain passes echo to steam whistles and the whir of flying wheels") and a Hollywood feature (without the steam whistles' echo, it was a silent film) with the same name. The narrative melodrama focused on construction of a sturdy all-steel crossing of the Copper River near Cordova, known as the Million Dollar Bridge.

No comparable epic would be written about the wooden trestle at Chitina, left to wash away.

Historians and politicians have found a variety of morals in this tale of an orphaned country. They have blamed labor organizers, greedy tycoons, rabid conservationists, or dithering bureaucrats. There is an explanation for every political persuasion. It is hard to dispute, however, that the scars of early abandonment profoundly influenced the resource-leasing policies that would find their way into the statehood act and the state constitution, and in the oil age make the orphan rich.

In November 1955, at Alaska's constitutional convention, four years before statehood, delegates heard a speech on that subject from the territory's long-serving elected delegate to Congress, Bob

Bartlett. He urged the founders to develop policies that would hold onto natural resources and generate revenues to support the future state government, avoiding the "ruthless plunder" that afflicted fisheries and mining in Alaska. He warned against those "whose only aim is to skim the gravy and get out."

"The Kennecott Copper operation was typical of a nineteenth century Robber Baron philosophy which still has its few advocates today," Bartlett told the convention. "Copper in the value of over two hundred million dollars was removed from the Chitina District; the area was high-graded with ores of lesser value disregarded. The operation was shut down in 1938. The tremendous production and investment left absolutely nothing of enduring value for the Territory and its citizens except a small ghost town, which has become a minor tourist attraction."

⟵ ⟶

The last train out of the Wrangells passed through a transformed landscape. A forest of second-growth spruce and aspen was filling in the valley after it was blackened by a 1915 fire started by loco-motive sparks. What was still wild waited for the train to go. The crew stopped at each little red section house, taking away tools but leaving a woodstove, cooking utensils, cans of food, and kindling, according to north country custom, for anyone who might come along later and need shelter in a storm.

Ethel LeCount, the nurse of Irish stock who fell kerflop when the last train left and remained to the end, wrote her friends she was sorry to see everyone go. She had grown to like the lonely but lively outpost. Forty workers who stayed to close up straggled out over the next few weeks on chartered airplanes, taking off from a small air-strip hacked out of a McCarthy Creek bluff near town. Bad weather delayed their departure. Snow turned to rain, with heavy fog. Ethel

LeCount spent two weeks writing in her journal, over and over: "The Irish are a moody race." On December 2 the sky turned blue and her plane finally showed up for a scenic flight to Cordova. By Christmas, everyone was gone except two caretakers and their families.

Down in McCarthy, a handful of people had watched the train cross the Kennicott River for the last time. The railroad tracks were their only real access. A few clung to hopes that the mine shutdown, like earlier ones, would prove temporary. The Great Depression would end. The price of copper could rise. The train might come back. But the following spring, at Chitina, when the wooden trestle across the Copper River washed out, no crews showed up to build a replacement.

A young railroad carpenter on the last train out, assigned to shut things down at each stop, later wrote about that ride. Al Swalling had worked nine years in the railroad's bridge and building department, having come north from Seattle at age nineteen. His job had required him to drive up and down the railroad on his own speeder car, maintaining the section houses, pump houses, depots—all the structures except the bridges. After the railroad closed, he would fix boats and leaking roofs in Cordova, then cross Prince William Sound to Whittier to build a secret tunnel for the military. That job led to building wartime docks in the Aleutians and then to a career as a major contractor and civic leader in Anchorage. He would be named Alaskan of the Year in 1998.

Half a century after riding the last train, Al Swalling wrote a memoir in which he described the mournful process of abandoning the Wrangells. "At each station or section house, when everyone was aboard and the engine watered, the train waited while I drained the railroad water tank, opened the various drain cocks in the mess halls and bunkhouses, extinguished all the fires, closed the drafts, then closed and secured all the doors and windows. It was a very sad and very long day."

# 2

# No Safe Place to Live

J IM EDWARDS ONCE told me that on the afternoon he flew to the Wrangell Mountains for the first time and spotted the ghost town on the valley floor, he knew he had found a home. He had been living there for thirty years when I met him in 1983.

That first flight from Cordova in his two-seat Taylorcraft took several hours. He never lost the thrill of his first impression, banking away from the Copper River into the wide valley of its biggest tributary, the Chitina. The glacier-fed rush of the river, the braided channels and gravel bars, miles of forest reaching to mountains on either side, it was a valley so big you could drop a small eastern state into it. Ahead, in the far distance, a defiant wall of white. To his left, the snowy summits of the Wrangells. The higher he flew, the bigger they loomed. The massif of Mount Blackburn, 16,390 feet, the fifth tallest peak in the United States, spilled a broad moraine-striped glacier into the valley. Just beyond the glacier's terminus, seemingly vulnerable to erasure by one short surge of ice and rock, a small but dauntless settlement was perched beside the outlet river.

"There was something that struck me right and I hadn't even landed yet," he said. "I thought, this is the kind of place I want to live."

Edwards was twenty-two and working as an electrician in Cordova, the small port on the Pacific that survived on fishing after the mines shut down. A diffident young man who liked comfortable checkered flannel shirts, he had come a long way from Newberg, Oregon, where his great-grandfather had been the town's bank president, mayor, and founder of the local college. Newberg expected Jim to take over the family's brick factory, whose red bricks had built big parts of downtown Portland. Instead, Jim joined the army, where he was aggravated at his superiors because they wouldn't do what the recruiters promised. When he got out, he went to Alaska. He learned to fly in Cordova and bought the used Taylorcraft, which he hand-propped to start, and flew at a top cruise speed of 78 mph. He needed to build up flying hours, and a local couple he knew, both pilots, suggested he follow the Copper River canyon. The mail route to Kennecott passed through the coast range and turned right at Chitina. They told him he could land at a small strip in McCarthy to refuel and visit the picturesque mining ruins. His friends had flown there for their honeymoon.

A Model T with wooden sides rattled up to the airstrip to see who landed. By 1953 the mines had been closed for more than a decade. The driver of the Model T, Bill Berry, was one of the few who stayed around. He was constantly striking matches to relight his roll-your-own cigarette, snuffed by his dripping nose. A short, agitated tinker in his seventies, he was known as Blazo Bill for his practice of starting fires in woodstoves without kindling. He invited Edwards for a cup of tea at the old hardware store where he'd taken up residence. The woodstove in the kitchen was cold when they walked in. Edwards recalled watching his host dump a number-three washtub off the top of the stove, twenty gallons of cold dirty water spreading across the floor: "I was looking around amazed, and Bill said there's a hole it runs down, no big deal." Bill Berry stuffed three big logs in the stove and threw in a match while spraying Blazo gas through a blow torch. Out of consideration for his guest and all the smoke, he refrained from smearing grease on the bottom of the teapot to make it heat up faster.

After tea, Blazo Bill drove his guest up to Kennecott in a speeder—a truck with a friction clutch and flanged wheels for following the old rails. Ascending the mountain, the wheels slipped where tall grass lay across the steel.

The great mill and company buildings beside the glacier made an impression on Edwards. "It was such a big place, with every building interesting. You can't even begin to see it all. . . . There you are with a sizable little town with sixty or more buildings with all this machinery and equipment and houses and warehouses full of stuff, everything just left for the taking."

Edwards was not sure how he'd make a living if he quit his job in Cordova as an electrician. There was no electricity in McCarthy. But he kept coming back, and in the fall of 1954 he bought a little house from a man named Vic Rhine, a spur-of-the-moment purchase as he passed through town on a moose hunt. The house came with a 1928 Model A Ford. The town's summer population, he calculated, had grown by 64 percent while he hesitated: it was now up to ten.

A few folks teased Edwards for paying $700, three times what they said other houses had sold for. Edwards told them he planned to live there year-round. They laughed. A lot of people say that when they get here, they told him, but they don't last long. It was a bit of prophecy he would pass along to the generation that came after his.

"You don't look at things in the same way out here as you do in the city," he said, years later, in a series of interviews about his life and times. "You just don't. It don't work. I've watched people come out here, and they get use of a cabin and they bring in some stuff. But they find out that it does get cold and that the paycheck does stop, and they discover it is hard to get in and out, and that water does have to be carried—uphill, almost invariably. People are basically lazy. They'll do what they have to do, but they get tired of it."

Jim Edwards aimed to be the exception. Vic Rhine and a buddy were drilling and blasting tunnels at a mining prospect at Glacier Creek, on cliffs above Chitistone Canyon. The claim holder was paying them by the lineal foot. In 1955, when Rhine crashed his plane and ended up in the hospital, Edwards flew out to the Glacier Creek strip and got his first mining job.

At summer's end, he hauled a few hundred dollars' worth of groceries from Chitina to his little cabin in McCarthy. He was determined to stretch his wages through the winter. He began a study of how many cups can be drawn from a single teabag.

He had time to think about the brick factory in Oregon. Jim had been an only child. His parents divorced when he was young. They shipped Jim off to military school, and his mother, Mary Doe, the granddaughter of a famous and wealthy New Hampshire judge, moved away to Florida. Now he was twenty-four years old, sitting in a ghost town in Alaska and thinking about starting over with nothing.

"I fixed up my house a little bit, but that first winter for personal reasons of my own I didn't want to do much of anything, so I sat there most of the winter looking out the window and just stoking the fire, cooking some beans and reading some books and more looking out the window. It was the best winter I ever spent—the most productive. It's hard to explain when you say you didn't do a damn thing but look out the window."

⇐——⇒

One of the things Edwards liked about his new home was the town's old-timers. Blazo Bill Berry was a multi-talented handyman who made excellent whiskey out of carrots. Edwards found him "funnier than the dickens" despite a tendency to brood about his enemies. Berry had been a skinny boxing champion in the navy, and one afternoon got in a fight with big Billy Howell, back for a friendly visit. Bystanders rushed to separate the fighters, both in their late seventies, rolling in the street, before they hurt themselves. Living at the old Watsjold hardware store, Berry locked himself into the windowless cold storage room every night so that Ernie Gercken could not sneak in and murder him. His years at Watsjold's store left a mark. "I thought of Blazo Bill a lot in my early days," said a woman who bought and restored the building years later, its kitchen walls still blackened by explosions, and turned it into the iconic Hardware Store.

In the time before the airplane, Bill Berry had all the local transportation angles figured. He once carried mail over the Wrangell Mountains on horseback to the gold rush camp at Chisana; in summer, he traveled along the farcically precipitous Chitistone Canyon goat trail and in winter over an all-ice route that ascended a glacier called Whiskey Hill. For treading above the firn line, Berry fashioned horse snowshoes from potato boxes. His truck provided McCarthy's private coal and ice delivery, and after the last train left, he operated the rail speeder to Chitina. Berry built a hand-pulled cable tram across the Kennicott River rapids when the rail bridge into town washed out. He drove a truck with the engine and drive train of a Model T but a body built of salvaged lumber, which he said flexed better than steel on the boulder-strewn glacial moraine where the town sat. The problem was the temptation to peel apart his truck in winter when he got cold.

Firewood was an obsession in those hand-tool days. The spruce forest around McCarthy, leveled for lumber and stovewood in boom times, was just starting to grow back. Standing deadwood was hard to find. Winter settled in at thirty below. Bill Berry had the only power saw, and it weighed, literally, a ton: the blade was powered by a sputtering, banging one-cylinder horizontal engine with a big flywheel and a thirty-foot belt. One winter when he would go away to trap on the Peavine, Berry noticed his woodpile in town shrinking. He drilled holes in the ends of a few stove-cut logs, filled them with .22 rounds, and covered the holes with wood putty. Then he notched the logs so he'd recognize them and put them on top of his pile. A few nights after he left on his next trapping run to the Peavine, visitors in town were awakened by the sound of gunfire and found Ernie Gercken standing in snow outside his cabin in long underwear.

A former Klondike man, Ernie Gercken had a bosky beard and wore long underwear with a stain that darkened noticeably as summer progressed. He was a widower. On the night of the big fire back in 1940, Ernie saved the life of Blanche Smith, who did laundry in the town. She had started out working in McCarthy in "the row" of shacks down by the creek, where children were forbidden to go. Blanche boasted of being "the first white woman" in the mining camp of Chisana, by which she meant the first non-Native, as she herself was Black. Blanche and Ernie got married and lived together happily. She passed away shortly before Jim Edwards arrived. Ernie buried her in the McCarthy Cemetery and said one day he would lie there beside her.

The town's small graveyard lay beyond the old railroad turntable. Trees were starting to reclaim it. Of the fifty or so plots inside the

Blazo Bill Berry and Ernie Gercken, feuding rivals, vied to be the last man buried in the McCarthy Cemetery.

fence, several graves were marked with brass plaques, others with rock piles or rotting wooden crosses. Some had finished going back to nature. A few were fresh. When the town was booming, they would dig a supply of beckoning graveholes in summer, to be ready on a first come, first served basis once the days grew short and the ground froze. After the last train, if you wanted to be buried there, it was helpful to die in summer. In the winter of 1948, a man named Brunswick had a heart attack while waiting for the mail plane. The German caretakers at Kennecott described in a letter home how they ran down to town to get wool blankets, "but there was no need for us to run back up. Brunswick didn't need any more help." A burial dilemma was averted when the man's son summoned a charter plane to take the body away.

But an intense freeze imposed a two-week weather wait, during which the out-bound cargo lay on a sled wrapped in sailcloth.

Ernie Gercken moved to Cordova in his last years, and Bill Berry may have imagined that, with his enemy gone, he would be the last old-timer ever planted in McCarthy's graveyard. Blazo Bill died peacefully—not incandescently—and was buried there with his buddies. A thin lead plate was wired to a post, stamped with the words: WILLIAM H. BERRY BORN NOV 1879 DIED AUG 1958.

Two years later, Ernie Gercken's body was flown back from Cordova, in accordance with his last wishes. His friends laid him to rest beside Blanche Smith, thus completing the last burial in McCarthy's cemetery. The ground was frozen, and they used dynamite to open the grave.

<hr />

A few of those who stayed behind in 1938 were happy to see the last train go. George Flowers was a sixty-six-year-old trapper living in a small cabin on the Lakina River, near Long Lake, fifteen miles down the tracks from McCarthy. He was glad to hear the great silence descend and see the animals come back into the valley. On July 10, 1940, in a typewritten letter to a friend in Fairbanks, he described the change: "This country is absluty dead there is nothing left there ar about 3 people in Kennecott and 3 in McCarthy these to small tonns is dead and gone ha ha."

George Flowers had grown up in a sharecropper family in Mississippi. He left the South on a freight train during the Klondike gold rush. In Seattle, a friend recalled years later, "He knew better than to, as a Black man, get into steerage" on a steamship, so he walked to Alaska. People remembered that around 1910 an emaciated Black man had shown up at the Ahtna Indian village of Mentasta, north of the Wrangells, his clothes and gear in tatters. The Ahtna people

Long Lake trapper George Flowers befriended children from Kennecott, including Richard Osborne (center).

passed the traveler over to a nearby mining camp on the Chisana River. The camp boss, a well-bred midwesterner named John Hazelet, gave Flowers clothes and food. He found him to be a kind and interesting fellow who played guitar. Hazelet and his wife and daughter stayed in touch with Flowers after that. Hazelet's grandson, Richard Osborne, was the teenager in Fairbanks to whom Flowers typed his letters, three decades later, signing them "your old Pal."

There were no jobs for Blacks at Kennecott, where flyers occasionally circulated to announce Ku Klux Klan events. Flowers found work at the small placer gold mines in the creeks, gathering a grubstake to settle alone on the Lakina River near Long Lake around 1920. He built a ten-by-thirteen-foot cabin of logs, axe-felled and notched at the corners, side walls so low he could stand erect only under the ridge pole. He learned to live off the land, hunting and trapping furbearers in winter and gardening and fishing in the summer, when bright spawn-red salmon swam up the Copper and Chitina and into his net.

Long Lake, a three-mile finger whose shoreside meadows and woods had a few farms and a tent resort with a park-like feel, became a summer retreat for Kennecott's managerial families—a place for weekend escapes from the thundering industrial scene they supervised. Richard Osborne visited often as a young boy. His father was chief steward at the mines, in charge of food service for hundreds of workers. His mother, John Hazelet's daughter, took Richard to the Lakina River to visit her old friend, George Flowers. The trapper had built himself a bigger one-room cabin by the bank of the silt-translucent stream. He worked sometimes as a track walker for the railroad, checking for washouts, and sold vegetables from his garden. When the Osbornes visited, he played guitar and served delicious fried fish. Richard Osborne, who would grow up to be a professor of genetics and anthropology at the University of Wisconsin, learned to cast dry flies from his Long Lake pal. He recalled a time when he cast and caught himself in the nose: "My father said, 'Oh my God,' and so George took me on his knee and he laughed and very gently worked that hook out of my nose for me."

Flowers was listed in census records as literate, but he had to work hard at writing. Stabbing at his portable typewriter, he would look through a Sears catalog for ideas when he couldn't spell a word. After the mines closed and the Osbornes moved to Fairbanks, Flowers wrote to Richard that he liked having the valley to himself.

*The few peoples that is left they seems to get along all write. for they knows what to do, some of them, make hay while the sun shine myself i make it while it is cold and snow. so pal i am feeling fine and helthy and dohring fine i caught moor fur last winter than i caught in 10 years i have a fine garden a big strawbery patch since the railroad left the country had got lots of moose . . . Oscar and Fagerberg are still here dohring nothing as usal Buddy the great chang that we have had here, it hasn't interfeared with my life or living one instent i think that i am better off.*

The letter ended on a somber note, however. In 1940, the troubles of the world were felt even at Long Lake: "Well pal what do you think about this great great i wont say wor i will say conflick or murder i thank it is wrong it looks like there is no safe place to live on earth."

⇐——⇒

From time to time in those first years after the mines closed, Flowers might hear a motorized speeder car rattle past on the tracks. Sixty miles of track to McCarthy were still intact. The territorial road commission had assumed maintenance of the track. Where the railroad trestle bridge across the Copper washed away, a small flat-bottom ferry plied the river. A Chitina businessman, Otto A. Nelson, operated a speeder car and ran groceries from his store out to McCarthy. The railroad had been formally abandoned after a hearing before the Interstate Commerce Commission—despite protests from small-scale miners and Cordova businessmen—and in 1945 the private company relinquished the right of way to the federal government. But the rickety railroad's days were numbered, as maintenance could not keep up with extreme forces of erosion, which included grizzlies tearing out rail ties in search of grubs. Track work was on an emergency-only basis. Fuel drums shipped to McCarthy on the speeder car lost as much as one-fifth of their contents sloshing out the top vents.

By 1953, when Jim Edwards arrived, the railroad had yielded to the era of the small airplane. The daring pilots of those planes, landing on glaciers and ridgetops and river bars, would provide new heroes in the Wrangells, as their "skyboy narrative," in the phrase of Alaska historian Katherine Ringsmuth, replaced the cowboy mythology of an earlier American frontier.

The valley's busiest commercial pilot had big ambitions for the region. Mudhole Smith had arrived in the Wrangells in 1938, new to Alaska and assigned to McCarthy by Cordova Air Service just as the mines were closing. With his young bride, he rented a one-bedroom house from the town's leading businesswoman, Kate Kennedy, who in mining days ran the town's high-class brothel and now lived in Seattle and had a lot of empty property on her hands. When he arrived, the town of McCarthy was five blocks long and two blocks wide, with some false-front buildings and wooden sidewalks and the occasional truck driving around horses in the streets. It was more impressive from the air, as seen by an approaching pilot. The landscape cast a valiant light on the puny settlement, its only tie to the world a pencil line of trestle across the glacier's roaring discharge.

The new Cordova Air pilot figured the closing of the railroad would be great for business. People who used to take the train would have to fly.

Smith learned to fly growing up in Kansas. During the Depression, he performed stunts and offered rides for a jaunty Midwest flying circus whose brochure advised: "Don't worry—your money back if we kill you." A job offer from Cordova Air brought the moon-faced young pilot north in 1937, and he had to pinch himself when he saw the country. From McCarthy, his mail flight to the coast took an hour flying over the top of snowy peaks in sunshine and twice as long when he flew low through the valleys under heavy gray skies. He learned to navigate the Copper River canyon without seeing the summits, marking his progress by ravines and railroad trestles.

Mudhole was an excellent pilot, despite the nickname he couldn't shake, pinned on him by a competitor after a minor early mishap at the Bremner Mine in the mountains south of McCarthy. His friends called him Smitty. His real name was Merle. When the town of Cordova, years later, named its airport after him, they could not resist adding "Mudhole" in quotation marks. Merle Smith would go on to play a major role in the affairs of Cordova and Anchorage as well as McCarthy and serve as an Alaska Airlines vice president. But in 1938, barely thirty and freshly excited by Alaska's possibilities, he had not yet sharpened his business sense on the hard realities of the country. The Alaska skyboys could not slow the area's decline and fall. Mudhole failed to foresee that once the railroad closed down his passengers would all be flying one-way tickets out.

That first summer in McCarthy, in 1938, Mudhole Smith glimpsed a possible future for the Wrangells in which the extraordinary geography was at center stage.

He flew a charter for Bradford Washburn, the famed Harvard mountain cartographer and explorer, on a photographic reconnaissance sponsored by the National Geographic Society. The convergence of the Wrangell, St. Elias, and Chugach mountain ranges was the crown of the North American continent, with seventeen summits taller than anything in the contiguous United States and the third largest icefield in the world, after Antarctica and Greenland. Much of it was still unmapped other than by Xs for the tallest features. It was terrain that brought out the peak-bagger in a scientist.

The previous summer, Washburn had staged an expedition out of McCarthy to the 17,192-foot summit of Mount Lucania, in the western Yukon, the tallest unclimbed peak on the continent. That 1937 expedition relied on a competing pilot, Bob Reeve of Valdez, who responded to a meticulously detailed inquiry mailed from Cam-

Bradford Washburn, doing aerial surveys of glaciers, took this photo of McCarthy in 1938. Kennecott lies beside the rock-covered glacier, at the base of the mountain left of center.

bridge, Massachusetts, with a five-word telegram: "Anywhere you'll ride, I'll fly." Flying Washburn's expedition supplies out of McCarthy that spring, Reeve set a world record for a high-altitude ski-plane landing, at 8,750 feet. The landing was more successful than taking off again: Reeve was unable to get airborne with the climbers' weight, so once they completed their climb, Washburn and his partner had to hike out through the unmapped mountains and glacial rivers, more than a hundred miles east to reach a lodge in Canada.

Now Washburn was back. He loaded his fifty-three-pound Fairchild camera into Mudhole's plane, removing the side door and strapping himself to the bulkhead. They soared above the braided

Mudhole Smith's Christmas card, probably from his second winter in the Wrangells, featured Cordova Air's Bellanca with skis.

*Season's Greetings from Alaska*

MR. and MRS. MERLE SMITH

Chitina River, which Washburn described in his journal as "huge and muddy—it swings in countless meanders back and forth across its wide, flat-floored valley." Mudhole flew the scientist around the Canadian giants, Logan and Lucania, then swung north to approach the cold Wrangell volcanoes from the White River valley and Skolai Pass. Bradford Washburn called this saga of fire and ice and the beginning of time as "the most interesting and spectacular glacier systems on earth."

A colleague of Washburn's from the Boston Museum of Science, Terris Moore, came to the Wrangells fifteen years later to set up a more permanent base for high-altitude scientific research. Moore, who had moved north in 1948 to become the second president of the University of Alaska, was a glacier pilot as well as a mountaineer. His achievements included the first ascent of 16,421-foot Mount Bona, in the nearby St. Elias Range, and a new high-altitude landing record of his own, on the summit of Mount Sanford. The scientific camp first established by Moore on Mount Wrangell, an active but glacier-clad shield volcano, featured at one point a geothermally heated camp that had to be abandoned by 1973 because the mountain heated up.

A second expedition during Mudhole's first summer in the Wrangells formed an equally favorable opinion of the area's splendors. McCarthy's pilot was chartered in August 1938 for three days to a government delegation led by Ernest Gruening, the director of the Interior Department's Division of Territories. Gruening, who would become one of Alaska's towering political figures, had started his career in the East, after getting a Harvard medical degree, as a crusading journalist, author, and editor of the *Nation* magazine. He was drawn into politics by his support for New Deal reforms, and Franklin D. Roosevelt liked him. His interest in Latin America and Puerto Rico got him the territories job, but he clashed regularly with his boss, Interior Secretary Harold Ickes, who considered Gruening an "ineffective busybody." Ickes couldn't wait to ship him off to the frontier backwater of Juneau, which he would do the following year.

Appointed territorial governor in 1939, Gruening would embrace the position for fourteen years and later serve two terms as one of Alaska's first two U.S. senators. On the 1938 trip, his second to Alaska for the territories division, he included a visit to McCarthy with two top National Park Service officials to assess the impacts of Kennecott's impending closure and the potential for tourism in the Wrangell Mountains.

A week of perfect blue skies proved ideal for showing off the region's physical virtues. One morning, Gruening took a thirty-five-minute ride in an ore bucket to visit the mountaintop Bonanza Mine. With Mudhole Smith as pilot, the trio later soared above the glaciers and mountain nunataks, the white backdrop of sky revealing itself as snow on ever bigger peaks. Things got a little dodgy, however, when the Bellanca started to stream black smoke and the oil pressure light flickered. As Mudhole later told the story, he kept turning the plane and pointing to distant sights so his VIP passengers wouldn't look back and see the smoke. During a lunch stop in Copper Center he found a drum of used crankcase oil and surreptitiously refilled the near-empty engine so they could make it back to McCarthy.

The visitors agreed that the scenery rivaled, even exceeded, anything in the existing national park system. Gruening, with a sonorous gravity that would become familiar to territorial constituents, told his superiors at the Department of the Interior that the vistas were more impressive than Mount McKinley's:

> I have travelled through Switzerland extensively, have flown over the Andes, and am familiar with the Valley of Mexico and with other parts of Alaska. It is my unqualified view that this is the finest scenery that I have ever been privileged to see.

The group proposed a national park with the vast Chitina River valley at its center. They even suggested a name: Panorama National Park. It might be possible, Gruening said, to preserve the Kennecott ore tram, rising three miles from the concentration mill to the Bonanza, and create an aerial ride for tourists like one he'd seen in Rio de Janeiro. Gruening's plain hope was to preserve the railroad line to Chitina, or to replace it with a road, and thereby save both settlements. As the environmental historian Roderick Nash observed, Alaskans in those days were more likely to think it was civilization, not wilderness, that was fragile and endangered.

A few months after his trip, in November 1938, with the last train departing, Gruening urged the president to act quickly and proclaim Kennicott a national monument, encompassing both glacier and mines. (The copper corporation had left behind a bedeviling orthographic ambiguity. The glacier and its river were named for the early Alaska explorer Robert Kennicott. But the company setting up alongside the glacier called itself Kennecott. Both spellings were used, at various times, for the geographic location of the mill town, finally resolving on Kennecott in the modern national park era.)

Alaska's non-voting delegate to Congress, Tony Dimond, who once worked in small mines in the Wrangells, did not object to Gruening's conservation proposal, so long as mining could continue. But Kennecott Copper balked at leasing its properties, not quite ready to surrender the chance of a profitable return; a follow-up government party hit a week of rain and fog in McCarthy and were considerably less impressed; and President Roosevelt wrote that he saw "no urgency" in the plan, given the approach of a world war.

The proposal was shelved. But the foremost Alaska politician of his time was not done dreaming up ideas for the Wrangells.

As George Flowers feared, the great conflict reached the territory. Trouble had been boiling through Kennecott's final years—the very morning of the last train out, the world woke to the horrors of Kristallnacht. Pearl Harbor brought war close. Japanese forces captured two remote Aleutian Islands and bombed Dutch Harbor. Military construction in Alaska was feverish. Work and money were everywhere. The Glenn Highway was built from Anchorage to the upper Copper River basin to meet the road that ran from Prince William Sound to Fairbanks. At the intersection, the town of Glennallen was born.

But the Chitina River valley, far from any line of fire, slipped farther into the past.

For a handful of Japanese, the valley had once been a place of opportunity and exile. When the mines were open, a Japanese crew—single men, barred by immigration laws from bringing their families to Alaska—ran the kitchens and the laundries. Richard Osborne, George Flowers's young pal, recalled a laundry foreman who befriended him. The laundry man, who spoke a little English, said he missed his children. He let the American boy follow when he walked out to the cliff in front of the concentration mill. The laundry foreman knew how to fold Japanese newspapers into beautiful kites with long tails. He would stand at the edge and fly his kites out over the ice. Sometimes, Osborne recalled, the wind would rise and tear the kite free, and the Japanese foreman would watch news from home drift away across the glacier.

Now the Japanese were gone and the copper mines closed. A few miners still worked the gold creeks on the upper Nizina River, where glacial tributaries thundered out of mountain canyons. A rough road from McCarthy reached Dan Creek and Chititu, but the bridge across the Nizina was doomed. Eventually gold mining would shut down as non-essential to the war effort.

The 1940 census for the upper Chitina River valley, taken in December 1939, showed two watchman couples living at Kennecott, forty-nine people in McCarthy, and another twenty-three in the surrounding area, from Long Lake to Dan Creek. A few babies, no older children. The town itself was disappearing, like so many old wooden towns, in flames. On November 6, 1940, Ben Jackson, the postmaster, went for a short drive after dark and returned to a sky lit orange by his burning drug store. Ben's wife, Ora, age forty-eight, had stayed in the kitchen to get dinner ready. Neighbors were battling the blaze, but it was hard to do anything with water at fifteen below. They dragged what they could to safety. The fire died out around three in the morning, having erased an entire business block, including the drug store and post office, a grocery, and the Alaska House, Kate Kennedy's former top-of-the-line lodging. Ora Jackson's body was never found.

When the second delegation of federal officials arrived the next summer to assess a possible national monument, they reported only a dozen or so people left. McCarthy, "instead of being one of the busiest little towns in Alaska, was a ghost town with the business center a charred ruins." The delegation's 1942 report bristles with bureaucratic put-downs, clashing with Gruening's sunny 1938 assessment to a comical degree, as the new superintendent of Mount McKinley National Park got back at the territorial governor for calling his park "on the whole relatively bleak." Scenery in the Wrangells, the Mount McKinley superintendent retorted, "was not impressive compared to many other sections of Alaska." He conceded a point about the weather, raised by tourists in McCarthy ever since: Gruening's group had a week of "gorgeous weather," while the second group visited for "a period of cloudiness and rain. . . . A more complete contrast for viewing the same locality can hardly be imagined." Even so, he saw no reason for the government to take responsibility for the region and particularly for the Kennecott complex, an "unsightly conglomeration of shapes, sizes and locations" that would have to be razed at great cost. The cost of simply replacing bridges so people could get there would be phenomenal. With no bridge across the Copper River, the existing alternatives for crossing at Chitina, by aerial tram or row boat, were, the superintendent deadpanned, "thrilling." As for the people of the region, all they wanted out of national monument recognition, he said, was new roads—"There was no feeling of appreciation for the beauty or interest of the country."

The attitude reflected perhaps the sourness of their boss, Interior Secretary Ickes, the powerful New Deal Democrat who had banished his rival Gruening to Alaska. Ickes visited Alaska the year Kennecott was shutting down and blamed the whole sad situation on human greed. He wrote about the trip in his diary, published after his death:

*Mining is more or less a gamble even in the best of circumstances, and a gambling spirit does not make for the building up of a normal American community with a background of agriculture or industry. People have come to Alaska to exploit a nonrenewable resource, such as gold or copper, and then take the wealth back to the United States in order to live an easy life.*

As territorial governor, Gruening was equally exasperated about the meager fruits of capitalism in the colonies. The problem, he told the legislature in 1941, had been the lack of taxes or royalties. He said the great mining venture paid its shareholders and built fortunes in New York but left Alaska with a "hole in the ground" and three towns in need of federal relief.

In 1943 the neglected railroad bridge across the Kennicott River that led to McCarthy finally gave way. The collapse began not during spring break-up, as on the mighty Copper River, but in an annual flood that gushes midsummer from an ice-dammed reservoir in the Kennicott Glacier, a phenomenon known to geologists as jökulhlaup, an Icelandic term. Eventually, Bill Berry's hand-pulled tram cart, dangling from a cable above the current, was the only way to cross the river in summer. With no bridge, more people left. The post office closed.

The old trapper from Mississippi, happy to see people move away, did not get to enjoy his peace for long. Approaching seventy, George Flowers broke through ice on his trapline. His feet froze as he made his way back to his cabin. Gangrene set in. By the time friends got him to Valdez, the hospital could not save his life. As a Black man, he could not be buried in the Valdez community cemetery. Richard Osborne, in an oral history years later, said the friends were told to bury him in the "Indian cemetery"—presumably the graveyard at the town's original Russian Orthodox Church. According to the curator of the Valdez Museum and Historical Archive, that property later became a laundromat and was then abandoned, with the rest of old Valdez, after the Great Alaska Earthquake of 1964 sent a tsunami sweeping across the docks and through the old town's streets, killing thirty-two people. The Indian cemetery was lost, along with the grave of George Flowers.

The railroad speeder cars were finally given up altogether after 1948 once the territory provided access for bigger planes with an improved airstrip on the open flats at May Creek. The airstrip was twenty miles from McCarthy, across the still-stable Nizina River bridge. The undulating tracks to Chitina could now be removed, perhaps to make way for a bulldozer trail and the beginning of another transportation era. The steel between McCarthy and Long Lake was pulled and sold for scrap in the 1950s. In the early 1960s, an entrepreneur walked on foot the rest of the way to Chitina, along track buckled from soil subsidence and permafrost melt, then spent several years tearing out those rails for shipment to Chile, bringing the railway age to an end.

The last load of Copper River rails was stacked on the beach at old Valdez in 1964 when the earthquake struck. The tsunami washed them away—or as the ghost town trope would have it: they were never seen again.

⟵⟶

While the people had mostly disappeared by 1953 when Jim Edwards arrived in McCarthy, their goods remained. J. B. O'Neill's store and Hubrick's photo shop and the Golden Saloon were jammed full of furniture, kerosene lanterns, and copper tubing for making moonshine—everything that had been hastily moved to safety during the 1940 fire.

Downtown McCarthy in 1954. Fire had cleared out a block of buildings.

Kenny Smith, the son of Mudhole Smith, was a teenager when he visited in the early 1950s, wondered who all these things belonged to. Archie Poulin told him.

Archie Poulin was a retired French-Canadian businessman who returned to McCarthy every summer. He had a bitter on-going feud with another returning miner, Henry Schulze—apparently something about a woman from copper-mining days. Both were short men, wiry and strong, with "fingers the size of sausages." Archie and Henry always checked, before flying on the mail plane, to be sure the other wasn't traveling that day. They spent their summers doing assessment work on mining claims, rolling tobacco on their porches, and avoiding one another. Their houses were a block apart, but they had specific routes for their daily walks leading out of town in opposite directions. If someone threw a party for the town, there had to be a Henry room and an Archie room.

Henry Schulze was friendly with visitors and with kids who remember him as "skinny as a stick." He was miserly, teased for stretching his supplies unreasonably—even his roofing tar, essential for patching leaks, he cut with turpentine. As late as the 1960s, he spent two years dragging wood up a mountain to build scaffolding so he could reach a remote green copper stain on Nikolai Ridge, only to find no ore: one stick of dynamite blew all traces of copper off the cliff. Many of his life's disappointments he traced back to Franklin D. Roosevelt, the president he blamed for the Kennecott mines closing. People recalled it was easy fun to touch off a tirade by saying something positive about FDR in Henry's presence. He had a hand-cranked phonograph in his house, and a scratchy record sung in the voice of an Italian immigrant: "Good old Franklin D. / he too a son of a beecha lika me."

Meanwhile Archie Poulin, a more flamboyant type—Henry Schulze called him "that pimp"—was trying to relaunch a hydraulic mining operation at Dan Creek using old steel pipes with high-pressure hose nozzles known as giants. Poulin and his older brother, George, kept their McCarthy cabin neat and trim, using a jack to shore up the foundation with salvaged bridge timbers. Each fall, when it was time to return to Seattle, Archie and George would walk up to the airfield, Archie wearing a dark-blue pinstripe business suit, and their friends would follow to await the mail plane. Jim Edwards was the youngest in the party. The friends would always say, "We'll see you guys next year." And Archie would reply, "Yup. Yup." And George would lower his pipe and reply, "Well, at my age, you never know, you never know." Every year the same sequence, until one year, sure enough, George didn't come back. But Archie lived to the age of ninety-six.

In the summer of 1953, Archie led young Kenny Smith on a walk around the blocks cleared by the fire that took Ora Jackson's life.

There were no weather-beaten buildings in this part of town, just young balsam poplars. The old man pointed to businesses that were no longer there—and, in one case, to a business that had never been there. Archie told the kid he ran a soda fountain that was lost in the fire. Kenny saw the broken marble countertop lying in the trees. The Alaska Fountain, he later learned, had been a pool hall and saloon all through Prohibition, switching to soda only when a discharge pattern of black smoke from an approaching train warned of a revenue agent arriving from the coast. "Turns out he was the biggest bootlegger in the country," Kenny Smith said years later.

Kenny was hanging around McCarthy because his father was now in charge of Cordova Airlines, the upgraded version of the Cordova bush plane service. Mudhole had tried to leave the Copper River country back in 1939, after his first year in McCarthy. Frustrated by the atmosphere of fatigue and inexorable decline, he accepted a job in Kotzebue flying for the pioneer aviator Noel Wien. In April 1939, Cordova Air's founder and owner, M. D. "Kirk" Kirkpatrick, flew to McCarthy and unsuccessfully begged Mudhole to reconsider. Picking up a passenger that afternoon, Kirk headed home toward Cordova, hit a spring snowstorm on the coast, swung into the mountains to approach Cordova from the west, and, flying low through the storm over the small islands of Prince William Sound, clipped off a wing on a tree. Kirk and the passenger were drowned, and Mudhole Smith, grieving, agreed to remain and assume control of the airline.

"All his life he wanted to see the country come alive," Kenny Smith recalled. Mudhole had purchased a big taildragger DC-3 passenger plane for Cordova Air. He was looking for ways to deploy the plane beyond his regular air route to Anchorage. In 1952 Kennecott Copper decided to lay off the German caretaker couple at the old mining camp that had so fascinated Ernest Gruening. Mudhole saw his chance.

"Dad knew Kennecott had been left wide open."

# 3

# The Ghost Mansion

T HE IDEA FOR Sourdough Tours came during a 1952 vacation to Southern California. Mudhole Smith found himself paying admission at Knott's Berry Farm to visit a replica frontier town. He thought people might pay to see the real thing.

History became the valley's new resource. In 1953, the year Jim Edwards first visited McCarthy, Cordova Airlines started flying tourists to May Creek in a twenty-one-passenger DC-3. Flights departed every weekend from Anchorage and stopped in Valdez on their way to the Wrangell Mountains. At the May Creek airstrip, Blazo Bill Berry waited in his carpentered Model T truck with benches in back. Mudhole had pulled strings with the territorial road commission to get maintenance on the twenty-mile road to McCarthy, across the Nizina River bridge. On busy weekends the jouncing caravan included a Model B Ford flatbed and sometimes a Dodge touring car said to have carried President Warren Harding in 1923 during his visit to Cordova, where Alaska crabmeat was slanderously blamed for the President's death by cardiac arrest in San Francisco several weeks later.

Mudhole Smith's business plan required a lodge in McCarthy where fly-in visitors could spend the night. He arranged for two men from Anchorage, Howard Knutson and Zack Brown, to renovate a wood-frame photo shop that once belonged to photographer Cap Hubrick. The home had stacks of photographic prints taken by Hubrick, who was known as Cap because he ran a ferry across the Yukon during the Klondike gold rush. In 1921 Hubrick had advised the Hollywood cameramen filming spring breakup on the Copper River for the silent movie based on Rex Beach's novel *The Iron Trail*.

The new proprietors dusted off the furniture in Cap's house and set up a kitchen. They hauled beds from the dorms at Kennecott into rooms above the Golden Saloon and across the street at Ma Johnson's hotel. They got a beer and wine license from the territory and reopened the saloon, which had a vintage pool table, a roulette wheel, and a windup phonograph that played dance hall tunes. When a visiting US marshal gave them trouble for serving whiskey to tourists without the proper license, Knutson said, they left the bottle open on the bar and a jar for voluntary contributions, which more than covered the cost of the booze.

Howard Knutson, who would one day be the valley's main bush pilot, a sought-after hunting guide, and the last man to mine copper at the Bonanza Mine, was at that point new to Alaska, a twenty-four-year-old Minnesota boy who never wanted to see another farm. He had come north with his wife, Adina, and traded his car in Anchorage for a little Aeronca Champ airplane. He bought a house in McCarthy, a block from the lodge. Then he parted ways with Zack Brown.

The battle that followed, though brief, outdid the seething feuds of the old-timers. Jim Edwards had a clear view, looking out the windows of his house in town next to the lodge. "The two women got to fighting. Mrs. Brown was in front of the lodge and Adina was in front of her house, and the two were screaming imprecations at each other from a block away. Shouting obscenities, really going at it. And then when one wasn't looking, they would run down the street and tear up the other's garden—kick the plants over, throw things out—it was a sight to see." He watched Adina taking flowers from the lodge's flower box while Howard stood guard with a .30-30 rifle.

Knutson went to the lodge to have it out, and Brown came the door with a rifle. Knutson tore the rifle away and struck Brown with it, resulting in assault charges. The charges were dropped, according to Knutson, when he went to see the US commissioner at his office in Glennallen, and the two men talked it over in the back kitchen over hot buttered rums.

Jim Edwards tried to stay neutral. On the one hand, he shared ownership of a chainsaw with Zacky Brown. Also, he was lonely and had a crush on the Browns' pretty seventeen-year-old daughter. The prospect of finding a wife in the Wrangell Mountains was beginning to weigh on the twenty-five-year-old. At one point he walked all the way from a mining job in the Chitistone Canyon to town, thirty-plus miles through creeks and two feet of melting snow, just to see the Browns' daughter during a week off. "We sat in her cabin and talked and that's all that came of it. It turned out a guy would be damned glad he didn't marry her." On the other hand, Knutson could be a charming as well as determined and might be good to know for the long term. "Howard and Adina were both quite powerful people in their own way—pretty aggressive."

Sure enough, it was the Browns who departed first, after a few seasons struggling to run a lodge with no plumbing. "I carried a lot of water in and out of that place," Delphia Brown recalled two decades later. Another couple, the Weinrichs, took over the lodge for Mudhole. Next to the Golden Saloon, they turned J. B. O'Neill's store

Kennecott in the 1950s, before the concentration mill roof was torn apart.

into a small museum, designating dry goods that had been left on the shelves as historical artifacts.

Oblivious to the backstage drama, hundreds of visitors passed through McCarthy on their way to see the ruins over the course of four summers. The two-day excursion, all-expenses-included, cost forty-nine dollars. The ghost town tours got a plug on the floor of the state's 1955 constitutional convention from Bob Bartlett, even as Alaska's delegate to Congress lamented the Wall Street plunderers who abandoned the town. Jim Edwards helped out one season, riding up to the mining camp with the tourists on wooden rail carts behind a Model T speeder: "I would take people through the buildings, wave my arms, and tell them about Kennecott." Sourdough Tours was a success.

Mountain vistas were part of the attraction, of course, like the spectacular mile-high icefall descending from the radiant white peaks of the high Wrangells. But few of the visitors hiked all the way up to see the best views from Bonanza Ridge, "naked and glacier-scarred" in the words of writer Katherine Wilson, who had visited in mining days. People came for the ghosts. The Sourdough Tours brochure focused on the intact mine ruins, invoking "the strange tale of how every soul pulled out on the last train—leaving their homes and stores, down to the last lace curtain intact—on the day the Kennecott mines closed down, never to reopen again." Visitors walked through workshops scattered with tools. Company memos tacked to the walls outlined shut-down plans. Homes still had carpets on the floor, kerosene in the lamps, bedding and utensils ready, and 1938 calendars on the wall. Kennecott had the hospital and McCarthy the jail, both strewn with personal records open for examination. In the old schoolhouse hung a portrait of President Woodrow Wilson.

All around Kennecott, nature pressed close, indifferent to the fading human presence in a way that felt cold or comforting, depending on a visitor's inclination. The silence inspired a long view of time's ravages and consolations. Such reveries, however, were likely to be interrupted by the crash of boulders sliding down ice on the glacier, a reminder that in these dynamic mountains even time was borne along swiftly.

A highlight of any Sourdough Tours visit was the gravity concentration mill, the muscular fourteen-story structure cascading down the mountainside, which nurse Ethel LeCount had described in a letter as "the big red mill that crouched like a great watchful lion on the hills above camp." It was the cathedral of the industrial town. Ore from the mines, four thousand feet above, was once delivered in aerial cars to the top of the structure, generating electricity all the way down with the tram car's brakes. The separators and ore crushers were the pounding heart of the Kennecott operation. Its gables, dormers, and chutes were intact, as was most of the original machinery, according to a later survey: two Buchanan jaw crushers, a Stevens-Adamson apron feeder, a Symons crusher, Hancock jigs, Colorado impact screens, Wilfley tables, a door thickener, ore bins, and sackers.

For contrast, the tourists would follow a path up National Creek to the elegant two-story honeymoon mansion of Stephen Birch. With its clear-fir floors, commanding glacier view, and big stone fireplace and chimney, the cliff-top home seemed a romantic toe-hold for permanent settlement of Alaska, its air of domestic tranquility at odds with the industrial brawn that made it possible. "It was perched a short way up the mountain and faced out at the most beautiful scenery in the world," wrote Jo King, who lived in McCarthy in 1955. She especially admired the fireplace, inset with covellite jewels of copper from the mine, the blues and greens and shimmering purple of what they called "peacock ore." The mantelpiece was a smooth slab of chalcocite, the mineral that built Birch's empire. When the first trains left the Wrangells carrying unprocessed ore of 70 percent pure copper direct from the mines—that was chalcocite.

The man for whom the mansion was built, Stephen Birch, was the visionary who made Kennecott happen—a pioneer capitalist and outstanding American, "born Anglo Saxon and self-made," in the words of Katherine Wilson's adoring 1923 portrait. Newly graduated from Columbia University and quickly weary of surveying tunnels for the New York City subways, Birch sailed to Alaska during the gold rush, talking his way onto an army reconnaissance crew. He was on hand in 1900 when the new copper discoveries were made in the Chitina River valley, bought up the claims, sold the package to the Guggenheims and J. P. Morgan, and was appointed president of the new mining company. Birch became known as a cool and taciturn businessman, inscrutable to colleagues and journalists, but the early miners remembered him as a guy who loosened up when he was camping in the mountains. On trips to the Bonanza Mine, he would pick up loose fragments of chalcocite and empty his knapsack into the ore chutes "to pay for his lunch." He was absent on a three-week Dall sheep hunt in August 1914 when word reached the mines of the war in Europe that would make his fortune.

By 1916, with the wartime price of copper sky-high, Birch was president of the consolidated Kennecott Copper Corporation and already using Alaska profits to buy mining properties in Utah and Chile. That year production from the newly discovered Jumbo Mine, whose deposit was connected inside the mountain to Bonanza Mine's, turned the Alaska diggings a profit of $20 million—nearly half a billion dollars in today's dollars.

That same summer, Birch married a wealthy, much-younger socialite from Minneapolis. Eager to show off his mountain of pure copper, he prepared for a honeymoon to Alaska by joining two state-rooms into a bridal suite on the passenger deck of the company's steamship *Mariposa,* outfitting his private rail car in Cordova with expensive luxuries, and arranging construction of the Kennecott home with its fireplace inlaid with ore. Plans called for the couple to remain in Alaska for a month. But his bride was unmoved, the visit lasted two days, the marriage was a tragic one, and Birch would return but once more to the mountain where his fortune was born.

The handsome home fell instead to use by a camp superinten-dent and his family and later by special guests. The last official party to sleep there was Ernest Gruening's Interior Department delegation in 1938. Those federal civil servants came because Stephen Birch, now chairman of the world's largest copper producer, headquartered in New York City, was preparing to shut down the Alaska operation, a coldly logical decision under the corporate ledger-keeping that had transformed American business in his lifetime. The one-time Alaska adventurer had been living alone for a long time in rural New Jersey, now a widower whose wife died young of cancer. Two years after closing down the Bonanza Mine, Birch died at the age of sixty-eight.

Abandoned with the mines, the rustic honeymoon mansion found new life as a ruminative destination for ghost town tourists. To Mudhole Smith's customers, confronted everywhere else by audacious machinery and workingmen's dorms, the copper hearth provided a potent symbol of the millionaires who benefitted from it all—a domestic-arts celebration of the mountain's riches, perhaps, or a haunting reminder of dreams that never came true.

<hr />

For sightseers, the flight to the Wrangells was an adventure in itself. The region had a reputation for aviation danger—its notoriety derived in part from a night in March 1948. The sky had been perfectly clear when a chartered Northwest Airlines DC-4, flying from Shanghai to New York via Anchorage, slammed into the side of Mount Sanford, the range's second-tallest peak at sixteen thousand feet. Residents of Gulkana reported seeing a fireball erupt a mile below the summit. All thirty people on board perished and the wreckage, in an unreachable snow cirque, disappeared into a glacier for fifty years. A legend grew that the plane was carrying gold bullion, though none ever turned up. The official Civil Aeronautics Board report blamed the crash on the northern lights, surmising the pilot had attempted to circum-navigate the mountain on a clear night, only to be confounded by a thin veil of clouds on the summit: "Such a layer of clouds would not only have tended to obscure the mountain but may have acted as a reflector for the Aurora Borealis which was observed to be particularly brilliant the night of this flight."

Residents of the Wrangells understood airplanes had become their main connection to the outside world. In addition to occa-

Howard and Adina Knutson, with Blazo Bill Berry on right.

sional weekend tourist flights, Cordova Airlines had the government contract to get mail to McCarthy—generally in small planes originating from Chitina. Seat fares on the mail plane were an economical way to get around. The McCarthy mail run included stops at May Creek and Glacier Creek and over the peaks to Chisana, Nabesna, and Northway, then back the other way to pick up return passengers. The mail pilot was often detained at the airstrips by those in search of news from outside and gossip from other mining camps. At Glacier Creek, the local miner sometimes left his windup watch at the mail drop with a request that it be set to the proper time.

In the days of Sourdough Tours, the mail pilot for Cordova Air was often Jack Wilson, who went on to become a well-known Alaska glacier pilot. A research glaciologist who commuted to the summit of Mount Wrangell later wrote that "to fly with Jack Wilson at high altitude in the mountains must be like flying with an eagle—he finds and uses thermal updrafts better than anyone else I have ever flown with." In addition to ferrying mountaineers and scientists to high icefields, Wilson spent years carrying exploration geologists and their supplies around the Wrangells. He said these passengers would talk his arm off with long words if he gave them any provocation. "Warning: people who know a geologist should steer the conversation to flying, the weather, football, even politics, but never rocks." He said his main interest in rocks was avoiding them, especially the local clouds full of rocks, which he called "cumulo-granite formations."

Wilson published a memoir, *Glacier Wings and Tales*, in which he described flying a load of dynamite to McCarthy. He broke the rules that day by carrying volatile detonators on the same flight as the explosives, lashing a box of blasting caps on the co-pilot seat of his Cessna 170. He couldn't carry human passengers with such freight, but the Hazardous Materials Manual didn't say anything about Zack Brown's cocker spaniel, returning from the vet. As he loaded up in Chitina, he was also handed a gunnysack holding a tranquilized cat, because the lodge needed a mouser. Wilson's story proceeds through air turbulence over the upper Chitina River, an awakened cat, an electrified dog, and "a maelstrom of dog and cat scratching, biting, rolling, clawing, barking, and yowling" that landed heavily on the front seat seconds after Wilson opened a window and flung out the blasting caps, narrowly averting an explosion that would have been heard in Canada. "If I ever have the opportunity to help revise the Hazardous Materials Manual, I will recommend that dogs and cats not be hauled simultaneously with other hazardous materials unless they are tied apart with choke chains and the pilot has been issued a sawed off baseball bat."

Jack Wilson had settled in Chitina with his wife, Jo, who was a pilot herself. Jo was what they called in those days a vivacious brunette, "a real looker" as Jim Edwards put it. She was already in her second marriage, and she wouldn't really settle down until she married Jack Wilson's friend, the hunting guide Harley King. As Jo King, she wrote a memoir of her own, *Bird in the Bush*, after Harley was shot and killed in the McCarthy murders in 1983.

In 1955, while Jack and Jo were still a couple, Jo spent the winter in McCarthy, caretaking the lodge for Jack's boss, Mudhole Smith. She was on her own much of the time, running the radio, feeding Mudhole's six packhorses, and trying to keep the canned goods from freezing. "There were more horses than people," she wrote. Her social life mostly consisted of visits with Blazo Bill Berry, who had a room at the hardware store filled with shiny copper tubing and bubbling liquids, "like Dr. Jekyll's kitchen." Berry would occasionally supply a jug of his carrot whiskey to their other McCarthy neighbors, Cal and Vi Aiken, because he was worried about the safety of their bathtub gin.

If Sourdough Tours was mining the past for spectacle, the local residents were mining it for more practical purposes. Furnishings from the cottages, offices, and shops at Kennecott outfitted the Chitina home of Jack and Jo Wilson. Jo found a fine set of Bavarian dishes in a mining camp cabinet. Jack brought back wood trim for the house, a front door, captain's chairs, and enough window frames for everyone in Chitina to build greenhouses. He outfitted his bathroom with a wash basin, toilet, shower head, hot water tank, and plumbing fixtures from the hospital. "The Big Rock Candy Mountain," he called Kennecott.

"What a bonanza it was!" Jack Wilson wrote. "There were tons of good stuff in those old buildings. There were dishes, furniture, household goods, lumber, hardware, everything a person could need. And it was all in perfect condition. What few residents lived in the area at that time took good advantage of this largess. And it vanished quickly as time went on."

Jim Edwards, living in a cabin in McCarthy and helping occasionally with the tourist business, kept two lists nailed to the wall: a

Kennecott's loveliest ruminative relic: the fireplace in Stephen Birch's mansion was inset with copper ore.

shopping list for the store in Chitina, and a scavenging list for Kennecott. He said he felt a bit guilty about the latter until an inspector from the Kennecott Copper Corporation helped him load a bathtub into his flatbed truck. "We don't want that stuff," the official told him.

Treasure hunting fit the mining town's mentality. Once again, everyone was happily depleting a non-renewable resource. As with any bonanza, rivalries and resentments developed. Taking-to-use was considered a higher priority than taking-to-sell. Locals felt proprietary when they saw tourists grabbing souvenirs. People who had lived there longer complained about claim-jumping by newcomers. Jim Edwards got sore at one neighbor for loading a flatbed carelessly and breaking dishes by the boxful, and at another who beat him to a treasure they'd discussed the night before.

"When you have a neighbor and you thought he was being friendly and you mention to him one evening that you got a bookshelf and now you realize you haven't got any books so I think I'll go back to Kennecott and get some books. And the very next day I drove to Kennecott, but I didn't go early—maybe midday. When I went up to the library, the books were all gone. The guy had heard me say I was going to get some books, so he went and got all the books himself. And he threw them down in the rain somewhere behind his house and just let them rot but he was going to keep me from getting them. This was part of the mentality that went on for years and years."

<hr />

And then, all of a sudden, the party was over. No Trespassing signs went up at Kennecott. No more tours. No more locals helping themselves. Private ownership had reasserted itself, in order to facilitate a more thorough form of plunder.

The man who put up the signs would be remembered in McCarthy, decades later, as the scourge of preservation, the ravening jackal who ordered the place burned down—or maybe just as the Visigoth who set out to sack Rome but got no farther than dismantling two roofs.

Ray Trotochau showed up in 1957 talking about tearing down the mill buildings and closing the mine entrances under contract to Kennecott Copper, who had grown anxious about liability. A photo of a Sourdough Tours group at Kennecott appeared in *National Geographic* magazine. Through J. B. O'Neill, the former McCarthy store owner living on Puget Sound, Kennecott management was introduced to Trotochau, a Seattle junk dealer. Within a year, Trotochau had assumed Kennecott's liability by purchasing the whole surface estate, approximately three thousand mountainside acres, "together with the tenements, hereditaments and appurtenances thereunto."

No record of the price paid has turned up, though subsequent owners said Trotochau made a down payment of $1,000 toward a purchase price of $6,000. Nor has any written record emerged of a side agreement to tear down the buildings at Kennecott, though that was what the new owner told everyone he had agreed to do.

Pleas from Mudhole Smith and Sourdough Tours were to no avail. The idea of a government buyout gained traction locally. Trotochau tore the rails out of the public right-of-way to Kennecott, cutting off access via the colorful old speeder cars. In 1960 federal officials said Trotochau had overstepped when he did this but deferred to the new state government, which sided with the supposed mining business against the tourist business. Eventually Sourdough Tours shifted the destination for its DC-3 trips to Dawson, in the Yukon Territory.

Ray Trotocheau's Seattle outfit, the Sultan Sawmill Company, professed to have mining experience, though his chief business seemed to be in mining scrap metal and antiques. He went to work stripping Kennecott for parts. Trotochau brought in a crew to pull furniture and brass and plumbing fixtures from the buildings. He emptied the general store of its merchandise, and employee cottages of their china and chrome-fitted cookstoves. The Victrola and Maytag in Nell McCann's red-and-white cottage were long gone. "Much of the intrigue associated with the abandoned mine was eliminated," Mudhole's son, Kenny, recalled. "I can attest to the suddenly bland appearance of the place."

The only copper extracted was peeled of high-voltage wires. But after a few summers, Trotochau began to consider the blue-green rocks lying at his feet. There seemed to be a lot of chalcocite and malachite and azurite left behind at the ruins of the world-famous copper mine.

One final mineral survey had convinced Kennecott no interesting commercial deposits remained underground. The corporation, now

Sourdough Tours carried visitors from McCarthy on railroad speeder cars.

a major international mining and oil conglomerate, nevertheless withheld subsurface mineral rights from the sale to Trotochau. (The picket-fenced company cemetery, along the wagon road below the tracks, was also kept beyond the junk dealer's reach.) But as for the spillage all around the mill and under the tram swing stations—and the tailings up at the Bonanza and Jumbo Mines, and slopes where the copper vein had been eroding out of the ridge for centuries—lawyers could argue about that.

Gordon Burdick, an Iwo Jima vet and former history teacher who had followed Trotochau from Seattle, spent the summer of 1959 carving a rough five-mile Cat road up switchbacks to the mines. Unlike his boss, Burdick had embraced Alaska mountain living. He spent his free time descending into the adits and shafts with a flashlight to look around. Four distinct mines were connected by long tunnels.

When an official delegation showed up later that summer, with the approval of Kennecott Copper, Burdick was the logical one to lead the tour underground.

The visitors were scientists and engineers from the Lawrence Radiation Lab in Livermore, California. They were looking for a place to detonate a nuclear bomb.

"The majority of the manways, crosscuts and accessways between shaft levels were completely solid with ice," the engineers wrote in their report—"much to the discomfort of those in the inspection party." Crystalline ice structures covered the walls and ceilings. "In some areas these ice stalactites and stalagmites had completely blocked the passageways and had to be knocked down by the party in order to explore further into the workings. The severe ice conditions in the mine made passage from one level to another rather hazardous as it was almost impossible to maintain footing while descending inclined manways."

The eight-page unclassified memo, distributed to officials with the Atomic Energy Commission, said nothing about a bomb. The report was presented as an assessment of the mine and supporting structures, with consideration for their reuse. Reuse as what, the authors did not say. They recommended using portable diesel generators rather than trying to restore the original power plant. They took note of the rough trails being bulldozed to the mines, "with very steep grades and many sharp turns and switchbacks. . . . It should also be reiterated that air travel and road transportation in this portion of Alaska is extremely inconvenient and in no way resembles the transportation comforts and ease of movement prevalent in other areas associated with our activities." Recommendations would follow, the memo concluded, in a separate classified report.

The visitors were in Kennecott under the auspices of the Plowshare Program, a secret government undertaking aimed at finding

Kennecott in the 1950s, with the future Kennicott Glacier Lodge in the fore-ground and Root Glacier in the distance.

peacetime excuses for setting off nuclear bombs. The project was launched in 1957 by the Atomic Energy Commission and led by Edward Teller, director of the Lawrence Radiation Lab. At a 1957 symposium in Livermore, a talk titled "Uses of Thermonuclear Explosives in the Mining Industry" pointed to the abandoned Kennecott mines in Alaska as a place where an explosion might be useful in removing the overburdened impediments of ice and snow. Over a twelve-year period that followed, thirty-five nuclear devices were exploded in underground industrial-application experiments. While the actual explosions were in Nevada, New Mexico, and Colorado, a number of projects in Alaska were studied, including blasting out a canal through the Alaska Peninsula at Port Moller and a harbor at Katalla, near Cordova, where early attempts to build a railroad port had been wiped out by a 1907 storm. The "peaceful" project that came closest to ignition was a five-bomb proposal to crater out a harbor at Cape Thompson, in northern Alaska. The nearby Iñupiat Eskimo village of Point Hope resisted, and several professors at the University of Alaska lost their jobs for helping villagers win the fight.

The visitors at Kennecott had come directly from Point Hope. One of the engineers who was there in 1959 explained, in an oral history years later, what they were looking for. At Kennecott, Raymond Harbert said the idea was to set off a nuclear device and flood the mine, then use electrolysis to extract copper from the water. The day before they climbed to the Bonanza, in late July, a foot of snow fell on the high peaks. "I damn near froze," Harbert recalled—he had only brought shorts and T-shirts. They went home and wrote up their reports and nothing was ever heard about it again.

Once the mad scientists were gone, Trotochau's crew went back to hand-picking ore. They loaded the rocks into jute bags left by the original miners. They tore up the rails down to McCarthy, so they could drive ore trucks along the railbed to the little airstrip dating from Kennecott days. The heavy jute bags could be flown on small planes to Chitina, where a road led out to the Richardson Highway. Kenny Smith had started flying the mail and could carry twelve of the hundred-pound bags if his Cessna 185 was returning from McCarthy empty.

Trotochau's crew also trucked ore across the Nizina's rotting trestles to May Creek, where bigger planes could land. One evening, Kenny Smith recalled, a wartime training plane known as a Bamboo Bomber, coming to pick up ore, buzzed McCarthy on the way in. The pilot whacked the tip of a radio antenna erected by Archie Poulin and landed at May Creek with a brass ball planted in its wing.

Dangling buckets, stooping over to clutch rocks, Trotochau's potato pickers were avoided by locals. People figured they were hired off Seattle's skid row, bums whose probation officers probably didn't know they were in Alaska. It was an unfair rap, at least for some. One of the more upstanding was Joey Lopez, a ranked middle-weight fighter who called Kenny Smith "kid." One time Smith was delivering supplies to the crew's likable manager, Frank DeCaro, who once surprised a gathering at the McCarthy Lodge by standing to sing "Old Man River" in a beautiful baritone. Smith asked DeCaro who ordered the heavy bag of red beans. "Joey wants to make a comeback," DeCaro explained. Joey Lopez flung hundred-pound bags of ore into Smith's Cessna with pride. DeCaro said they had a big guy on the crew who baited Lopez like a gunfighter in a western. Joey, much shorter, shrugged it off. Then one bright summer night, the crew was driving back to Kennecott after drinking at the McCarthy Lodge. Joey called out for DeCaro to stop the truck. The two men got out and squared off in the road. Joey danced around for a while, then cut the big guy to pieces. Joey Lopez later moved to Anchorage, Kenny Smith said, where he worked for the Plumbers and Steamfitters Union and brought boxers to Alaska for big fight cards.

The first load of Kennecott surface ore, trucked to the Tacoma smelter from Chitina, caused such a stir that operations paused—no one had seen ore this rich in decades, DeCaro said, not since the Alaska mines shut down. The smelter had to be recalibrated. Howard Knutson, who was helping fly out their ore, noticed that when Trotochau flashed a roll of bills, he always managed to drop a few. Knutson considered him a con man, "operating out of his hip pocket." The mining effort faltered. Trotochau left and people stopped getting paid. Trotochau's workers were known to track him down in the alleys of Anchorage's bar district to settle accounts. Knutson finally locked up a truck filled with jute bags of ore in Chitina and filed a lien over an unpaid air freight bill.

Meanwhile locals were relieved to see Trotochau make little progress on the one thing he'd promised: to raze Kennecott. They got just a glimpse, in 1961, when a crew dismantled the back half the general store, then attacked the roof of the fourteen-story concentration mill. Starting at the building's peak, where aerial trams once delivered ore from on high, workers peeled away boards and roof timbers, flinging them to the slopes below. It was a harder job than they expected, and having opened the historic structure and machinery to the ravages of rain and snow, they gave up. Thus it was left. For years after, visitors to Kennecott could look up in the sky, observe the stick silhouettes of empty rafters, and mutter the name, as a malediction against the planet's race to ruin: *Trotochau.*

Things could have been worse. Trotochau, back in Seattle and under business pressure, told Frank DeCaro to burn the whole place down—dismantle what they could and torch the rest. However, DeCaro stalled. He got the crew started on the roof of the mill building and saw to it that work crawled along until Trotochau gave up. "He didn't have the heart to comply," Kenny Smith wrote, years later, calling Frank DeCaro the man who saved Kennecott.

Before long, new owners came along and the tear-down mandate was forgotten. It was too late, though, for Kennecott's loveliest ruminative relic. Stephen Birch's honeymoon mansion had been gutted. The shell of the building still stood, but the copper hearth had been torn out by Trotochau's men, the fireplace shattered by picks and sledgehammers, the chalcocite mantel extracted, and the peacock ore shipped to Tacoma.

# 4

# Unaccompanied Miners

S OON AFTER YOUNG Jim Edwards moved to the valley, he found
work with the last of the independent copper prospectors.

Mineral exploration in Alaska was going corporate by the 1950s,
shifting to the search for uranium, silver, and, as always, gold—
though for all its busy sifting and grinding, the Chitina River valley
had never produced a lot of the latter. When it came to copper, the
better-financed explorers were mostly searching elsewhere for big
deposits of low-grade porphyry, like those of the open pits in Utah
that drew the Kennecott Copper Corporation south. Nabesna, on the
north side of the Wrangells, looked promising.

But a few individuals still hunted in the mountains for the enig-
matic kind of high-grade deposit that made Stephen Birch's fortune. The dream of another Kennecott would not die. Prospectors
followed the limestone-greenstone contact line over passes and
under glaciers, their vision tuned to inferences of cross folds and
fault lines that might yield the makings of the next Bonanza. Most

were looking for a quick hit: a hopeful discovery to sell to a bigger operation. In the case of a rangy Croat named Martin Radovan, however, the moment of hopeful discovery sustained him for a lifetime.

Jim Edwards flew to a gravel bar on the Chitistone River in February 1955 and hiked a mile up Glacier Creek on a freshly snowshoed trail to Martin Radovan's cabin. Over a dinner of wild sheep meat, potatoes, and fresh baked bread, Radovan explained how they would be climbing up into a high cirque every morning, four miles on snowshoes. After a storm, he said, it might take two days to stomp out a new trail.

Radovan spent decades probing these high mountain cliffs. One of his mining claims was known as the Binocular Prospect, because mining engineers once said binoculars were the only way anyone would ever get close. Not even European mountain climbers hired by Kennecott had been able to reach the oxidized green stains high above the Chitistone Canyon. Radovan got there by climbing straight up steps he'd chiseled in the rock. Occasionally he would visit his streambed claim at Dan Creek, the next valley down the Nizina River, to sluice enough gold to pay for his copper quest. His wife, Gussie, once lived in the Glacier Creek hut with him. She was the daughter of Norwegian immigrants from Seattle and met her hopeful and hard-working young husband in 1913, two years after the railroad was completed, when they both had jobs at a McCarthy roadhouse. Working in the big company mines was not for them. Radovan named one of his remote claims Augusta. After she died suddenly of a cerebral hemorrhage in 1944, he named his later claims after his animal friends—Bootsie the fox and a bear called Pongo Boy. Radovan's cabin yard was aflutter with camp robber jays, for whom he cooked up rice and raisins. He lived an austere life, except for a shot of whiskey every morning before climbing the ladder chiseled in the cliff.

Jim Edwards worked for Radovan on a narrow ledge high above a small glacier, cleaning out hand-dug "coyote holes" tight as animal dens. That first summer, Edwards was amused by the old man's bittersweet stories, how so-and-so didn't do something he should have. But in subsequent summers, when he heard the same stories recited word for word, Edwards concluded that muttering them in solitude must have been Radovan's principal entertainment during the long, dark winters.

Radovan was seventy-one the summer he showed Jim Edwards how to reach the Binocular Prospect. Edwards then led a visiting engineer and survey crew onto the face of the sheer cirque, following a ledge at the contact line between greenstone and limestone. They kicked scree off the ledge to make steps as the path narrowed to ten inches wide. Where the cliff face bulged, they had to crawl on hands and knees. In another place, a hanging glacier seven hundred feet above the trail dropped blocks of ice toward the ledge, "whistling like bombs, and they'd break into dust when they hit the trail," Edwards recalled. The survey crew made it past these obstacles and close enough to see, without binoculars, evidence of Radovan's work—his hand tools, a cotton mattress atop a boulder where he sometimes spent the night. But small rocks buzzing past like minie balls panicked the visiting engineer, who turned back without getting any closer to the putative ore body. Radovan was furious.

The old prospector kept working into his eighties and was in his nineties when he died in 1975, still expecting an assay to prove he had found a mountain of solid copper.

The other miners who paid wages to Edwards those first few years were looking for gold. "They were in their eighties and the country was rugged so you'd take a younger guy to pull you a little bit when you needed it. I did it because I had nothing better to do, and it was fun until I got into squabbles with them. These old guys were

Chitina valley prospector George Smock was the model for many Fred Machetanz paintings, including *High in the Wrangells* (1975).

cantankerous. Most prospectors live in a romantic dream world. All the mining deals I saw had something funny about them. My feeling was that they really didn't need to go prospecting, because they knew where the gold was. It was just a matter of convincing somebody to go get it, because they were already too old. And somebody who didn't see it there was pretty stupid.

"I remember setting up a stick on a post—we aligned that stick up perfectly with a nail, so that it would just point exactly where I was to go. It'd take me the whole damn day to climb up to that place, a dangerous steep cliff, climbing up through hard brush, scrambling, and finally get where he'd told you to just fill a sack with rock. You'd get it back down and he'd take a five-second look at it and throw it down in disgust, being angry at you for not coming down with a sack full of gold."

In 1956 Edwards found work with a bigger exploration outfit using a helicopter. As a consequence, he spent part of that summer working out of Chitina and living in the hotel. The former railroad town was barely surviving on its rough road connection to the Richardson Highway. The town's principal buildings were owned by Otto A. Nelson, a railroad surveyor and civil engineer who helped incorporate Chitina back in 1918, invested in its infrastructure, and good-naturedly presided over its decline, having made a tidy sum disposing of Kennecott Copper's local assets. The new "millionaire" poked fun at the ghost town tours of Kennecott by painting white cartoon ghosts on Chitina's old buildings. The hotel where Edwards stayed was called the Spook's Nook. A handout of eleven rules for guests included "Please do not stick hatpins through keyholes. A man lost an eye that way last year." Edwards was impressed by a sign in the dining room: "If you have nothing else to be thankful for, just look around and be glad you're not a cannibal."

When free time opened up that summer in Chitina, Jim Edwards decided to walk the old railroad route to the sea through the Copper River canyon. It was one hundred miles to Cordova. The impressive engineering feats of an earlier generation were fading like a dream from which the land was trying to awaken. But the tracks were still mostly in place. He crossed steep side canyons on rotting trestles held up by nothing except the steel rails. He came to one fast-moving tributary creek where he had to wade, lost his footing, and was swept into the icy murk of the big river. He could hear the hiss of glacial silt. He had been told the fine silt will fill your clothing and drag you under. He managed to loosen the shoulder straps on his pack and hold his rifle high and realized he was bobbing along like an ice cube, pleasantly enough atop his pack, which was buoyant from the plastic bags he'd sealed to keep his gear dry. He found himself gazing up at the mountain scenery. The current pushed him into an eddy on the far side of the river, where he was able to stand. He realized there was nobody between him and Canada on this side of the river, so he pushed back into the cold current and bobbed across to the railroad side, where he resumed following the abandoned tracks to Cordova.

Life in a ghost town had its entertainments. The tongue-and-groove floor of McCarthy's Arctic Brotherhood Hall was still stout enough to host occasional dances and movie nights. One summer Edwards helped a helicopter-exploration crew set up a bowling alley in the hall. They jacked up one end of the rotting foundation so the bowling ball would return automatically. Bowling continued until the Arctic Brotherhood Hall was torn apart for firewood by Ray Trotochau's crew.

By 1957, though, Jim Edwards had seen enough of McCarthy's bachelors. In addition to offering poor cannibal fare, they seemed unhappy and lonely. Whatever it was he was looking for in McCarthy, he concluded he would never find it if he had to keep eating his own cooking.

That summer he left to work at the Ruby Creek gold mine on the Seward Peninsula in northwest Alaska. Flying south from Nome at the end of the season, he spotted a pretty, young tourist from California on the plane. She was a tall brunette, with dark eyebrows and an avid gaze. He was too shy to say anything. At the airport in Anchorage they went their separate ways, to separate hotels. In their separate rooms they undressed and went to bed but neither could sleep. Restless, each dressed and went out to walk the city streets. Jim decided he wanted an ice cream cone, and there at the ice cream parlor he saw her again. This time he was braver. The next day Jim planned to go flying in his small plane and he asked if she wanted to come along. Maxine said yes.

⇐——⇒

A few of the solitary prospectors who drifted through the country in the 1950s and 1960s were figures with dogs and gold pans out of another century. Hard Calvinists hunting proof of their own self-worth, they worked remote claims and rarely appeared in town. Others were little more than con men, getting by on their knack for extracting grubstakes from hopeful investors (a skill useful at all levels of investment in the mining industry).

One practitioner of the mining arts who met both descriptions, depending who you talked to, was George Smock.

Old-timers described Smock as a mean sonofabitch, an outlaw and a loner whose snarling team of wolf hybrids kept strangers at a distance out in the woods. To feed his dogs, they said, he would shoot a moose, slit open the belly, and turn them loose. They said he broke the rules of the wilds—what kind of man mushes from one cabin to the next, during those war years when the valley emptied out, and takes the survival supplies left by miners and trappers? Smock carried a ketchup bottle of gasoline to start fires in deep subzero temperatures, and rubbed "coal oil"—kerosene—on his feet to treat frostbite. He spun yarns about coming to Alaska from Kentucky as a young man in 1911, though he didn't reach the Chitina Valley until World War II, at which time counter-yarns were spun about Smock having been escorted out of the Yukon by Royal Canadian Mounted Police after his trapping partner suspiciously failed to make it back to town. Later Smock made himself a home in a railroad cabin at Long Lake, where he shot grizzlies on sight and was said to have sued the government in the 1960s, claiming that underground atomic bomb tests on Amchitka in the Aleutians had made the lake's returning red salmon radioactive and caused his hair to fall out. He died in 1974.

But Smock had another side. He excelled at playing the colorful old prospector. He had a number of prospects, he told people, each one within about a year of paying out. Tourists in Chitina were drawn in by the dog team in his truck and a glimpse of some real gold nuggets. Some offered to invest. With his unruly white beard and granite squint, Smock certainly looked the part of a grizzled backwoodsman. So impressively grizzled, indeed, that the outlaw of the Chitina lives on today, in Alaska's museums and corporate board rooms, as the face of the state's idealized sourdough.

Fred Machetanz, the most famous Alaska painter of his generation, fell in love with Smock's face. Trained as an illustrator in the mode of the early twentieth-century artist Maxfield Parrish, Machetanz and his magic-hour oil landscapes had achieved true success by the mid-1960s, after decades of hard work and travel in the Alaska wilderness. He told an interviewer at the time that his goal was to portray the "romantic and authentic" aspect of the country. "Old Alaska is rapidly disappearing," Machetanz said, "and I want to preserve what I can before it too is gone. In a way I want to do for Alaska what Remington did for the Old West."

Maxfield Parrish had his wistful maidens, Frederic Remington his cowpokes, and Fred Machetanz would soon have scowling, bearded George Smock. Writing of himself in the third-person, the artist described meeting his archetype in the text for his 1971 portrait *Now Back in 98*:

> *The model for this lithograph was George Smock, a genuine 80-year-old Alaskan sourdough and prospector. The artist once saw a picture of George in a newspaper and thereafter for the next six years made every attempt to establish contact. Finally through a rather extraordinary coincidence, George was located and prevailed upon to come to our studio home, High Ridge. He drove into the clearing in his battered old pick-up decorated in a unique fashion with a magnificent set of moose horns atop the windshield. He climbed out and had scarcely introduced himself when he sat*

*down on a cut section of spruce beside the original cabin part of*
*our studio and without any prompting fell into this pose and began*
*recounting his life in Alaska. The moment he sat down the artist*
*wanted to do this picture of him and feels the title needs no further*
*explanation. George is a hard rock prospector and by the time this*
*lithograph was printed, was off staking a claim in the remote and*
*ruggedly lovely Chitina valley of Alaska.*

There is no indication that Machetanz knew the other side of his model's story. But at the time he wrote his description, the idealized sourdough was getting run out of the ruggedly lovely Chitina Valley by a posse led by his nemesis, the pilot and hunting guide Howard Knutson.

Knutson was another of the valley's outsized personalities, a man of intense friendships and enmities. He had been engaged in McCarthy since 1954 when he helped start the McCarthy Lodge. After breaking off that partnership with the butt of a rifle, he flew to Cordova to complain to Mudhole Smith and was offered an airline job, initially as a "baggage smasher" and later as a pilot flying the mail out of Chitina. He became a sheep-hunting guide and managed the hotel in Chitina, where his wife, Adina, was postmaster, and where they teamed up with Mudhole to buy the holdings of the aging Spook's Nook mogul O.A. Nelson.

He was also one of Alaska's best-known aerial wolf hunters, flying all over to collect the fifty-dollar bounties paid by the state. In 1968 he found himself at the center of controversy after he helped a filmmaker make a documentary on the wolf hunts, only to find out the finished film powerfully condemned the practice of shooting wolves from airplanes. It was better than using poison, Knutson protested. "The wolf is a truly magnificent, courageous, cunning, and vicious beast. He lives by his wits at all times," Knutson wrote in a letter to

Aerial wolf hunter and guide
Howard Knutson with his pet
wolf, Babe, 1969.

the *Anchorage Daily Times.* "The wolf is far too cunning to allow
himself to be hunted like any of our other game." As newspapers
filled with letters condemning the hunts, he brought home a wolf
pup and raised it into a gargantuan lap dog named Babe.

Knutson first got to know George Smock when he was running
the hotel in Chitina. Knutson warned his customers that Smock
was a con man, lest they agree to fill the colorful old-timer's sleds
or chartered planes with supplies for work at "secret mines" in the
Bremner River and Hanagita country.

The summer Smock met Machetanz, the old prospector had
hired four jobseekers, new to Alaska, to help him brush out a trail
and landing strip and get supplies to a remote cabin on claims in the
mountains south of McCarthy. Knutson warned the four of them,
including a father and son from Oklahoma, they'd never see a pay-
day. They flew out anyway. One month later three of them were back

in Chitina, discussing their escape with Knutson, tape recorder running. Conditions had been every bit as harsh as Knutson warned—canned sardines instead of the promised moose steaks, and Smock supervising clearing of a landing strip from a stump with his .30-06 rifle. Rather than work at gunpoint, three of them had fled into the wilderness. It took four days to get back, thrashing through brush to the Chitina River, then trying to cross on a spiked-together log raft that fell apart as soon as it spun into the big glacial cataract. They found themselves stranded on a gravel bar. The two younger men made it across the river by clinging to floating logs, leaving the father on the island. They hiked out to Chitina over several hot days and sent a helicopter back for the older man. The gravel bar where he was found had been dry at night, so he could sleep, but calf-deep in glacial meltwater every sunny afternoon when the river rose. In the taped session, the three made plans to rescue the fourth, who had stayed behind because he felt sorry for Smock. They discussed how many guns they should bring to deal with Smock's nine dogs and the man himself, who, they concluded, could be dangerous because he had "nothing to lose."

The fourth worker was rescued by float plane without incident. George Smock departed the remote camp soon after. Once he was gone, Knutson landed his plane on the nearby lake, determined to put Alaska's iconic sourdough out of business before somebody got killed. Knutson helped himself to dogfood from Smock's log cache, then hiked three miles to Smock's cabin. Finding no dynamite, a box of blasting caps would have to do. He made a blazing fire in the stove and threw in the box and walked out the door. Knutson was nearly back to the lake when he heard the explosion. But he saw no smoke and taking off realized the blast simply blew the fire out. The little cabin survived. Knutson didn't feel like walking all the way back to try again.

Jim Edwards and Howard Knutson worked in the mining trade together after Ray Trotochau sold the Kennecott property in 1962 to a Seattle businessman and an engineering-savvy oil worker. The price was reported at $6,000, plus some portion of the junk dealer's accrued debts. The new owners flew back and forth from Chitina with Knutson, who wanted to get in on the deal. And once in, Knutson brought in a pair of hunters he knew, both of them Anchorage dentists intrigued by that cavity in the mountain.

Thus began the most ambitious mining effort of the post-industrial period. The junk man with his hand-picking operation had not been thinking big enough, Knutson believed. The new outfit, calling themselves Consolidated Wrangell, took out bank loans and brought in earthmoving equipment, a sorting conveyor belt, an ore crusher, and a flotation separator. A key step was getting out from under the US price controls and export limits of the 1960s. Knutson said a special act of Congress, steered through by the new state's two senators, Bartlett and Gruening, let him double his price by exporting ore through Vancouver to Japan. He also benefitted from a good freight-haul rate on the Alaska Highway. Lynden Transport, a trucking firm that served Alaska out of Seattle, liked the ballast for its empty backhauls over a thousand miles of gravel road. One problem remained: getting big volumes of ore from McCarthy to the road-head in Chitina. Knutson needed a better airstrip.

Gold miners at Dan Creek, across the Nizina, didn't face such transportation problems. They could carry their gold to town in their pockets. The Nizina creeks also produced heavy little nuggets of pure native copper, which could be polished from their natural scuzzy green to gleam like kitchen pots. This was the source of the element that gave the river and the country its name. The Indigenous Ahtna fashioned the native copper into knife blades. Such nuggets didn't exist in modern commercial quantities, however, so miners collected them in jars as souvenirs—but also used them as indicators showing where heavier gold was likely to settle.

One Dan Creek gold miner in the 1950s did face a transportation dilemma when he dug up a boulder of pure native copper the size of a bathtub. His partners told him to get it to Anchorage to help sell stock in their mine. The copper nugget weighed nearly three tons, which happened to be the payload of a thirty-two-passenger DC-3. Mudhole Smith sent one of his planes to the Nizina airstrip with seats and floorboards removed. The pilot and miners calculated the tail-dragger's exact center of gravity and loaded the nugget with a block and tackle. They lashed it to the frame of the fuselage. Flying over the mountains, the pilot struggled to keep the airplane trim. The nose would sink until the pilot pointed the plane skyward and then the tail would drag him down. The DC-3 bucked all the way to Anchorage but landed safely. The nugget ended up at the log cabin visitor center in downtown Anchorage, and eventually at the University of Alaska museum in Fairbanks.

The original McCarthy Creek airstrip, built on a bluff like so many Cessna-sized runways in these mountains, was too short for big planes and exposed to prevailing crosswinds. The May Creek airstrip was bigger but too far away, over a road rough, with the Nizina River crossings ready to give out at any time.

In early 1965 Knutson took off from the McCarthy Creek strip in his Super Cub and flung rolls of toilet paper to mark a stretch of trees and clearings above town, near an abandoned boom-era outpost called Blackburn, where the valley floor starts climbing to

Kennecott. He tried to sort out who owned the land thus flagged, never an easy task in a ghost town. The state had set aside $15,000 in planning money for a McCarthy airport. Knutson convinced the state to give him the planning money to buy gas. The miners had walked and pulled their heavy equipment sixty miles from Chitina that spring before breakup, a gruesome struggle, though at least there were no longer rails in the way. With early-summer snow still shrouding Bonanza Ridge, they carved out a 3,500-foot airfield on the stony glacial plain and smoothed the runway with mine tailings trucked down from Kennecott. Because they ran out of gas, the new airfield's only flaw was an unnerving hump in the middle, which prevented planes at one end from seeing planes at the other—a problem fixed by the state thirty years later.

With the new airfield ready, Consolidated Wrangell got to work at Kennecott. They painted their equipment pale green, distinct from the barn-red and white trim of the old company buildings. Jim Edwards, who went to work for Knutson in 1965, extended Trotochau's switchback road to the slide area at Bonanza Mine. He climbed above the glory hole in a D-7 Cat to scrape ore off a ridge so narrow that when he pivoted, the front and back of the bulldozer hung over thin air.

The miners scratched copper from the surface piles, where they found a small untouched surface vein and snuck into the mine openings to scour out ore. Descending the mountain's 17 percent grade in heavily loaded dump trucks, Edwards held the door open in case the brakes failed. At one point, he lost a front-end loader off a cliff: Parked on the road below the mine, its engine was left running because the starter was faulty, and its bucket was dug into gravel because there was no emergency brake. The hydraulics eventually bled off, and the loader let loose, rolling to the first switchback as

Consolidated Wrangell working the ore left behind at Bonanza Mine, late 1960s.

Edwards jumped out of the way and watched it disappear over the edge.

The miners helped themselves to the empty oil drums lying everywhere. They loaded them with ore and welded them shut, so they could be moved easily and stored without fear of pilfering. The first flight from the new airfield, heavy with ore drums, was unexpectedly thrilling, according to Knutson and his partners. They said the aircraft was a boxy late-1940s vintage troop-transport glider outfitted with two engines. The YC-122 wallowed down the runway with its heavy load and barely cleared the trees. The valley fell away toward the town of McCarthy and so did the airplane. The plane couldn't gain altitude so it followed the canyons of the Kennicott and Nizina and Chitina Rivers. Knutson sat next to the pilot he'd hired for the operation. The pilot complained that the nose was too heavy and said the plane would fly better next time with two more barrels in the rear. He asked Knutson to watch for shallow lakes in case they needed to set down.

The bulk of the ore was hauled out that fall by Cordova Airlines on a DC-3, which flew consecutive loads to Chitina over several days. The ore-ferrying ended with the new airfield's first crash, when the DC-3 sliced its left tire on a rock as it landed. The plane pulled left, the propeller on the left-wing engine nicked the runway, the left wing caught a gravel berm, and the plane pitched off the airstrip and down into the trees. No one was hurt. Knutson and Kenny Smith flew to Chitina to retrieve a heavy rope that was being used for a ski lift, and a bulldozer towed the DC-3 back to the runway. A maintenance crew showed up two days later, with spare tires, propellers, and a gear box nose case and repaired the damaged plane enough to fly it back to Anchorage.

The 1965 mining operation was not profitable, and that winter the ore crusher at the Bonanza Mine was itself crushed by an avalanche. Consolidated Wrangell decided to retreat down the mountain and set up future processing by the gravity mill.

As the big operation paused in 1966, a smaller family venture got underway at the Bonanza. Alongside a few hired men, the two Knutson daughters, aged nine and ten, were deployed to pick up chunks of blue azurite and green malachite and especially heavy gray-green chalcocite. The rocks were still everywhere—you could work on a small pile all morning. Gayle, the oldest, found the biggest chunk that summer: a hundred-pound chalcocite boulder that had to be rolled down the scree to the processing belt.

Jim Edwards quit in a tiff over wages but not before getting a chance to marvel at the work ethic of the girls' mother, Adina. The first time Jim took Maxine to McCarthy, they spotted Adina Knutson at the Chitina airport. A short, powerfully built woman, Adina was bundled in heavy clothes and big boots and unloading boulders from the back of a truck. "I sure hope I'm not going to look like that as an Alaskan woman," Maxine said with a smile. The two women later became friends.

Edwards recalled with admiration Adina Knutson's management of the Bonanza operation: "Adina could outwork about six guys—with her two daughters, they could outwork ten men," he said. She was the fastest at sorting ore on the conveyor belt, "and then the minute they blew the whistle for noon, the guys would all kinda relax and say, 'Oh God I'm glad it's lunch time, I'm hungry, tired,' but Adina would jump off and run over there where a bearing had gone out and grease the bearing, shut off the machine, grab a gunny sack that was half full of ore and another empty one and start running up the hill to the bunkhouse, throwing ore into the sack as she went. She'd have it full by the time she got to the bunkhouse usually, tear inside and by the time the guys walked up to the bunkhouse she'd have a hot lunch prepared for them. And while the guys were finishing up their meal she'd be back out running around that hillside with a damn sack filling it up with ore. These sacks weigh seventy pounds when they're full, and it's a steep hill, and she'd be right back there on that belt, had the machine all started up and going before the guys got back from lunch. That was the way the whole system worked."

Modest though it was, the hand-sorting operation attracted the attention of lawyers for the Kennecott Copper Corporation, who accused Knutson and his dentist friends of stealing the company's ore. Knutson argued that ore spilled onto the ground was neither ore from the mine nor mine tailings, which were restricted under the land deed. He flew to Los Angeles in 1966 to meet with the lawyers, who agreed to a lease giving the international mining giant 10 percent of any Consolidated Wrangell revenue in the future. It was a better deal than the lawyers would get from Chile, where Kennecott had invested its Alaska profits, only now to have its thriving copper mines threatened with nationalization. While the lawyers dickered with Knutson over spilled malachite, hundreds of millions of dollars were at stake in South America. Accusations leveled by Chilean politicians echoed old attacks on the Alaska Syndicate: the owners had taken a fortune out of the country and left nothing behind. Full nationalization of the mine was finally enacted, helping precipitate a violent reactionary coup in 1973 backed by the Central Intelligence Agency. But even with the Socialists dead or in jail, the new military dictatorship never gave Kennecott its Chilean mine back.

Consolidated Wrangell geared up for another big push in 1967. This time they brought in short-bed dump trucks in partnership with Lynden Transport, the regional trucking company. The company owner's two young sons were among the drivers who braved the three-mile descent from the Bonanza that summer. The scream of their compression brakes could be heard five miles down the valley in McCarthy. The ore processing equipment—conveyor belt and screens and jig separator—were moved down the mountain. The miners built a dump-truck chute behind the top of the mill, where Trotochau had torn off the roof, to direct ore to the separators below. To make way for its sorting and loading operation, the miners bulldozed the original Kennecott superintendent's home and a three-story staff house where nurses and female office staff once lived upstairs, on a floor called No Man's Land.

Mudhole Smith's tourist attractions were in the way. The ghost mansion of Stephen Birch, already stripped by Trotochau, was consigned to a bonfire of clear fir boards, so trucks full of ore would have room to turn around. Human persistence also required burning down the bunkhouse up at the Bonanza, already half-capsized by gravity, to get at ore beneath the floorboards. One other building disappeared, but by accident: a trackside electrician's barn burned when a friend's kid, hired as a favor, poured gasoline into a hot running generator.

It was all for naught. Heavy rains in the summer of 1967 made the switchback road too dangerous. Even when it was dry, the easy pickings appeared to be too scarce, the price of copper too low, and the cost of transportation too high: half the expense of getting the ore to Vancouver was incurred flying it sixty miles to Chitina. Howard Knutson and his investors insisted, years later, they managed to pay off their equipment loans and Trotochau's debts. The Bonanza Mine "nearly broke the company," Lynden Transport said in a corporate history, which documents the company's prosperous recovery, as a major intermodal transport firm having nothing to do with McCarthy, in the pipeline era to come.

Except for one secretive effort six years later, which resulted in miners going briefly to jail, copper extraction at Kennecott thus ended with a shrug. But the investors in Consolidated Wrangell had been left with a valuable asset. They paid no property taxes on three thousand scenic acres in rural Alaska, where private land was rare. The forty-ninth state had been promised huge tracts of federal land, but Interior Secretary Stewart Udall had just imposed a massive land freeze. The state would get nothing until Native land claims were settled. Multinational oil companies, having surpassed Alaska's mining industry in political clout, had found oil deposits at Prudhoe Bay, whose scale were reminiscent of the copper lodes of Kennecott. Clearing title to the right-of-way for a pipeline across the state was going to require resolving all the other land-use conflicts. Conservationists wanted to be part of any political carving-up of Alaska. Meanwhile a new generation of settlers was headed north, looking for a place to escape the modern world.

All these outside forces would soon be brought to bear on the Wrangell Mountains. From now on, land ownership in Alaska would matter. The years of squatting in someone else's ruins were nearly over.

# 5

# The Hippie Hole

T HE FIRST THING Loy and Curtis Green noticed about McCarthy when they climbed out of the plane in 1967 was the sky—a dark preindustrial blue above the white peaks.

And the quiet. In Chitina, where they had lived the previous few years, a private generator ran twenty-four hours a day. To the Green brothers, it had been a noisy reminder of the two-car-garage civilization they had fled in one of the first waves of 1960s restlessness to reach the Wrangells.

Loy and Curtis were dharma bums from Colorado who carried copies of Thoreau and Whitman to the end of the road in Chitina. Their first job there was with Neil Finnesand, a Norwegian in his eighties who came into the country before the railroad. Despite freezing off two toes delivering the US mail to McCarthy by dogsled, the old Norwegian could still out-hump the brothers as they packed into his silver claim at Spirit Mountain. He insisted his claim was not yet "played out" and neither was he.

On the day the Greens flew to McCarthy, Fred Potts was their pilot. Potts came from wealth in Los Angeles and had once explored Afghanistan and lingered in the sands of Tangier with William Burroughs and Paul Bowles. Fred's wife, Dolly, was a sharp-cheekboned beauty who caused a stir in Chitina with her knee-high leather high-heeled boots, miniskirt, and holstered .44 Magnum. Her eyelids were tattooed with eye shadow. People said Dolly Potts had once appeared, smiling on a swing, on a Coca Cola poster. Fred was the chief pilot for FEPCo Aviation (which stood for Fred E. Potts). The schedule was limited: FEPCo generally flew only in early morning, before the mountain day breezes picked up. Much of his time was devoted to writing a critical study of classical music. Research for this, according to Curtis Green, consisted of playing an LP of Beethoven's Sixth Symphony, the first and second movements, over and over, while he made bullets. Every afternoon, when he had enough bullets, he stopped the music and stepped outside with his pistol for target practice.

The Greens were drawn to McCarthy by an employment offer from Gordon Burdick, a pot-smoking Cat skinner and raconteur who had remained in McCarthy after the departure of his sponsor, Ray Trotochau. Burdick had been a marine and fought in the Pacific and played basketball for Seattle Pacific College. Ever since leading the nuclear bomb scientists on their tour of the Bonanza Mine, he had been second-guessing the pillar-retreat strategy of Kennecott's engineers, convinced he could take out every other pure-copper-ore column left behind in the mines without the roof collapsing on him.

Burdick stayed busy doing annual assessment work on unpatented mining claims staked all over the country. He hired the Greens to help him reopen the wagon road up McCarthy Creek to the Nicolai claim, named for the Ahtna chief who pointed it out to prospectors. It wasn't a paying job, per se, as Curtis Green recalled in an unpublished memoir—more a promise of sharing in untold future riches.

Progress up McCarthy Creek on a little Caterpillar D-2 was slow, Curtis recalled. Mornings started around ten o'clock with strong coffee in town at the hardware store. Presiding beside a Queen Monarch chrome-and-enamel cookstove taken from the superintendent's house in Kennecott, Burdick rapped with Loy and Curtis about gold prices and the Vietnam war while his wife, Frieda, whose savings had bankrolled the mining venture, pushed him sarcastically to get to work. She called him Action Jackson. "Frieda would be bustling about, making lunch, in and out of the kitchen, pushing Gordon to get a move on," Curtis wrote. "The harder she pushed, the more he stalled."

"Basically Gordon made his living here for twenty-five years by talking. He never at any time produced anything," Jim Edwards later recalled. "Gordon mined a fraction up at the Jumbo, and at the Green Butte for a lot of years. Mined. I say mined. He was not really a prospector and not really a miner. He could get on a Cat and spend five years building a road that was already there to someplace that he didn't need to go to. He built that road up McCarthy Creek to Green Butte more or less several times over a fifteen-year period and never did have the road open. He got a series of backers that would put up money for two–three years, because he convinced them he'd make a lot of money."

The Nicolai claim had been staked and dismissed by earlier prospectors, and it wasn't until July that Loy and Curtis hiked up to the ridge with Burdick to see the deposit for themselves. With enough vision, or enough weed, it was possible to imagine a time-eroded streak of copper extending east from Bonanza Ridge and the Mother Lode Mine, rainbowing across the sky before reappearing across the valley in the Green Butte and Nicolai bluffs. Burdick tapped around with his hammer at the Nicolai, however, and declared the copper vein "pinched out." The campfire was unusually silent that night, but in the morning the boss declared it would be on to the Green Butte! Burdick, Curtis wrote, was a man who needed an El Dorado. "He was an interesting character," Jim Edwards said, "if you could detach yourself from the fact that he owed you money."

The Green brothers eventually bowed out, finishing the summer working for Consolidated Wrangell. In early winter, however, they quit and went back to the deserted Green Butte Mine, which they had glimpsed with Burdick. They settled into an old two-story log dormitory, patched a few leaks, and this became their home.

◄——►

That same summer of 1967, Les and Flo Hegland arrived in McCarthy. They were in their forties and though they shared a desire to plant themselves far from city life, they were not countercultural like the Green brothers. Industrious, religious, gregarious, abstemious, they hailed from small towns on the North Dakota plains. They bought a small frame house in town—the one Mudhole Smith once rented from Kate Kennedy, and later, the one where the Aikens made their bathtub gin. The Heglands bought it from Cal Aiken, a Cordova fisherman who later drowned in surf on the Bering River flats. The Heglands' ten-year-old daughter, Janet, was told that Aiken decided to sell after he got chased up a tree by an angry cow moose and froze his lungs, at twenty-below, waiting for it to leave.

The Heglands secured one of the only paying jobs in town, taking measurements for the weather service. They reported the data several times a day over a single-sideband radio. Les Hegland supplemented that income by trapping furs. Flo Hegland was a painter and a collector of antiques. After they flew a bright green Willys Army Jeep into McCarthy, they got in the habit of driving up to the new airfield to meet every plane. They would sort the weekly mail and hold it until people dropped by. In winter, if warm chinook winds brought rain and frozen ruts to the snowy runway, Kenny Smith's brother, Wayne, skipped the landing and air-dropped mailbags directly into the Heglands' yard. Handling the mail was a free, neighborly service, as was hosting nondenominational religious services in their living room. Both roles would continue until the 1983 shootings.

When they first moved to the ghost town, Janet Hegland pestered her parents with questions about other people showing up. She couldn't understand why there were so many empty buildings. They did have a few summer neighbors. Molly Gilmore, who had grown up in McCarthy long ago and was once queen of the Fourth of July parade, moved back in 1960 with her husband, Tom, still talking about how the Kennecott mines might reopen. But the Gilmores, and a few others, left each year after the beautiful colors of September.

That first year in McCarthy, Thanksgiving dinner in town consisted of the Heglands, Loy and Curtis Green, and the young family of Jim and Maxine Edwards. The table fare consisted of moose, bear, and mountain goat.

"Turkey, at a dollar a pound, was too rich for us," Maxine Edwards wrote in a letter to her aunt and uncle, "and this was better anyhoo."

⇐——⇒

Maxine Krussow married the man from the ice cream parlor before she ever saw where he lived. Jim Edwards and Maxine were wed at her mom's place in California. The next year they moved to the ghost town in Alaska. By 1967, after nearly a decade in the north, she was deeply settled into wilderness living, with its improvisations and drawn-out logistics and favors that take days to bestow. Jim had wooed her with a promise to carry two buckets of bathwater

Jim and Maxine Edwards, with their children Shelly and Steve, on the lawn of their house in McCarthy, 1966.

every day from the creek. By 1967 he had rigged a waterwheel in Clear Creek that pumped a steady trickle into a water tower made of welded fuel drums. This allowed them to have an indoor flush toilet and also generated a few light bulbs' worth of electricity. Having a family had given Jim a new pastime: inventing home conveniences.

They lived right in town, in a small house next to the McCarthy Lodge, with their two children, Steve and Shelly. Maxine tended a huge vegetable garden on the back lot and flower boxes behind a white picket fence in front. When Jim took Maxine into the claustrophobic tunnels of the Bonanza Mine, she said the frozen crystals on the walls looked like ice flowers. The lodge next door had struggled after the end of the Kennecott tours and for a few years in the late 1960s shut down altogether—a development that suited Jim fine. The town was so quiet, he wrote, he could hear the mail plane coming from fifteen miles away. He ran a single wire from town up the bluff to a crank box at the old airstrip, so any visiting pilot could ring a bell in the house for fuel or mechanical help.

Though he felt the Heglands' job reporting McCarthy's weather to the world was adding unnecessarily to the national debt, Jim Edwards got along well enough with their few neighbors, thanks in part to Maxine's kindness. She had been twenty-seven when Jim spotted her on the flight back from Nome. At that time she was working as a Pan Am flight attendant and using the privileges to travel extensively. Her mother was an indomitable German immigrant who raised Maxine in California as a single mom. A few years after Maxine settled in McCarthy, her mother came to visit. Jim Edwards was flying for Chitina Air Service that summer. His schedule was tight, and he asked Wayne Smith, his fellow pilot, to fly her up the Copper River canyon from Cordova. Jim would meet them halfway. Wayne landed the elderly lady on the Bremner River bar, a wide sandy flat often visited by coastal grizzlies seeking salmon. Jim will be along any minute, her pilot said, and took off. Jim was late and in a panic as he flew around a bend in the canyon and saw his mother-in-law in the distance, standing alone on the glacial sands with a red dress and straw purse like she was waiting for a city cab.

In the winter of 1961, right after his son was born, Jim flew out to Chitina to pick up a bulldozer and a load of supplies and a surprise present for his wife: her 1949 Chevy DeLuxe sedan, which they had driven from California as far as the highway could get them.

There was no road to McCarthy at that time. The pale-green Chevy had made it to the end of the Edgerton Highway, where it

Maxine Edwards managed a big garden behind the McCarthy Lodge. Elevated drums for irrigation were filled by a waterwheel in Clear Creek.

was parked in Chitina alongside an old D-4 cable-blade dozer with a slippery clutch that Jim had bought with a small inheritance. He proceeded to make the last journey from Chitina to McCarthy before the abandoned railroad tracks were torn out.

Edwards salvaged decking and logs from the washed-out railroad bridge and built a sled, on which he loaded the Chevy DeLuxe and drums of extra fuel. He crossed the frozen Copper River easily, dragging the sled behind the D-4, but the first half mile up the river bluff on the far side took a full day. He had to cut a sidehill trail with pick and shovel. Once he gained the elevation of the old tracks, he had just enough room between the rails to drive the Cat. Where the bed was washed out and tracks hung in the air he had to stop and chainsaw up some logs, building a ramp to climb out over the rails and detour through the brush. Some places this happened every few hundred yards, so his progress east toward McCarthy was slow. Broken rails stopped him, but he found that half a stick of dynamite would shatter the iron so he could proceed. It was so cold he kept the dozer running all night and his canned food froze hard as glass. At Chokosna the front track system broke. He walked twenty-five miles back to Chitina, passing multiple campsites in a single day's hike. He flew his plane to Anchorage, bought a replacement part, airdropped the part near the bulldozer, and landed on a nearby lake on skis. Resuming the bulldozer journey, he built snow bridges across ravines and crossed the Gilahina Canyon on a high trestle that buckled but did not give way. Finally he reached the frozen Kennicott River and presented Maxine with her Chevy, comprehensively dented but mechanically sound. He had traveled sixty miles in thirty-seven days.

Two winters later, he made that trip in reverse, this time with Maxine and two small children. The family wanted to visit Anchorage before the holidays. Most of the tracks had been pulled out for scrap since his last journey, leaving a rough roadbed with only a few miles at Long Lake still blocked by rails. He assembled a bulldozer-pulled train of sleds and the Chevy, where his family was kept warm by a woodstove in the back seat, stovepipe out the window. By the end of the three-day journey, the woodstove, D-4 Cat, Chevy, a truck, an airplane body, and an empty welding-oxygen cylinder were scattered along the route, casualties of one mishap after another, to be retrieved on the way home. After sliding on their butts down the snowy Copper River bluffs with their luggage and crossing the ice on foot, pulling three hundred pounds of frozen moose quarters on a sled, the family borrowed a pickup truck and made it safely to Anchorage. Edwards jauntily recounted the long tale in the *Alaska Sportsman* magazine under the title "A Christmas Shopping Trip."

⬥

With the tracks gone, plans were being drawn up for a railbed highway to McCarthy. The mere rumor of such a route stirred up the
community. People began to talk about McCarthy as if it had a
future, not just a past. That meant something to fight over. Local
feuds began to sort out along the lines of the Nixon-era culture wars.

In the summer of 1969, the empty McCarthy Lodge was purchased
by a barrel-chested bartender named Winnie Darkow, who was running the Drop Inn bar in Fairbanks. He flew down to look at the place
in his Piper Cherokee with his wife, Barbara, and two children. On the
flight home, he called for a vote on moving to McCarthy and every
hand shot up except his. "He said, 'This is the last time we're going to
do anything democratic in this family,'" Barbara Darkow later recalled.

Winnie Darkow and his teenage son, Adrian, loaded supplies into
a blue army-surplus ambulance and drove the rough, boggy route
to McCarthy in winter, crossing the Copper River on ice and laying
down their own boards to pass over the bridge above the Kuskulana
River gorge. The family soon had the lodge open to serve fly-in mineral exploration crews, visiting government employees, and hunters.

Darkow was a big believer in progress. The lodge owner kept
the runway clear of winter snow by pulling a broken-down grader
behind the blue ambulance. Darkow's renovating energies offended
Curtis and Loy Green, who preferred watching civilization recede.
Curtis wrote that he and the man with the moniker of a Dickens vil-
lain instantly recognized one another as natural enemies.

*I saw him as one of those loud and aggressive types that the anony-
mous author of The Desiderata, that 17th century piece of wisdom
that was so popular in certain circles at the time, advised one to
avoid as being vexatious to the spirit. But not merely vexatious—*

*something more sinister than that. A money-grubbing devotee of Mammon come to despoil Shangri-la and shape its future in his own image; one for whom the sweetest sound in all creation was the ring of his cash register opening its maw to receive yet another green-backed Yankee dollar from the fat wallet of one of the endless tourists that would soon be passing thru his portals. And not just in the summer time either. No, for in "Winnie World" even the winters would no longer be sacrosanct, for our quiet little village was to become a Mecca for recreational snow mobilers racing unobstructed throughout the country side, shattering the primeval silence with a ratcheting snarl of nerve-numbing noise from the netherworld.*

For his part, Winnie Darkow believed he could see through the Green brothers' artistic pretensions to their essential ne'er-do-well natures and made sure they lost their jobs as winter caretakers at Kennecott. Curtis concluded that Consolidated Wrangell owner Howard Knutson had been enlisted by Darkow to fight "against the environmentalist/hippie/Commie threat, of which we were so obviously a part."

Darkow was forming his own interest in the Kennecott workings. The Erie Mine, halfway up a cliff, was the most inaccessible of Kennecott's portals, left untouched by the surface-mining efforts of Consolidated Wrangell. There had been a flurry of activity at the Erie in the summer of 1938, the year the mines closed, over a last-minute find of a copper vein. In the summer of 1973, Darkow, his son, and a hunting guide named Guy George, who would later achieve local fame by killing a charging grizzly with an ice axe, set out with pick axes to quarry an exposed seam of chalcocite at the Erie. They claimed to have studied the records and determined the plug of copper they were mining had never been properly surveyed and claimed, so they saw no need to be secretive—the operation involved a lot of dynamite and a helicopter, rented for an afternoon, to ferry ore bags down from the cliff.

The courts would rule otherwise. The Kennecott Copper Corporation, deeply engaged by this time in international litigation over expropriation of its $300 million Chilean copper mine, took time to go after the Erie Mine thieves as well. The chalcocite helicoptered down from the cliffs was confiscated. Adrian Darkow and his father spent a few hours getting booked and released from the Anchorage jail. Adrian said later it appeared Gordon Burdick turned them in, after they rejected his bid to join them. The caper was settled with the help of Howard Knutson, who agreed to buy the purloined ore (less than a truckload) at auction, ship it to the Tacoma smelter, and pay Kennecott a fee. Knutson received a premium in Tacoma, where the smelter cleaned its kiln with the intense heat generated for the high-grade ore. He reimbursed the miners for their expenses, after taking something off the top for his troubles.

Meanwhile the environmentalist/hippie/Commie threat had established a beachhead deep in the Wrangells, where the Chitistone River flows into the headwaters of the Nizina. Spruce Point had once been an overnight roadhouse on the trail up the Nizina and over a pass to the Chisana gold fields. The valley's first back-to-the-land commune flourished in an old cabin there in the summer of 1970, as the chief pilot for FEPCo Aviation hosted a group gathered around a "prophetic type" named Loping Bear, who retained his name even after Dolly Potts killed a grizzly near the camp with her bear pistol. According to Curtis Green, the site was inauspicious for settlement because Fred Potts didn't trust the water and insisted on hauling five-gallon jugs in his plane from Anchorage, more than two hundred miles away. Before long, Dolly and the rest of the commune moved away, leaving a young long-legged mate for Fred who had taken the name Belphagore, after Fred's favorite horse.

Not long after, Frieda Burdick gave up on her investment in Gordon and moved out, declaring her husband "so crooked he had to screw his pants on in the morning."

In 1971 long-haired college students arrived, notebooks in hand, deployed to the Wrangells by an environmental studies program at the University of California, Santa Cruz. But it was the arrival that spring of an outlaw who called himself Raven, and the excavation of the hippie hole, that marked McCarthy's coming of age as a 1960s-culture end-of-the-road town.

⊂—⊃

Raven wore a feather in his black cowboy hat and decorated his .44 Magnum holster with a beaded peace symbol. Two skulls, dug out of the McCarthy Cemetery, sat on a table by his bed, with candles burning in the eye sockets.

His real name was Ron Cole, though nobody called him that. He was a marine vet in his thirties, who had gone to Korea as a teenager, slight but tough, with a prominent Fu Manchu mustache. In the spring of 1971, he showed up in McCarthy with a pigtailed girlfriend barely out of her teens, a new buddy named Jim, and several hundred marijuana starts. Young Jim had just inherited land in McCarthy and received a nice insurance settlement. Passing fat joints around the hardware store with Loy, Curtis, and Gordon Burdick, Raven laid out his plans for Jim's money: a five-story resort lodge built out of logs, with a full basement devoted to year-round cultivation of top-quality weed. He said pot was practically legal in the libertarian north (though the eventual Alaska Supreme Court decision allowing personal consumption of marijuana was still a few years away). And McCarthy had a long and respected speakeasy tradition.

Les and Flo Hegland took an immediate dislike to Raven, who was making a strong impression on their fourteen-year-old daughter.

A drug dealer known as Raven stole two human skulls from the town cemetery.

But at first, with hundred-dollar bills from the insurance settlement fluttering around town, there were few complaints. Loy Green recalled that Winnie Darkow, the town's leading law-and-order advocate, happily accepted Raven's money while serving as his unlicensed air taxi, flying the entrepreneur back and forth to his truck at Chitina.

Gordon Burdick used his bulldozer to dig out the foundation for the marijuana lodge. The hole had to be deep enough to support a log structure of several stories. Curtis noted drolly that this was the only foundation work Burdick ever undertook—and it was for someone else's castle in the air.

Jim and Maxine Edwards lived across the street and observed that the "hippie hole," as they dubbed it, was being excavated on a lot the hippies didn't own. Jim Edwards, who kept his hair cropped short, not as political commentary but so it could be cleaned with a wash cloth, looked on the new developments with bemusement rather than horror.

"There was a guy sitting out front of a tent with an Indian-type headband around his head and smoking marijuana, two young girls scurrying around taking care of his needs—he was just looking at the sunshine," Edwards recalled. "This was in the days when people had general resistance to 'hippies.' I would go to Cordova or somewhere and continually meet somebody who'd say 'Do you got any hippies out there?' as if it were some disgusting thing that might have happened to us like the plague descending on McCarthy."

Eventually Raven and Darkow had a falling-out, and the law was waiting to pounce. They had been watching Ron Cole since his drug-dealing days in Cordova. A uniformed state trooper flew to McCarthy with a couple of plainclothesmen and hauled Cole back to town for an expired driver's license and a few parking tickets. By the time he got back to McCarthy, his buddy Jim had split for South America, leaving an empty hippie hole in the middle of town.

Raven told young Janet Hegland he was high on mescaline when he dug up the skulls in the graveyard. He now turned his menacing energies to pilfering old implements from other buildings as he guarded his marijuana plants. The supervisor of the Santa Cruz college program recalled an afternoon at the hardware store when two earnest undergraduates posed questions about modern-day mining practices to a gregarious and obviously stoned Gordon Burdick, while Raven glared out the window behind a nearby curtain with a rifle across his lap.

Trouble was brewing and everybody seemed in the mood. Darkow played sheriff and kept Les Hegland on edge about what the hippies might pull next. Les yelled at Jim Edwards for transporting Raven on the mail plane. Jim replied he was a common carrier open to all. "Les has lost his head," Edwards wrote. "I guess he has been hating so much it has ate him up."

Things boiled over in late summer when Raven's fourteen-year-old daughter came to visit. Raven approached Darkow in the street, gun in beaded holster, and said, "Okay, Winnie, it's just you and I." Flo Hegland called the troopers about six-foot-tall pot plants her husband reported stumbling upon. A lodge employee, stopping by the Hegland house to pick up mail, overheard Flo's radio call, and warned Raven, who slipped out of the hardware store with his daughter and disappeared up McCarthy Creek.

The troopers waited in town for a day before departing with Raven's girlfriend and his pot plants. A vigilante committee was formed by Darkow, but the small posse, in the blue ambulance, decided not to follow Raven into the ambush zone of the steep-walled McCarthy Creek valley.

Days later, participants in the Santa Cruz program were hiking near the Bonanza above Kennecott when they spotted Raven and his daughter coming over the knife-edged ridge. The two had ascended a sheer face on the opposite side, above the old Mother Lode Mine. The students let out a yodel in greeting. Raven waved his rifle, later telling them it was good that he recognized the yodel or he might have shot. He was carrying a transistor radio to listen for a message from his lawyer on Caribou Clatters, the bush-message show on Glennallen's AM station.

"He spent about two weeks up there without food, really roughing it," Loy recalled later. "Then he made his way clear around the back of McCarthy Creek, skirting the glacier and coming into McCarthy the back way." People met that night at the hardware store to hatch a plan. They didn't support Raven's drug lifestyle, they said, but at least he wasn't a hypocrite. "He was desperate," Loy said. "It was fall of the year and it was really getting cold. We figured we can't have him staying here, somebody was going to get killed. Not by Raven, but by the posse. They were the dangerous ones."

Loy put Raven's daughter, disguised as a Santa Cruz student, on the mail plane. They didn't want Jim Edwards to get in more trouble for piloting fugitives. A Super Cub pilot with connections flew out from Anchorage soon after to grab Raven. But two weeks later, in early October, the fugitive returned in a pickup truck over the rough road the state had started improving, with girlfriend and daughter, to collect all the mining-era booty he'd left at the hardware store. Unfortunately for him, it snowed that night. When Darkow spotted their footprints, the three took off in the Chevy pickup, splashing across the freeze-up trickle in the Kennicott River and bouncing toward Chitina. Darkow grabbed his son and Les Hegland and they flew to the Collinses' airstrip at Long Lake, fifteen miles away, where they were reinforced by an Alaska State Trooper plane. The fugitive ran into the woods and was caught. Having the troopers there helped. When Hegland got back to town, his daughter recalled, he realized his shotgun hadn't been loaded.

It was rare for an event in the Wrangells to merit newspaper attention, but an eight-inch unbylined story of the arrest, under the headline "The Law Swoops," reported that a state trooper plane landed on the road in front of Ron Cole's car to block his getaway. The story said the suspect was chased down in the woods by troopers, the pilot, and "other citizens." That was as close as the *Anchorage Times* got to using the word vigilantes. The October 14, 1971, story provided this background: "Cole was wanted for possession following the alleged discovery of marijuana being grown in a garden at his cabin in McCarthy."

No mention was made of graverobbing and human skulls. Les Hegland led the troopers to the cemetery, where they found two holes in the ground and had to guess which skull belonged where.

Tomb-robbing was rather a way of life in McCarthy, but Raven had gone too far. Things turned out badly for Ron Cole's own cranium. A few years later, in a forest north of Anchorage, a sow grizzly attacked him before he could draw his pistol. His new wife, Darci, who was twenty-one, took the mirror off the wall before helping him into their cabin. The bear had torn off his face. Cole came through with a glass eye surrounded by scars and a bear-attack story that won the Alaska Airlines "Alaska Brag Contest" in October 1975. The airline ran a newspaper advertisement celebrating the winner, with a photo of smiling Darci and a tagline that read "Nobody knows Alaska like Alaska knows Alaska." The prize was quietly revoked shortly thereafter, once the airline learned of the winner's recurrent role as defendant in major drug cases. *Alaska Magazine* published his story anyway, in 1976. "She was trying to eat my head, and from the pain I was sure she had succeeded," he wrote. "I tried beating her with my hands but it was like trying to break rock."

One year after his bear story appeared, Cole was charged with shipping half a ton of marijuana to Alaska—in sealed fifty-five-gallon oil drums, like the drums of chalcocite that Howard Knutson once flew out of McCarthy. At the time, it was the biggest marijuana bust in the state's history. Ron Cole reached the end of his road in 1981, in a big home on the Anchorage hillside, when a cocaine dealer who owed him money shot him through the head, and Darci too. In the Anchorage papers, narcotics officers described the deceased male victim, age forty-five, as "one bad Jose" who went by the name of Raven.

*Bridge*

# THE PROSPECTOR TYPE

*In the summer of 1985, as the lost decades began settling into memory, Jim Edwards sat for several weeks of recorded interviews with Jenny Carroll, who had come to the Hardware Store as part of the Alaska Wildlands Studies program. She was gathering material for a master's degree in anthropology at Stanford University. Carroll would move to McCarthy after she finished school and serve as director of the Wrangell Mountains Center (1987–92), thereafter remaining tied to the community.*

*In the following passage, taken from the transcript of Carroll's interviews, Jim Edwards recalled one of his early contemporaries, a lonely mountain man who seemed driven by some terrible, inexplicable thing.*

"MARK GOODMAN CAME IN HERE IN THE EARLY 1950S, BUT HE really wasn't around McCarthy much. It wasn't like he was a resident, he was just in and out of the valley. And he is still alive, in lower Tonsina. He's a heavy drinker. He sorta lost interest in living. Drinks with the idea that it will kill him. It's a wonder it hasn't already. He's been in the hospital with severe alcohol poisoning. In earlier days he was better. He's drank ever since I knew him but not so bad. He'd go out in the hills for some months and he was kind of a prospector. Had a dog that went with him. I don't know what became of the dog when he went on a drinking spree but most of the time he was calm and pretty sober—the dog was pretty much the same. Real quiet, easygoing dog that stayed with him pretty well. Good companion for him because he was the prospector type.

"When I first knew him in the early 1950s he would come into McCarthy for a day or two, chartered in after he drank all his money in Chitina. I don't know where he got his money. He'd been in the service during the war, maybe he'd been wounded and got a pension. He is five or ten years older than me, but he looked older than that because of his heavy drinking. To me and my wife he was always nice and polite. Easy going and quiet. Apologetic for his presence, especially if he'd been drinking the last time he'd seen us. He had a reputation when he was drinking of being real belligerent, a wild man. He'd get into awful fights and I wondered if he had an underlying need to put himself down. Can't ever tell why in those situations. But when he got into a bar where he could meet fighter types, why he'd stir up fights. Sometimes he'd get hurt when people beat him up real bad. He got into a fight one time and went out in the street—oh, some kind of trouble down there, maybe even shooting, I don't know. And he got hit by a car when he went staggering into the street in Chitina.

"We liked him. He was extremely capable out in the woods. He would come to McCarthy where there was no road. He would be in town for a day or so getting his act together, and I have a scene in my head where he went out the back door and into the alley and down the street and past Joe Summer's house, and that road leads up to McCarthy Creek. Maybe it was December or November, and I remember that scene yet—I looked out into the backyard and saw him go by—his dog walking along beside him, his rifle slung over his shoulder—an old ratty rifle and a little bitty sled he was dragging behind, a five-foot-long wooden sled with a couple runners under it.

The Erie Mine ruins gaze out at the Root and Kennicott Glaciers.

On the sled he had an old cheap sleeping bag, just thrown down on the sled, a small duffel bag half full of clothes, a small cardboard box full of groceries, lid partly open, a fruit box—the kind twenty-four cans of fruit come in—and it wasn't full, and he went down the road out of town to go prospecting in the hills. And this was in the days when nobody else was around, maybe six, eight people in McCarthy and nobody in the hills in those days. He went off up McCarthy Creek—a foot and a half of snow—walking out of town on snowshoes. All his equipment looked cheap and shabby—coat old and shabby—maybe a blanket thrown on the sled, but not much—going off in the middle of December. Didn't come back from the hills until March, out at least two-and-a-half, three months. I don't know how he made a living out there—

"When I got to the point of flying commercially here, I flew him around a number of times. By that time, fifteen years later, he was a little older but he was still doing the same thing—going out into the woods and spending the winter or summer, several months at a time. Come to me in Chitina and say he wanted to go to May Creek or Glacier Creek or to Peavine Bar. He had a deal out there later where they paid him to watch one of the camps when they closed down for the winter. They'd pay him to caretake it. He didn't have to stay there all the time—he could go prospecting so that was a good deal for him and he had shelter, a tiny bit of food and a little salary—at least a place to go. But in the years before I don't know. There must have been cabins out around he stayed in but what he did to eat I don't know.

"I would take him places in my airplane—of course I tied it in with the mail run a lot of times, because I could take him on mail flights to May Creek and then he could charter to some gravel bar he wanted to go to or to Glacier Creek or somewhere for just a few dollars more. They don't do that now.

"Sometimes the load would be such that I'd have to leave him off somewhere for a couple of hours and come back and pick him up 'cause I had other passengers or whatever. It was no problem for him. "I'll be here." I'd be back anywhere from two hours to two days. I'd leave him off at May Creek and I'd come back. He'd be sitting there by the cabin, a little fire about six inches in diameter and a pot of coffee on it. He was completely capable. He was here doing that stuff in the '70s when Ben was here with his college program. There were a number of people here who thought it was quite a joke. There was a student here who had been hiking around and he met up with Mark and he took it upon himself to give Mark a lecture on how to get along in the wilderness. Mark I guess just sat there and listened to him.

"Mark wasn't the belligerent type anytime I ever knew him. Maybe the fighting in bars was an outlet for him. As the years went by he drank more and more and he got to the point where they told him he better quit it or you'll die, and he said, "I want to die, I have nothing to live for." He wasn't interested any more. This was in later years. I saw him in Chitina four years ago in a cabin. It's hard to visit with a guy who drinks all the time—there's not much there. He was a nice guy though. He did his work patiently and reasonably well and he did what he was asked. It was funny to watch him work—his clothes were shabby and often a cuff would come off his pants and be hanging down under his shoe and of course I run around like that myself. He was a good worker—people liked to have him work for them because he was a good fellow, didn't argue or squabble about it—like me, I argue, I think I got my own idea how to do things and the thing I heard about him somewhere—I never really got to talk to him about this—somebody told me that he had been in the war and had been on a troop ship across the Atlantic and been torpedoed. So maybe he was in the war and in the battles in Europe. I never talked to him directly about it. We talked about general things and stuff—but I heard he'd been wounded and maybe he was on his way home on the troop ship when it was torpedoed and sunk so he was wounded and paddling himself out there on a raft trying to save himself. Must have been a tough thing and maybe that scared him. I don't know. Hard to say. He's still around, somewhere in lower Tonsina."

# PART TWO

Here's to Alaska, here's to the people
Here's to the wild and here's to the free
Here's to my life in a chosen country
Here's to Alaska and me

JOHN DENVER, "ALASKA AND ME"

# 6

# Wrangell Mountain High

I N THE SUMMER of 1972, the year after Raven and the hippie hole, it seemed like the whole world suddenly got interested in McCarthy. The town swarmed with a fresh crew of UC Santa Cruz students, national leaders of the Sierra Club, reporters from down in the states, including a writer for *National Geographic*, exploration geologists, and political activists arguing over the economic development freeze on 120 million acres of federal land, including a group that called itself Alaskans for Alaska. Congress was debating how to build the Trans-Alaska Pipeline and whether to set land aside in Alaska for new national parks. Meanwhile the state, feeling flush with new oil money, sent surveyors to prepare for a two-lane gravel highway into the heart of the Wrangells.

"At stake was not only the future of McCarthy, but the vast untouched wilderness that lay beyond, and it all centered around the question of access," wrote Curtis Green, who had been living in the area with his brother for five years. "It is as if we were catapulted overnight from obscurity onto the front lines of the environmentalist battlefield. Why, most of the folks around there had never even heard the words environmentalist or ecologist only a year or so previously."

The big moment came in midsummer when the Secretary of the Interior, Rogers Morton, landed in McCarthy for lunch. Morton, a former chairman of the Republican National Committee, had been appointed the nation's land and resources chief after President Nixon fired his predecessor, former Alaska governor Walter Hickel. The official entourage arrived in two planes. Curtis Green recalled the guest of honor: "Secretary Morton, white haired and avuncular, perched majestically atop the lodge jeep, surrounded by a bevy of buxom blondes—who graciously dispensed box lunches, courtesy of Uncle Sam, to the hoi polloi—puffing on a huge cigar, as if he thought he really was somebody."

The town's reception was commandeered by Sumner Putman, a local hippie pilot, who pedaled his bike out to the airstrip in a Superman shirt and offered his one-speed as transportation for big shots only. "Are you a big shot?" he asked Deputy Undersecretary Jack Horton. "A very big shot," replied Horton, a former navy pilot, Rhodes Scholar, and All-American lacrosse player from a ranch in Saddlestring, Wyoming. The smiling Horton rode to town on Putman's handlebars.

Sumner Putman lived on a pastoral slope of Fireweed Mountain, a short hop in his plane from the ghost town, though his home had ghosts of its own. The sylvan meadow had been a hayfield back in railroad days, when the valley raised its own beef and fed hundreds of horses and when it seemed a lasting community could take root. Horse-drawn mowing tools still lay hidden in tall grass around the small tin-roofed log cabin where Putman and his wife lived. The original farmers, a solitary couple named Jones, abandoned the homestead after their only child, Willie, enlisted during World War I and was killed a few weeks after he got to France.

At the top of the sloping hayfield, Putman had started work on a geodesic dome cabin, many of its dihedral angles later constructed of stolen plywood campaign signs for Congressman Don Young. Putman commuted to McCarthy in a souped-up iridescent-blue Piper PA-14 that he called the Mystery Ship. One of the mysteries was how the plane managed to fly off the side of a mountain. He had installed leading-edge slats on the wings so he could be airborne at a wind speed of twenty miles per hour and was skilled enough to land on the meadow aiming uphill, a maneuver that required balloon tires, a hot arrival, and a willingness to rebuild the plane from time to time.

The hippie homesteader had a practical side. One summer a nuisance black bear, drawn to his compost pile, tore an exploratory hole in the side of the Mystery Ship. Annoyed, Putman patched the hole and went to town, where he found sheep hunters weathered-in at the lodge. He flew a restless hunter to his home, hosted him overnight to comply with same-day-airborne regulations, and kept the bear meat and $400 for "lodging."

An anti-war marine veteran who had served in Vietnam, Putman was a prankster—he would later be arrested in Fairbanks for painting "Yankee Go Home" on Alyeska Pipeline vehicles and ticketed for flying a loop under the suspension bridge in Juneau. He was finally settling into a career as a part-time legislative staffer in 1981 when he was killed in a midair collision over Bristol Bay, along with his passenger, the son of famed movie producer Dino De Laurentiis, who was filming a documentary about the salmon fishery. They were flying low over a bluff toward the water when a plane taking off from the beach struck them from below.

But on that summer day in 1972, Curtis Green wrote, with the Interior Department big shots' planes sitting on the McCarthy runway, Putman put on a "stunning display of aerial acrobatics in his outrageously painted psychedelic Super Cub, while Winnie Darkow shook his fist at the heavens and roared imprecations at the 'show-off hippie son of a bitch,' and somebody somewhere in the crowd turned up the volume on a tape deck playing Peter, Paul, and Mary singing 'If I Had a Hammer.'"

By 1972 Alaska had come to represent, for the nation's burgeoning environmental movement, the final refuge of the once-wild continent. The discovery of oil, and the burst of urban development that came with it, made protection of Alaska's remaining wilderness an urgent political cause across the Lower 48.

Rogers Morton's staff at Interior had been given two years to survey all of Alaska and decide which public land to set aside for possible park, refuge, and wilderness designations, and which to leave open for development and state and Native selection. Under the Alaska Native Claims Settlement Act, which passed Congress in December 1971, some 80 million acres had been quarantined for their conservation potential under section 17(d)(2). These became known as d-2 lands—the raw material for Alaska's new parks and wildlife refuges. The process of settling their fate would dominate Alaska politics during the 1970s. The map of Alaska's future was being drawn, with a clock ticking: the d-2 withdrawals would expire in seven years.

The Wrangell Mountains were an important feature of those withdrawals. They had been admired for their national park potential since territorial days. Ernest Gruening, who pushed for a park when Kennecott Copper departed in 1938, later urged the government, as a US senator, to build a "national park highway" over Skolai Pass. To promote the area, he came back in 1967 and induced his friend, the Alaska artist Fred Machetanz, to paint a series of Wrangell Mountains landscapes. Machetanz, who was taken by the landscape but had not yet fastened his eyes on the outlaw prospector George Smock, was given free rides on US Geological Survey helicopters operating out of May Creek. Sometimes Senator Gruening came along for the ride. Machetanz described one such trip—possibly to Lost Butte in the Kuskulana River valley—that led to his painting *Mt. Blackburn, Sovereign of the Wrangells*:

> *About twenty miles east of Chitina an opening in the mountain range to the North exposed this view of Mt. Blackburn from almost base to its summit. I hastily asked if I could be let off to study this lovely view for a potential painting. Fortunately there was a rock butte which extended above the solid forest beneath and on this I was deposited while the Senator and his group flew around until later afternoon when they returned. By then I had made many color notes and sketches which culminated in this painting of Mt. Blackburn, 16,500 feet high. The perpetual snowfields on top move downward to form the many glaciers surrounding this greatest of all the Wrangell's peaks.*

The artist's raptures didn't reference the rain and low clouds that thwarted many of his trips. To the pilot in Chitina, Kenny Smith, Machetanz grumbled about the long drive from Palmer and wondered where the senator got the idea he was a landscape painter.

Ed MacKevett, the USGS boss at May Creek, whose job was to assess the mineral potential of the proposed national park, said he worried at first about a camp visit by the politician and the artist. He was relieved when they required little helicopter time. Gruening, MacKevett said, "was an excellent story teller and also had a thorough appreciation of the scenic wonders of the Wrangells and the nearby terrain. . . . Both [visitors] contributed to the routine camp chores." A local man, Walt Holmes, a maestro of blasting gold-bearing gravel with high-pressure water hoses, lived near May Creek and dropped by in the evenings. "It was particularly enjoyable to listen to the senator and Walt Holmes, one of the best natural story tellers that I have ever met, trying to outdo each other during the evening cocktail hour. The senator drank gin or vodka."

Gruening's proposed national park highway would start in Cordova, follow the Copper, Chitina, and Nizina Rivers to Skolai Pass, then descend the White River into Canada, hooking up to the Alaska Highway somewhere to the north. It was an old-fashioned way of engaging the wilderness—build a road, so that people could see more of it!—which found no great enthusiasm in the federal bureaucracy until Hickel became Interior Secretary under Nixon. In 1969 Hickel proposed a Wrangell Mountain Scenic Area: 10.5-million acres managed for multiple use by the Bureau of Land Management, not the National Park Service. But Hickel's effort was resisted by state politicians, who wanted no such restrictions on their ability to select acreage under their statehood grant and who underestimated the conservation pressures to come.

The federal Bureau of Outdoor Recreation studied making the Chitina River a protected Wild and Scenic River. One problem: the Alaska Power Authority had plans on paper for a Copper River hydroelectric project. A 1,400-foot-high dam in Wood Canyon, below the town of Chitina, would back water all the way up into the Nizina River canyon. Such a dam, never built, raised plenty of unanswered questions, particularly regarding the river's heavy silt load and the need to provide fish passage for the thriving Copper River salmon runs.

The Wrangells popped up again in Washington, DC, in 1972 when the Nixon administration, marking the hundredth anniversary of Yellowstone, the country's first national park, proposed a new park in Alaska as a "gift to the American people." The Wrangell Mountains made a likely candidate for a quickly assembled offering because the maps had been studied so much. The so-called Alaska National Park would have encompassed seventeen million acres of the Wrangells, with an emphasis on recreational access rather than wilderness. There was talk of a similar effort on the Canada side of the border. Feverish planners predicted half a million annual visitors to such a park by 1985 (more than six times the number who visited the eventual park in 2016). The centennial effort soon collapsed, as many Interior officials preferred to ignore the standalone Alaska National Park and instead slog through the ANCSA d-2 lands process, in the decade ahead, in hopes of a bigger prize: new parks and wildlife refuges all across Alaska.

The lofty goal was to preserve wild landscapes. The fate of a small anachronistic community, surviving in the Wrangell Mountains due to historical accident, was not a national concern, nor something that much troubled conservationists. The people of McCarthy would set out to change that.

❮——❯

That same summer of 1972, an amphibious Grumman Goose landed at Glacier Creek, on the upper Nizina. Down from the passenger seat climbed a wealthy San Francisco doctor whose influence on the future of McCarthy and the surrounding region would be huge but largely behind the scenes.

Edgar Wayburn had recently completed his second term as president of the Sierra Club. Having led the successful fight to create Redwoods National Park in California, he turned to the preservation of Alaska. On a 1968 flightseeing tour of Alaska with high-ranking federal officials, he had been bowled over by the majesty of Mount Blackburn and the Wrangells. "Around us rose a spaciousness and absolute silence that sucked the breath from our lungs," he wrote in his autobiography. He compared the Nizina River canyon, with its Mile High Cliffs, to Yosemite and marveled at how the "turbid glacial streams seemed to defy gravity and flow in several directions." He winced to see derelict school buses in the mountains nearby, abandoned by miners, and he softly regretted Kennecott and McCarthy as "indelible marks on the landscape." He feared for the future. Outdated homestead and mining laws, he wrote, "which most people associate with the nineteenth century and Manifest Destiny, were still being used with full force in one of the earth's superlative wilderness regions."

Wayburn's passion and personal fortune would help drive the Sierra Club through the coming decade-long fight to wrest an Alaska parks bill from Congress. After the struggle to piece together surviving tracts of old-growth redwoods, Wayburn was out to protect more than token amounts of land. Success was by no means certain, but an alliance of conservation groups known as the Alaska Coalition proved able to draw on the swelling environmental concerns of the 1970s to run an innovative national grassroots campaign in the districts of swing-vote congressmen from both parties.

Wayburn was also the key figure who had helped grubstake, through the Sierra Club Foundation, an Alaska environmental studies program, early in 1971, at the University of California, Santa Cruz. Given all the big Alaska issues coming down at once—oil development, Native land claims, wilderness conservation—the timing seemed perfect for a study of land-use planning on a gigantic scale. In an era of heightened environmental awareness challenging the traditional resource-extraction ideology of the frontier, the program would ask, in the words of founding professor Richard Cooley, "Can the state of Alaska learn from past mistakes in other areas?"

The Santa Cruz field program was the source of the college students who began showing up in McCarthy in 1971. Wayburn himself had pointed to the Wrangells as a likely focus, given the potential changes that a new road to McCarthy would bring. The first students soaked in the long sunlit evenings and asked questions about wilderness and the role of human communities. Must people always be a destructive force? Could nature and community coexist, sustainably, in a way that might provide lessons for sustaining our endangered planet? Could a new national park somehow serve in helping sustain this rustic way of life, as part of what was being protected in Alaska?

The awestruck students backpacked and camped in the mountains, interviewed the locals, ate communal meals at the Hardware Store, and roughed it all summer in an atmosphere of enchantment. During the decade that followed, McCarthy became the scene of what one leader recalled as "a Midsummer Night's Dream version of an environmental studies program." The national conservation movement began to hear about the community of McCarthy, Alaska. And the students, some of whom returned to live in Alaska and even in the Wrangells, would contribute an off-kilter streak of green politics and introspection to a ghost town that was starting to think abandonment not such a bad fate after all.

⟵  ⟶

As Curtis Green wrote, all conversations about the future came back to questions about access. Attending the ribbon cutting for a new bridge across the Copper River was one of the first actions Ben Shaine, a Berkeley graduate student, took when he arrived in 1971 to set up the Santa Cruz field studies program.

For thirty years, the open river at Chitina had complicated access to McCarthy. In winter, ice could support a bulldozer. In summer, a rowboat or canoe was sometimes at hand. During freeze-up in fall, however, when the river was full of fast-moving slush ice, there was no good way to cross.

That was the situation confronting Jim Edwards one autumn after traveling sixty miles overland from McCarthy. He had a dental problem that the files in his toolbox couldn't fix. Arriving late in the day, he found the Copper River freezing up sooner than expected. There was too much moving ice for a boat. He looked up: a quarter mile of steel cable left by the railroad's long-decommissioned engine-driven tram was suspended above the floes. Edwards climbed the abandoned tower on the McCarthy side. The cable, rusted and sagging, spanned to a cliff on the far shore. He looped a heavy chain over the cable, rigged a seat harness on a plank of wood, pulled on leather gloves, and started across. To move forward, he had to lift his weight with one arm and push the chain forward with the other. It was almost easy at first, sliding downhill, but halfway across the river he saw that he had underestimated the difficulty of the climb. Pushing up toward the cliffs, he could move only an inch or two on each shove. It grew dark, the temperature sank, and his strength drained away. He did not want to be remembered as the dead fool dangling above the Copper River. When he reached the opposite tower, he collapsed on the platform, his gloves worn through, his jacket shredded. He slept through the cold night, and his body was black and blue for days.

Now the new crossing of steel and concrete at Chitina was about to transform access in and out. A road would come next. On the McCarthy side of the river bulldozers had left a rough gravel lane when the rails were torn out and the ties pushed aside in the early 1960s. A sturdy pickup truck could sometimes negotiate the washouts and beaver ponds as far as the Lakina River—and when the rivers were low, or frozen, continue all the way into McCarthy, sixty miles from Chitina. The state Department of Highways was planning to widen the gravel road to two-lane federal standards, build bridges across the Lakina and Kennicott Rivers, and usher in a new age of easy access.

"It should be realized that the growth and development of all areas of Alaska is irrevocable," was the assertive phrasing used by the state in a plan for the new road. Environmental impact statements were still something new, and this one, by the state Department of Highways, occasionally read like a travel brochure. It explained how the valley would benefit from a mining and tourism boom. The Department of Economic Development even pitched in a paragraph about converting the trams above Kennecott to ski lifts.

The road-building enthusiasm of Democratic governor William Egan's administration was being resisted by state and national conservation groups. They had sued over an effort to build a similar highway south from Chitina, to Cordova, over that leg of the abandoned Copper River & Northwestern grade. In 1972 the federal courts said if the state planned to use federal highway funds to build these roads through wild country, it needed to do a full environmental impact study, under the three-year-old National Environmental Policy Act.

The study forced a pause and an opportunity to record for posterity attitudes about building a road to McCarthy. Opinions were divided, but the deeper into the mountains you traveled, the more opposition you were likely to hear. The new bridge across the Copper River and the immediate prospect of easy access for America's pickup campers and Winnebagos alarmed residents of the upper valley far more in the summer of 1972 than the idea of Rogers Morton turning the mountains into a national park. Everyone understood that McCarthy was the way it was because it was hard to get to. Residents were starting to think of isolation as their last nonrenewable resource.

⋖──▸

The Santa Cruz program published a report that endorsed the region's potential as a national park and objected to further highway spending, calling the road an $11 million subsidy to create a handful of mining jobs. "Uncontrolled development of resort-type facilities and vacation homes near Long Lake, at McCarthy, and Kennicott could occur," the students wrote. After two summers in the valley, the school group shrewdly framed improved access as a danger to the town's lifestyle, saying a road would bring the need for "people management" to a place that cherishes its laissez faire lack of rules.

Curtis Green submitted testimony from McCarthy on behalf of a group called the Chitina Valley Residents Association. The group consisted of his brother, Loy, Jim and Maxine Edwards, some landowners at Long Lake (who would be the first to encounter travelers over the road), and a handful of absentee deed holders. "If the road is being built for our benefit—to make travel in the valley easier—the Highway Department could better spend its money elsewhere," Curtis Green wrote, insisting the existing "primitive access road" was sufficient. "The physical isolation and absence of a highway constitutes a large part of the reason we choose to live in the Chitina Valley." He said tourists who manage to make their way this far deserved to be rewarded with a visit to a truly different place, "not just another overcrowded, littered, 'tourist attraction.'"

On the other side of the argument were many Chitina area residents, small-time miners, and absentee landowners, some of whom said they hoped to build retirement homes in McCarthy. Howard and Adina Knutson, running the Chitina Hotel, signed a petition backing the road, which would improve access to Consolidated Wrangell's unsubdivided land at Kennecott. The Darkows, who owned the McCarthy Lodge, wanted to see a road built so they could sell out for a good price, and the Heglands joined in, taking a position anti the anti-roaders. But the usual booster voices for highways, development, and opportunity were not ringing loud in McCarthy. In their written comments, road proponents took this lack of local enthusiasm to be un-Alaskan and vaguely un-American.

Phil O'Neill, a pro-road miner working at Dan Creek, offered the novel argument that a road would prevent vandalism rather than promote it. In his view, road opponents wanted to close the area to everyone except "the undesirables, as is the case now, we have a large colony of the hippy types on the Nizina River, another colony, or commune, I think they call themselves, in the McCarthy area, and more coming, these characters have their own aircraft, fly in their own dope, and raise their own marijuana, the old mining sites and homes they have not taken as for their own use, they have vandalized to the point of complete destruction, so until we get some roads in there so the state troopers can get around there is absolutely no chance to preserve the historic old mining sites, or preserve much of anything else."

Jack Wilson, who had moved his glacier pilot business from Chitina to Glennallen, suggested that if the government insisted on creating a wilderness area for hippies, the area be limited to the Skolai Basin, at the crest of the Chitistone Trail: "This would make a few hunting guides mad, but speaking only for myself, I would let them have this beautiful part of our country if they would quit hollering about the rest of it." As was often the case in the Wrangells, there was a feud hidden behind principles. The previous summer, Wilson had flown to Skolai Pass to pick up Santa Cruz backpackers and made a dangerous landing: the high-country airstrip had been dynamited by a White River guide trying to keep other hunters and guides from getting access to sheep habitat he considered his personal realm.

The local back-and-forth over the road, which can be followed in comments accompanying the 1973 environmental impact statement for the Chitina-McCarthy Highway, quickly became wrapped up in the national conversation about the future of the forty-ninth state. Miners accused the anti-road side of trying to stall development so the Wrangells could be made into a park. They opposed locking up the country in wilderness-only zones. The Santa Cruz report responded that miners wanted to lock up the country in bulldozing-only zones. They published photos of improvised zigzag bulldozer routes up the sides of local valleys. That prompted Johnny Wilson at the Peavine claim to bulldoze "SIERRA CLUB GO TO HELL" into the broad gravel bar at the mouth of Chitistone Canyon, where Edgar Wayburn's amphibious plane had landed. The bulldozer graffito with hundred-foot letters was an essential scenic flyover for VIP tours on all sides of the issue for years, until flooding in the braided river washed it away.

If that erasure made a point for those who considered alarms about bulldozer devastation overstated in this rubble-strewn land, it also made one of Ben Shaine's points about reasons for preserving the landscape. The defining theme for the national park, the Santa Cruz report said, would not be nature's timelessness but rather nature's everlasting erosion, loss, and rebirth: "Whereas the mesas and canyons of the Southwest are imposingly monumental and stat-uesque, the Wrangells are strikingly mobile and ever-changing in an equally classical and enduring sense."

Change wrought by glacial rivers was one thing. Change wrought by speculators and developers was another. Fervent believers in evo-lution, the college-educated environmentalists were never Social Darwinists: Alaska's future needn't be surrendered to "irrevocable" forces of American progress. That message struck a chord with some of the locals. A gristly streak of resistance in the state's political makeup grew more pronounced during the years of hearings, law-suits, and debates over construction of the Trans-Alaska Pipeline, whose route passed through Glennallen and skirted the Wrangells on its way to Valdez. "The irony is that some of us are trying to make Alaska into a replica of the society we came up here to escape," a visiting journalist was told in 1970 by the Republican majority leader in the state senate, a bush pilot guide from Naknek named Jay Ham-

Bulldozer graffiti by placer miner Johnny Wilson was a regular feature of fly-over tours during the debate over new national parks in Alaska in the 1970s.

mond. Congress would approve the pipeline right of way and construction permits in November 1973 under pressure from the Arab oil embargo. It was a decision greatly welcomed in much of Alaska, to be sure, especially in the urban money-making areas. But even there, some wistfulness was apparent about the coming transformation of the "last frontier."

Local sentiments veered from the national conservationist program on one point: the Chitina River valley's residents did not propose to relinquish their homes to federally protected grizzly bears. Why couldn't settlement and wild nature coexist? The Santa Cruz vision of an ideal and humane middle landscape was later picked up by the noted environmental law professor Joseph Sax in a consulting report for a local group. He said Alaska's new national parks could also be lifestyle preserves. The UC Berkeley professor advised the National Park Service to take a "light touch" and consider that visitors would be fascinated to encounter several dozen families living "on their own at the edge of the managed world":

> *The combination may have no equal on the American continent. Here in a single place three intertwined eras in Alaska's history lay almost literally one atop the other—the pristine wilderness, the intrepid exploitation of mineral wealth, and bush Alaska in its authentic late-twentieth century form. There is not an iota of fakery here. . . . Visitors who come here will go away with a sense of the real Alaska, and perhaps with less misunderstanding of the state and its aspirations. They can see how people live here, the heritage they bring to their lives, how they relate to the natural world and to a vast public domain.*

Improbably, it was a "light touch" decision that opponents of the McCarthy road forced from the state in the summer of 1973. Governor Egan's administration opted for a quick fix—what engineers called a pioneer road. A get-something-nailed-together homesteader mentality would put off until another day high-strung arguments over a permanent highway. Using state maintenance funds, which allowed planners to ignore federal engineering requirements and environmental studies, the state graded the gravel railbed, fixed a few stream crossings, and tacked up wooden bridges across the Lakina River and the twin roaring channels that poured out of the Kennicott Glacier.

Late in the fall of 1973, the bridge into town opened and a person could finally drive from Anchorage—or Seattle—to McCarthy.

Winnie Darkow had fought for a road with the kind of speculative energy that powered centuries of westward expansion. At long last, his lodge might be worth something. That fall the first people to drive across the bridge knocked on the McCarthy Lodge door. It was almost midnight and they wanted hamburgers. The lodge owners complied, only to hear complaints about the buns. "They were not happy because it was not like Anchorage," Barbara Darkow said. "The next day, Winston went to town and put the lodge up for sale."

◄———►

The rough pioneer road into the Wrangells emitted an irresistible call to the personal-adventure motor fleet of pipeline-era Alaska. McCarthy residents never forgot the stream of recreational vehicles crossing the bridge in the summer of 1974, prowling the town's two streets and squeezing up the road to Kennecott. Abandoned autos were ransacked for parts by antique car buffs. Local residents, who had been picking through mining-era leftovers for years, used the word "looting" for the first time. Les Hegland confronted visitors at the bridge and took back items from their trucks. He emptied houses in McCarthy and hid things away in his shed so they wouldn't leave the valley. Jim Edwards hated to step outside because of the "wall-to-wall Winnebagos." He moved his family across the river.

McCarthy's motor tourist era didn't last long, however. Partway through the first summer, Hidden Creek Lake let loose its annual jökulhlaup flood, and the new highway bridge across the Kennicott River suffered the same fate as the old railroad trestles. Wooden pilings in the east channel were staggered or washed away. The state tied the remaining pilings together with a steel I-beam but soon designated the structure for foot traffic only. The next summer's flood damaged the west channel bridge as well.

Also washed away, in those pipeline years, were some underpinnings of old Alaska politics. In 1974 voters chose the Naknek bush pilot Jay Hammond as their new governor. Unusual for an Alaska politician, the bush Republican was skeptical of big construction projects, especially when they were forced on unwilling rural "beneficiaries." State enthusiasm for additional road and bridge work in the valley faded. The McCarthy highway project was set aside.

In 1977 the Hidden Creek Lake flood took out the east fork footbridge altogether, washing it onto a gravel bar downriver, where a fight over reclamation rights broke out. Access into town reverted to the rudimentary hand tram, a splintery platform, built in the 1950s by Blazo Bill Berry, suspended from a cable across the river channels. At first there was no return rope, and not every visitor had the means to summon help in the traditional way—by squeezing off three rifle shots. One alternative was an hours-long detour on foot up to the glacier and across the moraine-covered ice. Another was to go away.

When the first jökulhlaup washout occurred, two German tourists visiting McCarthy in a rented Mercedes found themselves stranded. They walked across the half-fallen bridge, caught a ride back to the Anchorage airport, and left the key in the Mercedes hoping someone would return the rental car to the city once the river froze. The Mercedes remained in the Wrangells, however, with its key in general circulation. For several years the Mercedes served as McCarthy's public transportation system, and as a reminder: flotsam beached by the high-water mark of tourism.

＊

Loy Green was so disgusted by the brief tourist boom of 1974 that he left town. He got an artist's commission to paint a landscape at the remote Tebay Lakes, in the mountains south of the Chitina River. He camped there that summer with the hardy old prospector from Chitina, Neil Finnesand, his former employer, who was still doing assessment work on his Spirit Mountain claims. The two of them cruised the lakes in a leaky boat with a touchy outboard. Loy Green later described how they nearly perished:

*Well here we are on the far end of the lake, and at this point the water is channeling into a stream moving into a river, about two hundred yards away is a waterfall. Of course I got too close to shore and sheared the pin on the propeller. It is necessary to raise the motor, I set the oars to hold and control the boat, and DAMN, one of the locks breaks out. The stream has us. At this point the current is gentle but it is easy to see that it will increase quite rapidly. This water is a clear blue, we can see the bottom. It is about waist deep. We both understood the situation. I say, 'Neil, we gotta hold this fucking boat!' Neil glanced over the side once more and said, 'I'll hold her' and over the side he went. Grabbed the boat, braced himself, and indeed he held her. I raised the motor, replaced the pin, started it. Neil pulled himself into the boat and home we went. Neil Finnesand, at that time, was ninety years old.*

◁──▷

In the fall of 1975, after the road bridge had washed out, one of the biggest stars in American music flew to McCarthy and wrote a song about the place.

John Denver spent a rainy September week at the McCarthy Lodge with a large film crew that included—according to folklore handed down through generations of forlorn McCarthy bachelors—several attractive and exuberant females. Three years later the documentary they produced, *Alaska, the American Child*, appeared on ABC television and joined the national debate over Alaska's d-2 lands. The movie blended a soft political message ("Alaska is our past, living in the present—what a luxury to have this second chance") and romantic sentiment ("Where the rivers are still running free") and music ("American Child is a Call of the Wild..."). Denver, a pop-country troubadour famous for such songs as "Country Roads" and "Rocky Mountain High," narrated the film as if dictating an excited letter home, leaving it to the soaring landscapes and major-chord progressions to close the political argument. "The words and pictures created a huge 'armchair' clientele for Alaska's wilderness," wrote historian Roderick Nash, who said the film played an important role in the national conservation campaign.

As its title suggests, the movie could be a bit condescending to the people of Alaska. Yet Denver couldn't have been more admiring of the two Alaskans who served as his traveling companions in the film. They were a pair of sideburned and mustached bush pilots who told Denver tales of flying and hunting and the ways of the North. The movie does not make note of the leathery pilots' day jobs: Tony Oney and Hoppy Harrower were both on leave from their Anchorage dental practices. In Alaska, flying dentist hunting guides are a thing. Every fall Oney and Harrower blacked out their schedules to guide in the Wrangells, whose slopes were renowned for producing the finest big-curl Dall sheep trophies in Alaska. For hunters, Dall sheep are an especially demanding quarry. Harrower (who got his nickname in dental school when he broke his foot and threw away his crutches because of all the stairs) wrote a short memoir of their hunting exploits, detailing the record-book scoring of curl measurements. Tony and Hoppy landed airplanes on precipitous ridges with the dexterity of practitioners accustomed to working in tight spaces. They also guided polar bear hunts up north in early spring, ingratiating themselves to the nearby Iñupiaq villages by providing free dental care.

The movie follows Denver and his pilot buddies to the Arctic and Bristol Bay before they reach the Wrangells. The tiny mountain hamlet of McCarthy was presented as something great from the American past. Local residents welcome him on-camera and tell their stories. The singer would go on to write "Wrangell Mountain Song" for a later album: "If you think they're wild it's just because they can't be broken."

John Denver (left) performs for locals and his movie crew at the McCarthy Lodge during his 1975 visit.

Jim Edwards wrote his father that he brought the family one night to hear "this singer or movie star or whatever he is." It was a special family event—most nights at the McCarthy Lodge, during the film crew's visit, were considered too rowdy for young children. The lodge owner had sent her own kids, aged five and seven, across the river for the duration of filming. Edwards came away unimpressed by the performer who, one month later, would be named Entertainer of the Year at Nashville's Country Music Awards ceremony—"I did not think he was so hot really." Edwards told his father he'd heard one night there was "a half-orgy ending up in a beating, and couple of girls leaving town in a hurry."

One scene that nobody filmed occurred on a night when Denver and his crew crowded the saloon inside the lodge. Two locals who had been bickering got in a loud argument. One of them, the bartender, drew a knife, and the other pulled a .44 and fired. As the film crew rushed out the door, the bartender staggered to the floor in a pool of blood. Fake blood, it turned out: Jimmy Galzinsky was firing blanks and the bartender was in on the spoof. The point, according to later explanations, was either to reclaim the pool table from the movie crew or to give them a taste of their own fake movie reality.

The movie's star was upset by the staged shooting. In contrast to the movie's dreamy portrayal of the remote hamlet, Denver wrote in his 1994 autobiography, *Take Me Home*, that the visit to McCarthy was "one of the direst moments of that trip." The town's few dozen inhabitants "all seemed to spit nails when they talked." A few days after the locals "had a good laugh" at their expense, "it became a volatile situation. One night, one of the jokesters turned edgy, feeling one of us had gotten too interested in his girlfriend. The next day we finished up and got out of there, maybe none too soon."

Scenes that did make the final cut featured short speeches in the McCarthy Lodge about Nature and Freedom. The climax was an antic chase scene around ghost-town Kennecott in speeded-up slapstick style, with Tony Oney pursuing Denver down long rickety staircases and up exposed chimney ladders, as if it were a Buster Keaton training film for personal-injury lawyers.

In his book, Denver described Kennecott as "a wild streak of industrial violence" that "just sits there, brooding in the night." It might seem odd that a movie about preserving Alaska's wilderness would linger amid the frontier ruins of industrial capitalism, but the allegorical setting actually suited the times. The conservationist's fundamental truth, about the environment winning in the end, presses itself constantly upon a visitor's imagination in the Wrangells, there being no greater illustration than Kennecott itself. Juxtaposed against the propulsive boosterism of Alaska's modern oil boom, in which Alyeska Pipeline had replaced the Guggenheim Trust, Kennecott's ruins provided an almost religious tableau, a place where spiritual reassurance might be found in the atmosphere of decline and fall, in the inning when nature bats last.

Another oddity of the film was the starring role of the two hunting guides, who might easily have been cool to Denver's conservation message, given the hunting politics of the day. It was tough enough to be an Alaska guide in the 1970s, even for flying dentists. New guides were moving in, competing for space, and Dall sheep hunts were especially contested, being difficult, expensive, and attractive to high-end clients. There were bitter fights between traditional horsepacking outfits and short-trip fly-in guides, and disputes over certain high cirques and spike camps considered proprietary under an old code of honor that not every Johnny-come-lately subscribed to. The state was trying to sort out exclusive guide areas. Now a new national park threatened to close some hunting areas altogether—"taking up all the best land," as Harrower put it years later. Talk of a park brought a rush of hunters to the McCarthy airstrip every August, hoping to take a trophy off MacColl Ridge before it was too late.

Tony Oney and Hoppy Harrower said later they didn't foresee how a movie extolling Alaska's natural virtues might turn out to be so political. Yet they warned Denver away from accepting an offer to be grand marshal at the Anchorage Fur Rendezvous after the film showed, saying his life could be in danger. Their surprise at the film's pro-conservation stance seems a bit naïve, given the raging politics of the d-2 decade. But it may also be they could see the opportunity reflected in John Denver's wire-rim spectacles. In addition to being bush pilots and dentists and hunting guides, Oney and Harrower were partners with Howard Knutson in Consolidated Wrangell. Ten years earlier, they had been part of the failed effort to barrel up the last scrapings of copper and fly them out to Chitina. They had approached the mining venture with an old-fashioned single-mindedness, bulldozing structures like the Birch honeymoon mansion that got in the way of their trucks. By 1975 the mining camp owners were adapting, adjusting to the idea that resource extraction was no longer the future of the frontier. Oney, Harrower, and Knutson reformed their partnership that winter as the Great Kennicott Land Company and made preparations to survey Kennecott as a subdivision.

The big unanswered question in this business plan was what would become of the massive industrial edifices and the mountaintop mines. Hostility to the national park planners could be counterproductive: the best solution was probably a buyout by the federal government to preserve the historic landmark (minus the historical edifices we tore down—sorry!). In the meantime, the new park, even though it would cut back their sheep-hunting territory, would attract home buyers too starry-eyed to discern where the mine tailings ended and the glacial moraine began. One year after John Denver's visit, the cottages and offices and small warehouses featured so picturesquely in *American Child* were offered over the counter in Anchorage and snapped up in just a few weeks.

⇐——⇒

Similar land-buying pressures were starting to be felt down the mountain in McCarthy. But land titles in the old boomtown were more problematic. Ownership was difficult to trace through oral agreements, expired leases, and titles lost in a January 1949 fire that destroyed the Chitina recording office. There was a story about paper records blowing out of the back of a pickup truck as it drove through Copper Center. Deed holders had disappeared, and a few squatters accepted down payments from tourists for cabins they were occupying. Local conversations turned on fine points in the law of adverse possession. A claim jumper posting fliers about how he owned the town was run off by Les Hegland with a shotgun. And now, even as John Denver was filming in Kennecott, a new con man was advertising and selling lots in McCarthy based on a forged deed.

Much of the problem stemmed from the fact that McCarthy had never been staked as a federal townsite. The town had grown up, instead, on a private homestead. And the family that owned the homestead had left Alaska.

# 7

# Family Secrets

PAUL BARRETT, THIRTY-FIVE, a Harvard Law grad and a successful Seattle attorney, was taking depositions for a civil case in Washington, DC, on the afternoon in 1975 when he learned that his family owned a ghost town.

His father, Laurence Barrett, was the supervisor of Snoqualmie National Forest in Washington State. His grandfather, John Barrett, had been, in Paul's memory, a gentle and hard-working manager of a small apartment building in Tacoma.

John Barrett always had an air of mystery, however. In the brick basement of his apartment building, a private room was padlocked. The children had glimpsed a desk and boxes and a single bed. Their grandmother told Paul and his sisters to keep away from that dingy room. But their grandfather sometimes left candies on a shelf by the door, and the kids kept coming back.

Paul's grandfather died in 1961, when Paul was in college. And now, fourteen years later, he received a long-distance call from his father. Laurence Barrett needed legal help. Somebody was trying to steal the family ghost town in Alaska.

Of the many questions that leaped to Paul Barrett's mind, one of the first was: "Alaska?"

John Barrett went north to seek his fortune one year before gold was found in the Yukon. "The bears in Colorado were well thinned out and mining wasn't what it used to be," he explained to a reporter years later. It was 1895 and he was twenty-three. Barrett was one of the lucky few who were close at hand when they struck the Klondike. He jumped on the first boat headed up the river from Circle City, Alaska, the next spring. Outside Dawson, he found some gold on a stream called Sulphur Creek and years later told the newspaper reporter a dubious story about sharing a cabin that winter with Jack London.

On return visits to Colorado, the sparkling Doze sisters caught his eye. They were identical twins, and practical jokers, and it took him three visits to figure out which was the one he wanted to marry. Josephine Doze was eighteen and raring to go. John and Josephine traveled through Alaska for several summers, prospecting in the Fortymile River country. Eventually they settled in Bremerton, Washington, as John continued his summer expeditions.

In 1906, following reports of a major copper find, he scampered to the Wrangell Mountains and uncovered a streak of chalcocite ore in the next valley over from the Bonanza. It would be known as the Green Butte prospect—the dreamed-of extension of the Kennecott diggings. The mine developed its own tram and two miles of drift tunnels, but it never paid off.

For the next four decades, John Barrett would continue to poke around Alaska's mineralized belts. But his moment of genius, in July of 1906, had only peripherally to do with copper. That summer,

John and Josephine Barrett during their early years in McCarthy.

while Stephen Birch was in New York organizing the Alaska Syndicate, Barrett staked a homestead at the toe of the Kennicott Glacier. He calculated that any train collecting ore from the future Bonanza Mine would have to back up the side of the glacier to get to the mill. Locomotives would need a flat place to turn around. His 296 acres was the only flat space for a turntable and freight siding.

The following summer, when railroad surveyors saw what he'd done, Barrett agreed to lease some of his land to the Copper River & Northwestern. The railroad built a depot and crew quarters. In 1913, two years after the tracks were finished, Alaska's last gold rush brought stampeders on trains north from Cordova. They disembarked on Barrett's land and prepared to set out on foot across Chitistone Pass to Chisana (pronounced *Shushanna*, and spelled that way on Barrett's street map). Commerce boomed. Barrett quickly surveyed a townsite on a corner of the homestead. He named his new town, like the nearby creek, after James McCarthy, a well-liked prospector who helped stake the region's first copper claims and drowned when his horse bucked while fording the Tonsina River.

As tents and wood-frame buildings sprang up, Barrett leased lots and, once he'd gained title, sold them to the leaseholders, hoping to promote further growth. Josephine moved back north, and the couple settled into a town of well over a hundred people that had become the region's supply center and, for Kennecott's isolated miners, a social outlet where the nation's Prohibition laws had little influence. Johnny Barrett, as he was known, had nothing to do with the alcohol or prostitution. He sold land and insurance and ran a water distribution business. He tried to develop the Green Butte Mine. He stayed busy prospecting, hunting, gardening, and exploring. He guided the Bryn Mawr alpinist Dora Keen on first ascents of Mount Blackburn's east summit in 1911 and 1912, and she named a hanging glacier after him. The Barretts put up money for the town's recreation hall and donated land for a school and a baseball field. Josephine climbed Donoho Peak and drove alone to the Green Butte Mine for lunch with her husband. Josephine's brother from Colorado, Al Doze, came north and staked an adjacent homestead along McCarthy Creek.

Things seemed fine until 1921, when a fire burned out part of the business district, including the McCarthy Hotel, the town's finest. The town would rebuild, but the price of copper was down after the war, and production was already declining. The historian of the town's boom days, M. J. Kirchhoff, noted that John Barrett "must have suspected that McCarthy had seen its brightest days" because at that point he deleted several undeveloped blocks of his townsite, restoring them to his homestead. The Barretts sent their son, Laurence, away to high school in Seattle.

In the 1930s, Josephine moved full-time to Puget Sound to be near their son, who had finished college and was entering the US Forest Service. John spent his winters with her but continued his summer work at Green Butte and some Dan Creek gold claims. Not until 1943, turning seventy, did he give it up. After that, he drank coffee with other pioneers in Tacoma and swapped stories. He told a reporter he planned to return to Alaska "as soon as the way is open." The way never opened again.

Laurence Barrett, by this time married with three children, scraped together money for John and Josephine to buy a Tacoma apartment complex. Laurence's wife, Florence, was not happy about the financial strain of supporting her in-laws. The deed to a ghost town in Alaska seemed pitiful compensation. Despite being married to a forester, she was not moved by tales from the northwoods. Indeed, Florence and Josephine, strong-minded women who did not always see eye to eye, found common ground in their unsentimental appraisal of Alaska as a malign influence, a land of grandiose and thwarted dreams. The two matriarchs maintained what was effectively a conspiracy of silence in the presence of the children, keeping the very existence of McCarthy a family secret.

If Alaska came up at the dinner table, Josephine would say, "No one wants to hear your old stories, John." The aging pioneer descended quietly to his basement lair to handle business—the rare question arriving in the mail about some deed or old lease. In 1954 he sold four railroad buildings to young Howard Knutson, who advised him in a letter that the right of way and buildings had reverted to Barrett ownership after the railroad was abandoned. Up in Alaska, they still needed Johnny Barrett. The padlock keeping out the grandchildren also kept Josephine from throwing his old papers away.

Paul Barrett's little sister, Patsy, heard more about Alaska than her brother because she still lived at home when their grandfather's dementia first uncorked the stories. Patsy remembered being warned to look sharp as she left the Tacoma apartment building because a grizzly bear was lurking outside. After John Barrett died in 1961, Laurence started making periodic business trips to Alaska. Grandma Josephine waved away Patsy's curiosity about where he was going. The place they once lived had rotted away, Josephine said. There was nothing more to see.

In 1975 the secret came out. Three years later, after Josephine died, it emerged that her feelings about the ghosts of Alaska were more complicated than anyone realized. Laurence revealed to everyone a second family secret: in 1920, at the height of McCarthy's success, his mother had run off with another man.

The clues were there in John Barrett's old postcard collection, which Patsy held onto. For years, while John managed the affairs of the town in Alaska, Josephine had traveled through the states. Travel could be very social in those days. Her favorite thing about Alaska, she said later, was the voyage north every year on the steamships—days and nights of dancing and music and food. There were postcards to John from Lake Louise and Carlsbad Caverns and Yellowstone. On one of these trips, she fell in love with a man named Bill.

John, heartbroken, granted a divorce to his thirty-seven-year-old wife. Bill and Josephine married and settled in San Diego. Laurence was sent away to school. McCarthy burned in 1921, and John withdrew his undeveloped lots from the market. The future looked bleak to the town's founder.

One year later, his rival suffered an aneurysm and fell dead.

Along with the postcards, Patsy found two telegrams from 1922: one sent to McCarthy, and the reply:

*Dear John, Bill died. What do I do now?*

*Dear Josephine, Come home.*

John and Josephine were remarried at the Chitina Hotel in 1923.

Florence was appalled that her husband had withheld such an important story. Josephine Barrett had loomed so large in all their lives. Laurence apologized, saying he'd promised never to tell. The family kept its secrets.

In 1976, the year Laurence Barrett retired from the Forest Service, Patsy had proposed a family trip to Alaska to trace her grandfather's footsteps. She was a public health researcher at Berkeley, married with her own kids. Laurence was delighted, and Florence was enticed to go along by the prospect of a summer with her four-year-old granddaughter. The family traveled to Skagway and on to Dawson, following John Barrett's route to the Klondike. Finally they made it to the Wrangells, to see what remained of the Barrett family's town.

The drive to McCarthy on the rough pioneer road in 1976 was arduous. Patsy recalled her mother in the back seat, alternating between "Slow down!" and "When are we ever going to get there?"

A happy surprise awaited them. The sky was blue. White summits gleamed. The continent's biggest mountain wilderness reached in all directions.

Patsy's husband, an urban planner, was the first to snap to attention. "This is the most amazing place we've ever seen," he told Laurence.

Patsy's father proved to be well known around the town, or what was left of it. It turned out Laurence had been visiting since 1965, when Howard Knutson got in touch about building the new McCarthy airstrip. There was more to do these days—sorting out land ownership, quit-claiming deeds to people who had bought cabins from non-owners, and quieting title to reclaim abandoned lots for the family. Laurence sold a few lots to young people who seemed genuinely interested in building and staying. He kept a sleeping bag at Les and Flo Heglands' house.

McCarthy now had a dozen or so year-round residents and was growing again. The Barretts had arranged to stay in Archie Poulin's house. They still owned at least a third of the town, including, arguably, the very streets, given that McCarthy was laid out on a homestead and not a federal townsite. Patsy watched her father treat locals with the deference of an outsider, which struck her as ironic, since he was probably the only person around who actually grew up there.

During the years of absent Barretts, shady deals and mistrust had grown. There had been a few flim-flam sales—ghost town transfers haunted by phantom title records. Those who knew McCarthy in the 1960s and 1970s—Jim Edwards, Mudhole Smith's son Kenny, the Heglands' daughter Janet, the Millers at the Lodge—said Laurence Barrett brought back the handshake deal.

"He told us those were Alaska values he learned from his father," Patsy said, years later. "Like my grandfather, he was so kind and gentle and honest—I came to think that these values must have come from living the good life in Alaska—but, of course, one cannot generalize from a sample of two."

Laurence spent a good part of that 1976 visit traipsing through the woods with Patsy's husband, clearing brush in search of property corners. Les Hegland had alerted him that the flim-flam artists were back. Laurence was fighting them in court.

Somebody was selling surveyed lots off the homestead owned by Al Doze, Laurence's uncle. The sellers had a notarized warranty deed from Tacoma purporting to prove that Alfred Victor Doze sold them the land in 1975. Uncle Al, however, had passed away in Mesa County, Colorado, in 1955.

Laurence Barrett took his complaint to the Alaska State Troopers but was told it appeared to be a civil dispute. He was advised to get a lawyer.

Laurence's son, Paul, was familiar with the courtrooms of Alaska. He had handled cases in Anchorage as a commercial litigator from Seattle. But he knew nothing about his own Alaska roots. As far as he could now determine, his great-uncle's McCarthy homestead had never passed properly through state probate. He opened an ancillary probate in Anchorage court and, on behalf of his grandmother Josephine, Al Doze's sister and heir, sued the Copper Valley Investment Corporation.

The faraway outpost of McCarthy encountered its first bold pipeline-era hustle in 1974, when a Nevada businessman named Carl Pool showed up at the McCarthy Lodge to set up a rest-and-recreation facility for pipeline workers. He claimed to be representing the Fluor Corporation, but it emerged on further questioning by the lodge owner that Pool and the two business associates accompanying him—Candy, age eighteen, and Michelle, age twenty-two—represented neither Alyeska Pipeline nor its pump station contractor. As an independent venture, it emerged Pool had made arrangements to buy a "palatial" facility in McCarthy, but upon inspection the palace proved to have holes in the walls. Pool proposed instead to base his operation at the lodge, flying workers in a DC-3 during their time off from Valdez and handing over a 40 percent cut. In the 1920s, such a proposal would have not been out of place, at least in certain parts of town. But Candy, Michelle, and Carl Pool were sent dismissively back to the runway. Two weeks later Pool and his wife, both in fact low-level Fluor employees, were arrested in Valdez on charges of transporting females for immoral purposes, at which point they were ordered back to Nevada by that state's probation and parole department.

In 1976 the Barrett family's adversary, the Copper Valley Investment Corp., was the brainchild of an Anchorage businessman named George Brown, former right-hand man of the locally famous strip-mall developer Pete Zamarello. Amassing and losing several real estate fortunes during Alaska's early oil-boom years, Zamarello had already been convicted of tax evasion and drawn multiple lawsuits; he would later be convicted of bank fraud. In 1973 Brown and Zamarello had shepherded a scheme to sell raw land in the Matanuska Valley to wealthy Arab businessmen, telling the *Anchorage Times* that their investment firm had obtained a six-story office building on London's Hyde Park. The investment firm wound up getting sued by investors from the Middle East who claimed they'd been sold worthless swampland.

George Brown turned to the Wrangells. He stopped first at Chitina, investing in the hotel and other buildings. Two years later, the state sold off those same properties, by court order, to satisfy a lien against Brown. By that time, however, he had moved on to the Doze homestead in McCarthy.

In court, Brown's lawyers treated Paul Barrett like a Seattle big shot trying to push Alaskans off their land. The Superior Court judge handling the case was a conservative no-nonsense jurist named Ralph Moody, whose territorial law career stretched back to World War II. He was unimpressed by the "protect-us-locals" line. Barrett won a quick agreement bringing sales to a stop. Settlement talks were soon underway.

The case was complicated because money had changed hands, and new deeds were recorded. Some of the buyers had been business associates of George Brown's, including Duncan Webb, an Anchorage attorney about to be disbarred and convicted as an accessory to a notorious local murder of a gambler and massage parlor owner named Johnny Rich.

The biggest new owner of Doze homestead lots was right there in McCarthy: the miner and Cat skinner Gordon Burdick, excavator of the hippie hole. Burdick was the one who first clued Brown into the vacant Doze land and the 1949 fire at the recording office in Chitina. He advised Brown he might be able to get the land cheap if he could find Doze's relatives. When Brown came back with a story about finding Doze himself in a nursing home, Burdick was skeptical, according to his daughter, Kathy. She recalled her father wringing his hands nervously. But then he told George Brown about the Green Butte Mine, where Burdick had staked a number of new claims on the theory that the original claimants, including Paul Barrett's grandfather, had missed the good stuff. Brown traded Burdick twenty acres of the Doze land for a stake in the Green Butte.

Now they found themselves together in court.

One person surprised by this unfolding legal dispute was Doug Pope, owner of a disputed lot and a lawyer himself. Neither a local, exactly, nor an associate of Brown's, he had bought five acres from his captivating friend Gordon Burdick and encouraged other friends to do the same.

Doug Pope grew up in Fairbanks and would go on to prominence in Alaska not only as a lawyer but a writer and member of the state Board of Game. In the mid-1970s he had a ponytail and beard and had just returned from law school with an energy for adventure of the sort that was bursting all over Alaska in those days. Pope had spent his college summers hunting for a place off the road system where he and his friends could build a back-to-the-land homestead and prepare for worldwide economic collapse. They looked in the Southeast and along the Tanana River, in the northwest on the Ambler

John Barrett, the town's founder, maintained his ties in later years and kept them secret from his family.

and Kobuk Rivers, at Lake Clark and around Kachemak Bay. Pope discovered the Chitina River valley through his high school buddy, the brash tie-dyed pilot Sumner Putman, now living in his dome on Fireweed Mountain. "It's like another country back in there," Putman's wife told Pope, enticingly.

Gordon Burdick was one of the most entertaining bullshitters Pope had ever met. He had that eyes-on-the-prize squint of the old miners. Burdick claimed his dog, Rusty, a golden retriever with streaks of gray around the mouth, could smell copper underground. Some of his stories turned out to be true. Burdick once described going into the woods at thirty below to rescue an accident victim. They had to wait for daylight, so he made a fire under a dead spruce tree. The fire climbed through the dead branches, and Burdick realized the supposedly dead tree was green when its needles torched like a rocket. The woods lit up, and the mountainside above, and for thirty or forty minutes they were warm. Then the dark and cold descended and he walked over and torched off another green tree, and thus they made it through the night. Doug Pope didn't believe him, but Burdick took him for a ride over Porphyry Mountain in his Piper Cub and pointed out the stand of burned-out spruce.

Burdick produced some "jeweler grade" ore from the Green Butte and convinced Pope to truck it to Anchorage, where the pile remained for years in Pope's backyard. Burdick's meal ticket in those days, Pope realized, was getting investors to take options on the Green Butte prospects. The fact that Burdick was squatting in a house in McCarthy but claimed to own it should have been a red flag to someone in the legal profession, Pope conceded later. Pope was nevertheless drawn to giving Burdick a little cash and helping with legal advice on those expired mining options, in exchange for five acres of Burdick's land along McCarthy Creek.

Pope now found himself in front of Judge Ralph Moody, representing the interests of Burdick—and all those who had bought from Burdick, including a few friends Pope had invited in.

Like his father before him, Laurence Barrett was sympathetic to settlers. On May 20, 1977, he agreed to allow bona fide purchasers, who had been unaware of the fraud, to keep their land. Some parties disclaimed interest and walked away, including Anchorage lawyer Duncan Webb, whose troubles had deepened when his own defense attorney, in closing arguments at the murder trial, explained away certain inconsistencies by referring to his client as a "pathological liar." George Brown returned to Anchorage, where he developed a subdivision in a Knik River floodplain that led to state consumer-fraud charges and a 1978 court order to pay back $1.6 million to landowners.

The Doze-Barrett settlement would drag on eight more years. In the end, the Barretts gave up fifty-five acres without compensation. Twenty of those acres went to Gordon Burdick, who continued to sell lots that had no access except through adjoining Barrett land.

Doug Pope got to keep his five acres. Most of it now lies in the wide rocky bed of McCarthy Creek, which rerouted itself in an epic flood during a 1980 typhoon. Pope kept his surviving sliver as a reminder of a lesson learned from a pair of swindlers who, he came to realize, were perfectly matched.

"George Brown had traded land he didn't own for rights to a mine with no copper," Pope recalled. "Burdick and Brown were both scammers. The difference was Burdick believed his scams were real."

In the summer of 1977, having negotiated the initial Doze homestead settlement, Paul Barrett finally flew to the Wrangell Mountains to see the family secret for himself.

His grandmother would have been disappointed to watch Alaska exert its malign influence once again. Paul Barrett's blissful ignorance about the place gave way to obsessive curiosity. He asked questions of everyone he could find, including J. B. O'Neill, the former McCarthy storekeeper in Seattle who had stories about John Barrett. Laurence Barrett lived to the age of ninety-four, but long before he died, his son had taken over close personal supervision of the family's Alaska interests. Paul Barrett and his wife and children made long summer visits to McCarthy, where he attended to town affairs and eventually rebuilt his grandfather's horse barn into a comfortable second home. The Barrett family was back.

# 8

# The Ghost Town Gazette

I N THE SPRING of 1975, Melody Webb Grauman, the National Park
Service historian preparing her definitive account of the Kennicott River valley's industrial beginnings, sent a memo to park planners calling attention to the town of McCarthy. It was, she said, a
rare window into a way of life that was supposed to have disappeared
long ago.

Her greater subject was preservation of the valley's human landscapes, scars and all. Mostly, this meant appraising the abandoned
city of timber and iron beside the Kennicott Glacier. The structures
at Kennecott—of relatively recent construction and remarkably pre-
served in the dry, cold climate—had a vividness already faded in
older ghost towns of the American West. A powerful sense of place,
like Kennecott's, was an essential precursor to the sense of loss such
places aroused. By 1975 Interior Department officials, like Gruening
before them, had come to appreciate the narrative value of the ruins'
rise and fall. The pristine wilderness had a human story.

Ghost towns like McCarthy-Kennecott had become tourist attractions across much of the American West. There was a beguiling absence in those scattered tombstones of expansion, communities crushed by depletion of resources or cruelly distant economic forces, bypassed by new throughways coursing powerfully across the continent's empty spaces. History moved on, but places left behind could stir the soul. A travel boom in the 1920s first drew attention to the West's ghost towns, as the birth of automobile tourism coincided with a wave of nostalgia for disappearing pioneer days. A second, more fervent craze, with guidebooks and landmark-preservation efforts, got underway in the 1950s. This was the period that inspired Mudhole Smith's Sourdough Tours flights to May Creek. Americans in the age of the atomic bomb seemed to enjoy making these "pilgrimages to nowhere" and pondering that enigma of ruins, from Rome to Bodie, California: is this where we've been, or where we're going?

There even developed a small but stimulating body of academic scholarship around the symbolic landscapes of ghost towns, in which old-timers' tales become "tropes" and failed schemes leave a "palimpsest of human intentions." The repetitive boom-and-bust story lines ignite bookish disputes—are the ruins tragic monuments to human endeavor, as the classical school would have it, or, in the framing of revisionist historian Patricia Nelson Limerick, places where we can "learn from the landscape of failure"? Meanwhile philosophers consider the "neo-romantic malaise" of ruin-obsession, or the liberating "radical perspectivism" that comes from watching nature, disrupted, reassert control.

To all this, the ephemeral towns maintain their stony silence. Philosophers, like tourists and local historians, are left to unpack the things they carry.

In Alaska the Kennecott ghost town invoked an especially powerful story, given the state's vulnerable resource economies and its engrained historical fear of becoming a ghost state. Alaska's map was pocked with deserted mining camps (and abandoned canneries, their local salmon runs mined to depletion), with names like Poorman, Cripple, Woodchopper, El Dorado, Eureka, and Sunrise. None were on a scale like Kennecott or told a story so complicated. The Wrangells had hardly been a "landscape of failure," not for the eastern financiers who built the railroad. But the local promise that came with great investment was not redeemed. The ghost town as a sanctifying symbol of what's been lost is almost an essential counterpoint, in the Alaska imagination, to the boomer-builder mentality. The historian William Cronon, later president of the American Historical Association, published in 1992 a classic essay, "Kennecott Journey: The Paths out of Town," in which he marveled at the freshness of the ruined factory town—"its haunting could almost have begun yesterday"—and how it felt more like the West than the North. "The past of these people is written in the marks they made upon this land," Cronon wrote. "If one wanted a case study for thinking about environmental change in the West as a whole, one could do a lot worse than to make the long journey to Kennecott."

One important task of the environmental historian, Cronon wrote, is to explore "culturally constructed" boundaries between people and nature and to locate in those boundaries "the paths out of town." Cronon concluded his essay movingly, with a description of escapees from the urban world who came now to gaze past the symbol of romantic decay into a world they saw as civilization's opposite, a "wilderness that is culture's creature, the place where nature and history have met and turned, and turned again."

In 1975, with the national debate over Alaska's d-2 conservation lands in full voice, Melody Webb Grauman advised that it was not too late to include a historical component in a future national park. The Kennecott mining camp could be saved, she said, if the desire were strong enough. "The interpretive possibilities are mind-boggling, as are the expenses of preservation," she wrote in her planning memo. Elsewhere in the Chitina Valley, the last surviving trestles, blackened by creosote and age, could evoke the railroad for future visitors.

But she called special attention to the living town of McCarthy. The community's way of life was a rare thing, she said. And in 1975 it was on the threshold of change. There seemed to be nothing, she said, that could stand in the way.

*The town, as it is now, provides a unique Alaskan historical experience. A near ghost town with buildings fallen into disrepair captures the feeling of a long ago past. However, the hotel without modern conveniences and the lifestyles of the town's citizens allow a glimpse into that past as an on-going present. The individualism and independence of the townspeople will probably spell the end to this experience. Without restrictive covenants, new buildings will destroy the town's character; without concern for historic preservation, the town's original buildings will fall into ruins; and, without population control and management, the improved accessibility and proposed park will have a dynamic and detrimental impact on the town.*

◁——▷

Even as Grauman wrote about discovering the past in the ongoing present, demographic trends were accelerating the pace of change. McCarthy was seeing the first stirrings of a reverse migration, after decades of watching the tide of life recede—a return of humans attracted by the absence of other humans. "What a luxury to have this second chance," John Denver said in his movie. Of these "neo-pioneers," as some academics had taken to categorizing them, not altogether disparagingly, only a handful had the skills to persist in

By 1974, McCarthy was starting to attract a new generation of settlers.

the severe conditions of the Wrangells. They had to learn to live with less, in weather and isolation more extreme than back-to-the-land settlers faced in Vermont or California. Bonnie Morris, a young seamstress who moved to McCarthy in the mid-1970s, liked to quote an early sourdough: "Just tell me what you need, and I'll tell you how to get along without it."

Bonnie Morris brought with her a copy of Gary Snyder's translation from Chinese of *Cold Mountain Poems*—"Who can leap the world's ties and sit with me among the white clouds?" Many years later, she recalled being one of those drawn to the Wrangell Mountains by the spellbinding landscape, whose distance from the modern world fed a quest for renunciation and spiritual uplift. They came to immerse themselves fully in wilderness, not as a scenic backdrop but as a force flowing through their daily lives. But there were practical, less romantic reasons, peculiar to the area's history, that made the Kennicott River valley a destination.

For one thing, there was no living Alaska Native presence, which elsewhere in Alaska could make a back-to-the-land movement feel like an invasion. The valley had once been home to people associated with the Ahtna chief Nicolai, who maintained a sheep-hunting camp on the middle Nizina, at the mouth of Dan Creek, and a winter camp on the upper Chitina, at the mouth of the Kiagna River. There had never been a central village, though, because the country was hungry and the Ahtna had to keep moving around. After the death of Nicolai and construction of the railroad, outlying sites were abandoned. Western communities rarely gave much thought to the absence of their Indigenous antecedents, and so it was here with the valley's first ghosts. The Ahtna were still around, of course, having settled full-time down the valley in the village of Taral, on the Copper River, where red salmon could be dipnetted in midsummer. In the 1920s, the local Natives crossed the water into Chitina to attend a territorial school. But half a century later, when the land claims settlement act gave the Ahtna rights to select nearly two million acres of federal land within their traditional homeland for a Native-shareholder corporation, the mountains and valleys of the upper Chitina were off limits, having been withdrawn for national conservation purposes.

The land was not off-limits to settlement, however. Another more practical consideration for the neo-pioneers was a relative abundance of private property. Most of Alaska was still in the federal domain. But in McCarthy, an envelope for development was a legacy of mining days, what with the Barrett property in town, the mine worker cottages at Kennecott, and abandoned private farms across the Kennicott River, which flowed from the old bridge pilings down to the Nizina and Chitina Rivers, and soon became the center of new activity. Hundreds of empty acres of state land on the far side of the river were sold off at an outcry auction in Copper Center in 1963.

The reverse migration started slowly. In the 1960s, nobody at all moved to that sold-off state land across the river. Most of the owners were in Anchorage or Fairbanks, content to dream "someday" about their piece of remote Alaska. Some stopped making payments and turned their lots back to the state. Empty private homesteads like the Holtet farm, where the valley's blacksmith left his tools and a buckboard wagon, sat waiting for someone to come back and resume the backbreaking labor.

Then Alaska's oil economy started to churn. With the new bridge across the Copper River in 1971, the pressure-cooker atmosphere in town grew, what with Raven and the hippie hole, Gordon Burdick's schemes, Winnie Darkow's lodge, and the road controversy. Fred Potts left the country, putting his air taxi permit up for grabs, and in the dispute between Darkow and Howard Knutson that followed, a Fairbanks pilot trying to set up in McCarthy told Curtis Green: "I thought folks living in the country were supposed to be mellow, but everyone around here is wound up tighter than the E string on a violin."

In 1973, just as the bridge into town was being completed, an older couple, the Lancasters, bought the small robin's-egg-blue Mezzerini house, along with the town's only package-store liquor license. Slim Lancaster had been a local moonshiner during mining days and long dreamed of returning to the valley. He had once run a rest stop along the wagon road to Kennecott and went to jail after his still upstairs boiled over, dripping hot liquid on a federal marshal who had stopped for pie and coffee. Miners quickly took up a collection to bail out their favorite bootlegger.

Slim Lancaster's return meant trouble for Curtis Green and his brother, Loy, who had settled into the Mezzerini house after getting fired as Kennecott watchmen. They found themselves abruptly cast out and blamed Slim's wife.

"Slim was a very pleasant, easy-going fellow, but his wife, Peg, who obviously wore the pants, was another story altogether," Curtis Green wrote in his memoir. Peg Lancaster settled into the town's "bubbling cauldron of controversy, conflict and intrigue," according to Curtis, "as delightedly as a suburban matron stepping into a hot tub. There was no way that that fancy lady was going to live in the little hovel that her unassuming husband had bought, so with dizzying speed they (i.e. she) bought out the Edwards and moved into their place. Jim and Maxine had for some time toyed with the idea of selling out and building over on Swift Creek on the other side of the Kennicott River where they had land, but they must have been stunned at the abruptness with which that future arrived. . . . So in one of those delicious ironies that Life so obviously loves, teetotaler Jim Edwards's house became, for a while, the McCarthy Bar and Liquor Store. But Slim didn't stick around long to enjoy it. He died of a heart attack within a year of moving in. At least he realized his dream, however briefly. May he rest in peace, he certainly deserves it."

Jim Edwards recalled a similar version of events that summer, how they sold out to the Lancasters—"we saw these people and realized they had some money"—and later how Slim died and Peg moved on, selling the house to the McCarthy Lodge. It made sense, he said, putting the two buildings under common ownership. He'd had to fight with the lodge all the time, living next door: Winnie Darkow tried to claim ownership of the family shed by adverse possession, asserting he'd stored things there for years while Edwards stood "idly by." Jim had to get a court order to defend his property.

And so it was that, just as the bridge into town opened, however briefly, Jim Edwards and his family, declaring themselves tired of friction in town, became the first to jump into the empty land across the river.

Jim Edwards had been preparing for years, staging materials at Swift Creek on eighty acres bought at the state auction. Town life was wearing him down. For the next two years on the west side of the river, Jim and Maxine and their two children lived in a red Kennecott-era railroad shack that Jim had dragged to their land behind his bulldozer. They called the place "Shacky." In summers, the children bailed out: Steve had a bed in a 1960 VW bus; Shelly, in her "playhouse," a child-sized cabin built by her dad.

On a forested bank of the cobblestone river flats, Jim worked slowly on their wood-frame home. He carved trees into roof beams with a ship adze and suspended rafters with iron salvaged from a railroad bridge. He bought the three-story Mother Lode powerhouse in town, which was full of building materials, including 153 weathered bricks to line the wall behind his wood-burning stove. "We still might have to clean a little more efflorescence off of them," he wrote in 1976 to his father, the Oregon factory owner, with whom he kept up a lively correspondence. "Wish it was your brick, but these are here."

When it was time to build stairs, Jim devoted three days to studying the angles and available materials. Jim explained to his son this was why he chose to live in the Wrangells—to have time to think things through.

Once they moved into the big house, Jim bulldozed a long flat space through the forest and planted it with grass. He tended this airstrip like a golf fairway. He built a shop using tools and steel and heavy vises hauled from the mining camp in a flatbed truck named Rigormortis, which was itself assembled from the parts of several abandoned vehicles. He invented a tracked snowmobile the same way, a decade before the first Ski-Doos were available, improvising with salvaged leather belts and skis and an auto frame. Impressive in concept, the prototype proved too heavy to move in the snow. But that was the way he liked to build things, one idea following the next—his inventions had the same rambling nature as his storytelling.

A hot tub—cut out of a heavy iron boiler from the Mother Lode powerhouse—failed because the local spruce and alder didn't burn hot enough to warm the metal. His waterwheel was more successful. After the state sent someone out to make sure there were no migrating salmon, Jim dammed Swift Creek and built a tall wheel to generate electricity, adding a compressor when the initial system couldn't kick-start a freezer motor. He told friends he built the dam so he could run a freezer for ice cream, which you could hand-crank using glacier ice in summer but could never keep for long. He liked ice cream with bits of pralines and chocolate.

Maxine managed the home—correspondence-schooling the kids by kerosene and Coleman fuel and electric bulb, baking and cooking, playing Chopin and Christmas carols on a piano dragged in behind the cable-blade D-4. She kept a special set of dishes for company. Her garden produced long orderly rows of vegetables for canning and deep ranks of flowers around the cabin. She got an early start on planting by pouring hot water into an old car radiator that Jim buried under the flower beds. She brought a thermos and ginger cookies on woodcutting expeditions. She took walks exploring for wildflowers. An old wagon trail bumped along the riverbank to their place, through spreads of pink river beauties, purple vetch, and puff-brained dryas. They drove the road slowly in Rigormortis, or walked, kicking big rocks out of the way.

The family went on expeditions to explore the region—gold sluicing at Dan Creek or camping on a mountainside above the Nizina, where Jim tried to measure the movement of a rock glacier.

His eyes lit up like a child's whenever he found his favorite fossil: *Pseudomonotis subcircularis,* a bivalve shell dating back to when the Wrangell mountaintops lay on the ocean floor. Jim published several droll stories in the *Alaska Sportsman* magazine about their life in McCarthy. Jim got the byline, but the amused tone of shrugging understatement closely resembles the voice in Maxine's surviving letters.

"One of our neighbors here ran out of wood four or five days ago. I don't know what they've been burning, but evidently they're finding something—probably feeding the old abandoned house next to them through the stove," Maxine wrote her aunt and uncle in December 1968 before the family moved across the river. "There are five others living in town this winter, besides ourselves. So we don't have to worry about getting trampled in the pre-Christmas rush anyway. It sure is quiet out here. If it weren't for hearing the neighbor's chain saw every now and then, you wouldn't think there was anyone for miles around."

Seven years later, she wrote Jim's father, now remarried in Oregon, from their new homestead at Swift Creek. That winter, she wrote, they were "the only ones over here on this side of the river—us and the coyotes. We hear them howling and a-barking out on the airstrip some nights. The moon has been so bright these past few nights. It illumines the snow and the spruce trees so pretty. The ice on the creek outside the door makes all kinds of weird creaky cracking sounds. And then the house will pop and snap real loud all of a sudden like they do in the cold. I don't know what causes it. Love, Maxine."

Over time, the isolation began to weigh on her. In 1978, with the kids away in Valdez, boarding with friends to attend high school, she left the homestead for a job at the principal workplace of the Copper River basin: the pipeline pump station in Glennallen. Her goal, she wrote her father-in-law, was to make money for a family vacation to visit relatives and friends on the East Coast. She worked seven weeks in a non-union job, planting trees and grass along the pipeline route gouged from the Alaska Range to Valdez.

"I admit I've enjoyed having such luxurious meals fixed for me, having my bed made, all the fresh fruits, sauna baths, movies that I could ever want," she wrote from the work camp in a letter to her in-laws. She worried about fitting in her jeans after all the New York steak and prawns and crab and pineapples flown from Hawaii. As for negative aspects, she cited "all the rough talk, pot smoking, drinking, etc. There sure is a lot of that . . . I inhaled so much cigarette smoke cooped up in buses riding back and forth to our job sites, which sometimes took up three hours of time each day." The camp was full of lonely men, but she'd had no unwanted advances. "It is a very subtle thing these men are watching for, and I have tried to communicate that I want no part of it."

The work itself was physical but unrushed. "Have had lots worse things to handle right at home. Harder work too, at times. We had a lot of poor transportation, and vehicles would break down and we've spent hours and hours just sitting around waiting for stuff to be repaired. Whole crews sitting around, getting paid 11–16 dollars an hour. It is so unreal. For lack of a $5 part. I could write a book about it."

Jim Edwards was not happy having Maxine gone, though often enough he had gone away for work himself. He could see how the solitude might be getting to her. If she had more company, she might be less restless. He told Kenny Smith, visiting from Anchorage, that he had started hoping for neighbors.

⟵——⟶

There were a few other people around the valley, but most lived some distance away. Cliff and Maureen Wright were across the Nizina near

May Creek. Once in a while they came to town, and everyone would gather at Tony Zak's to play music on a cassette deck and watch Maureen belly dance. The Wrights divorced after nearly dying from heavy metal poisoning. The problem was traced to a natural arsenic seep in their drinking water source, a rusty, sulfur-smelling creek that never froze. The mail plane pilot saved them when he stopped at May Creek and observed their pallor.

Closer at hand were the Wassermans, a young couple who showed up the west side of the river in 1974. Eric and Joan Wasserman were college graduates from New York City who moved to Alaska to live in the bush. They found out about McCarthy one night when Eric was hitchhiking in Anchorage and got picked up by Sumner Putman. The hippie pilot described how he liked to take a small hit of acid, soar high above the Nizina River, cut his engine, and drift in wide descending circles until he got to fifteen hundred feet.

Eric was tall and dark-bearded. Joan, sunny and brown-haired, wore a headkerchief as they worked on their gambrel-roof log cabin. "Everything you did, you appreciated it. You were doing everything for yourself," Joan later recalled. They learned on the job. They didn't have a drawknife to peel house logs, and Eric went to see his new neighbor. Jim Edwards pulled open a drawer holding six drawknives and invited Eric to help himself. "He showed me his pipe wrenches. He had them from six inches to six feet. I assume they all came out of Kennecott." Jim struck some people as irritatingly stubborn, but with Eric he was generous with time and tools. His reputation as a skinflint was legendary—asking for hot water at the lodge as he withdrew a dried-up tea bag from his shirt pocket, or turning off the propane before the beans were done and letting them finish with residual heat. That he had a small portfolio of stocks, and occasionally passed along to Eric a *Wall Street Journal* sent by his father via mail plane, added mystery.

Maxine enjoyed having Joan Wasserman for a neighbor. Maxine took Joan berry-picking in the fall, and in early summer to a secret grove of white wildflowers surrounded by purple ones—albino lupine. Joan found it hard to keep up with Maxine, who chewed coffee beans for energy. Joan thought Maxine was a good partner for Jim because they were both Capricorns and loved nature. When Joan was pregnant and broke her wrist, Jim flew her to Glennallen in his plane. The Wassermans played dominoes with the Edwards kids when Jim and Maxine came to visit. "Joan had just baked bagels when we got there, and also some yogurt and cookies, so I guess we timed that right," Maxine wrote to Jim's father. "Have you ever eaten bagels? They're good—kind of a hard roll. I think she said you boil them in water, before baking them. I think bagels are Jewish."

Another young woman welcomed into the valley by Maxine was Bonnie Morris. Bonnie was a skin-sewer of leather and fur. On winter nights, she made parkas on a treadle sewing machine in a little cabin by headlamp. When she first arrived with her boyfriend in the fall of 1977, lugging a box of books on Taoism and Sufism and old Rex Beach novels, she was struck not so much by the isolation as by the community, and in particular the handful of tough and savvy local women, in some ways playing traditional women's roles but also liberated by the need to take care of everything on their own. Bonnie had grown up hearing Alaska stories of "wrestling grizzly bears and striking it rich—very male-oriented fantasies." The women, she saw now, were unsung heroes. They could operate a Caterpillar, roll a fifty-five-gallon drum of diesel onto a porch, shoot a bear off the porch and skin it—but they also had an artful way of turning a social visit into a tea party, unlike their laconic and insufficiently appreciative husbands. Bonnie noticed these women often stayed isolated from one another if their husbands didn't get along. Yet they provided moments of grace in the wilderness. She was thinking of Flo

An adventurous spirit led Bonnie Morris to the Chitina River valley in the 1970s.

Hegland, Frieda Burdick, Fran Gagnon, Cora Andersen, a few others, and especially Maxine Edwards.

That first winter, Bonnie Morris and her boyfriend, Kelly Bay, set out to build his cabin. Bay, who would one day found Wrangell Mountain Air, the park's main backcountry flying service, was at the time a young pipeline worker with a 1961 Ford pickup and a Homelite XL 12 chainsaw. He bought a piece of the old Doze homestead along McCarthy Creek, ignoring warnings from Les Hegland and Jim Edwards not to do business with Gordon Burdick. He later had to hire an attorney and benefitted from the land settlement offered by Laurence and Paul Barrett.

Kelly and Bonnie set up a canvas ten-by-twelve-foot wall tent that October and commenced to cutting logs. They were hoping to make quick work of the cabin. The temperature soon plunged to forty below and stayed in that vicinity for five weeks. It was an exceptional cold spell, even for the upper Chitina valley. Joan Wasserman had her picture taken next to a thermometer that read minus sixty-four. It was impossible to keep a wall tent warm, especially with nothing but young green second-growth for firewood—Bonnie could sit on the woodstove. The only escape from the temperature inversions that locked down the valley floor was to climb to a friend's angle-station cabin along the old tram lines above Kennecott, where it might be fifty degrees warmer. By midwinter, all Bonnie could think about was their next meal and their clothing—the frozen laundry, stiff as cardboard, took up half the tent. The new cabin's walls were still only two logs high.

A decade later, Bonnie Morris recalled what those pioneer women meant that first winter.

*About mid-way into the winter I found that I was crying a lot and that I was overwhelmed, feeling like I'd bit off more than I could chew, and yet I felt really committed to this project. It was going so slowly and it was so hard I felt like I was really starting to lose it. I remember thinking that I'd go over and visit Maxine Edwards and take the day off. So I made a thermos and took a little rucksack and I had bunny boots. I remember walking across the Kennicott and I didn't know much about ice then, or crossing ice, or how to read ice with running rivers under it, and I went through slush ice along the side and got a little wet and had water in my boots. It was pretty cold in January and the days were really short, so it would have taken the whole day to walk over there. I'd have to spend the night and then come back the next day. It was a two-day journey because we had such short days—not like it is in the summer.*

*So I get over there and I was wet, tired, and cold and ragged out anyway, and I got over there and their house had a sense of order, where you thought it was always like that. I had no idea they started with brown chore gloves in a big alder grove and cleared it and built it. So I walk into this nice home and I remember there was this big three-decker chocolate cake sitting on this glass cake plate with a glass lid and Maxine asked, "Do you want a piece of cake?"*

*I'd been cooking on a Coleman stove so I said of course, I'd love a piece of cake. And I felt I was too dirty to sit in any of their furniture. And she served it on a little china plate with a little china teacup and she could kinda see my state. So I had the piece of cake and I looked up at her and I said, "Maxine, when you first came out here, did you ever cry?" She looked me right in the eye and she said, "Cry? I couldn't stop crying for five years after I realized what I'd gotten myself into."*

*I sort of burst out crying and laughing and thinking how I was getting this big lump in my throat and the tears just started pouring out and I said, "Oh, I thought there was something wrong with me."*

<figure>❮——❯</figure>

In 1978 a new neighbor family appeared near the Edwardses' place, and it was as if they had been sent by God.

Rick Kenyon, a Florida gunsmith and airplane mechanic, said he felt called to Alaska in 1976 to do the Lord's work. With his wife, Bonnie, and their ten-year-old son, Rick Jr., the family moved first to Valdez, a small and sinful port in the midst of the pipeline construction boom. They moved on to the mountains, where their first stop was Long Lake, west of McCarthy—the lakeside "resort" that had been home to the Black trapper George Flowers and the grizzled outlaw prospector George Smock.

The valley had never had a church, even during the peak of industrial mining. Rick Kenyon knew progress would be slow—preaching the Resurrection might be tough in a ghost town. "He's going to plow some rocky ground," Jim Edwards predicted to Curtis Green.

The Kenyons built a log cabin that first summer at Long Lake for Hank Hoffer, who owned the old Oscar Anderson homestead. An absentee owner, he let them stay that winter. Rick Jr. would happily recall jigging through the ice for lake trout and grayling. But Bonnie Kenyon found her first season of wilderness isolation to be very complicated socially.

Hank Hoffer was feuding with Cliff and Jewel Collins from Cordova, whose fly-in summer place on the lake was surrounded by colorful summer gardens. The Collins family had bought the old Fagerberg homestead in 1961 and seemed to have inherited the Fagerberg-Anderson feud in the process. They bought the transplanted railroad depot from George Smock and built their home around it. They used a rebuilt pump-action speeder on the tracks toward Chitina until the rails were removed. They held a fly-in breakfast every Memorial Day, where as many as thirty planes showed up from all over the state, friends of Cliff's through the Civil Air Patrol. The Collinses seemed perfectly nice, but because she was living in Hoffer's cabin, Bonnie Kenyon didn't feel free to socialize with them.

That left Jo and Harley King, old-time Alaskans who kept their food supplies safe from bears atop a cache built of logs, which showed up as a silhouette against the northern lights like a painting on black velvet.

Harley King was a well-liked hunting guide, at one time a bounty hunter for wolves (a career phase he shared with the conservation-minded Republican governor Jay Hammond). Harley was known for his easy smile, flashing big white teeth, and his laconic pipe-smoking wisdom. He was slowing down now due to heart trouble.

Jo King had not slowed down. During her years in Alaska she had worked as a fish spotter pilot, an air taxi pilot out of Bethel, a flight instructor, and an air traffic controller. As the first woman controller in a rural Alaska post, she fought the undermining efforts of her station chief and later wrote about it. One day in Cordova, she was the last person to talk to Alaska's most famous disappeared airplane—the twin engine Cessna 310 that vanished in 1972 carrying Congressman Nick Begich of Alaska and House majority leader Hale Boggs of Louisiana. Jo knew the pilot and had not been impressed by his recent article in *Flying* magazine, "Icing without Fear." Over the radio she warned him of heavy icing conditions as he flew east toward Juneau and oblivion.

Jo King had learned to fly as a kid in Colorado and moved north after the war, not yet twenty. The closest she could get to planes at first was a job as a stewardess for Pacific Northern Airlines. In that era in Alaska when men outnumbered women, she soon found herself engaged to three men at the same time. She married one, but it didn't last long. Her second husband was the glacier pilot Jack Wilson. She married Jack's hunting partner, Harley, in 1963, and they were living happily on their homestead at Long Lake when a disconsolate Bonnie Kenyon arrived in 1977.

*I walked through the woods to Jo and Harley's cabin. Jo was alone; offered me a cup of tea. We sat at her table and I broke down and cried. Honestly, I wanted to go back home. Jo let me cry and then looked straight into my eyes and said, 'No, you can't leave! You are needed. This place needs the peace you bring.' I'll never forget those words. They have helped encourage me many times over. I went back to our little cabin refreshed and encouraged that I was right where I was supposed to be.*

Jo King had some land along the river in McCarthy she was willing to sell to the Kenyons. It had been given her by a wealthy admirer back in the 1950s when she lived in Chitina.

Jo had been married at the time to Jack Wilson. Those were the days of raiding Kennecott to outfit their home and drinking carrot whiskey with Blazo Bill. Chitina was an emptied-out town, too, but more populated than McCarthy with its road connection and a small number of Ahtna Native families. Living in Chitina, Jo became a close friend of O.A. Nelson, the eccentric who painted white spooks on the town's buildings. O.A. was in his seventies, tall and thin with intense blue eyes, and he dressed in work boots, suspenders, and a transparent green bookkeeper's visor, like a "good-natured tramp," Jo later recalled, "like an impoverished old sourdough down on his luck." Visitors would ignore the cackling old man in the hotel lobby, and Jo loved being there at the moment when they found out he owned most of the town.

In addition to painting spooks alongside O.A. Nelson, Jo helped him put out a sardonic local newspaper, *The Ghost Town Gazette*, from 1956 to 1959.

*You will probably notice some mistakes in spelling and grammer in this paper. We put them there intentionally, we like to please everyone, and some people like to look for other peoples mistakes.*

Nelson was a well-read engineer and wrote biting columns, under the pen name Chief Ghost, mocking the Alaska statehood movement as a lot of self-important "moaning wind and flapping sheets." News items included an account of two unnamed "pugilists" from lower Tonsina who loaded up on "branch water" and "soon discovered an issue that could not be settled by arbitration." When a letter

O.A. Nelson, owner of Spook's Nook and editor of *The Ghost Town Gazette*, at Chitina's post office in the 1950s.

showed up asking the postmaster about local churches and business opportunities, O.A. replied with this description of Chitina:

*We never had a church and perhaps that is the reason the town is going to hell. The Indians live on fish and rabbits and the rest of us live on scenery and hope.*

O.A. had to leave Alaska for six weeks to attend a funeral so he put Jo in charge of the post office, hotel, and store. The Chitina Cash Store had a reputation as a place where one could "browse among the cobwebs" for dry goods pulled two decades earlier from the

Kennecott store and as the workplace of a clerk named Klaus, an eighty-year-old Swede who might take twenty minutes to total up a simple shopping bill, recording each can of food in a ledger book in long-hand Swedish, then translating as he fumbled over ounces and pounds. He moved so slowly, Jo said, he couldn't keep his self-winding watch from stopping. Many store items had to be retrieved from high shelves with a claw on a pole, and Jim Edwards said a customer needed to allot one minute per item:

> You had to have plenty of time on your hands and you couldn't get frustrated. It took forever. It was the funniest thing. I remember one time everybody in town was buying chickens. O.A. Nelson had gotten in a case of frozen chickens and somebody went down and bought a chicken. Pretty soon another person came and bought a chicken and then everybody ran down. At the end of the day, O.A. came in and said 'How's it going, Klaus?' and he said, 'Oh it's going good today. I sold that whole case of chickens already.' Come to find out he'd been selling them for 65 cents a chicken rather than 65 cents a pound. O.A. wouldn't have thought that it was anything but funny. Gosh he was an old man with a million dollars.

When O.A. returned from his trip to the funeral, Jo lectured him angrily: Why hadn't he told her about all the money? She had opened the safe and it was so full of bags of gold she couldn't get it shut again. A desk drawer was crammed with bills of all denominations; she had mailed an insured bundle of $18,000 to the bank in Anchorage. O.A. thanked her and rewarded her with unpatented gold claims on Dan Creek and old homestead deeds near McCarthy that might be worth something someday. Later he made headlines in Seattle when he tried to deposit twenty-six pounds of gold dust in person at the National Bank of Commerce. They hadn't handled that kind of customer from Alaska in decades, and after the reporters left they had to send the gold to San Francisco for proper weighing.

The caustic hotel owner had a reputation for being condescending to some of Chitina's Ahtna Native residents—and even physically violent if Native drinking was involved. One former resident who grew up in Chitina during the Depression recalled that Nelson was "very strict on separation" and insisted that most Natives stay at the Native end of town so they didn't become "a deterrent to the tourism industry."

But the town's biggest landowner had done well by Jo King. After O.A.'s death in 1962, and an amicable divorce from Jack Wilson, Jo set out to restake O.A.'s mining claims on Dan Creek. She enlisted Jack's old friend Harley King to help pack in camping gear—a business proposition that ended in a marriage proposal. Jo's mother in Colorado, after she met Harley, offered advice: "Guys like that don't grow on trees, you know."

It was some of the Kennicott River land from O.A. Nelson that Jo King sold now to the Kenyons, bringing new west-side neighbors to Jim and Maxine Edwards.

Bonnie Kenyon and Maxine became friends. On mail day, they often walked together to the airstrip to meet the weekly mail plane. Rick curbed his missionary instincts around Jim and they got along fine. Harley King came from Long Lake to till the Kenyons' garden. Rick erected a shop where he rebuilt Harley and Jo's Super Cub. On Sundays in winter, the Kenyons crossed the frozen river to attend Bible study at the Heglands' new house by the airfield, which featured an indoor bathroom.

In the future, the Kenyons would assume the role of Sunday worship hosts, fulfilling that sense of mission that drew them north.

Eventually they built the valley's first church, on the island between the two river channels. They also published a newspaper, the first successor to *The Ghost Town Gazette*. Rick felt the community needed a watchdog to keep the National Park Service in check. The *Wrangell St. Elias News* would have an improbable and rich twenty-two-year run, in a town with a few dozen year-round people, as a bimonthly publication combining lighthearted Chitina valley gossip, century-old reprints from the *McCarthy Weekly News*, and effusions from a political cauldron bubbling with old-time religion, gun rights, and manifest destiny.

This future as leading citizens would never have come to pass, the Kenyons believed, if God had not intervened to spare Bonnie on the day of the shootings that took the lives of so many close friends. They would always miss, with a ghost town sadness, those first neighborly years, before the park and all its tensions, before the murders, when old-timers and neo-pioneers were building the sense of place that is the essential precursor to a sense of loss—when they took tea with Maxine Edwards, made do with Harley King, bowed heads with Les and Flo Hegland, and rested the future in hands more sure than their own.

# 9

# Aggravating Circumstances

I T IS A truth universally acknowledged that a crew of workingmen in possession of a good fleet of heavy equipment must be looking for earth to move. So it was that an outfit of out-of-work loggers from the Pacific Northwest, having obtained patented mining claims in the Nizina mining district, upon arriving in the Wrangells with their bulldozers and backhoes, resolved to build a Cat trail up Dan Creek that would become, for young Gary Green, a street literally paved with gold.

During the summer of 1976 Gary Green was living in the old Chititu mining camp, a few miles down the Nizina. His buddy from Kennecott, Tim Nash, a powerful pick and shovel man, was helping him divert Chititu Creek for ground-sluicing. The loggers told Green they had been chased to Alaska by northern spotted owls. Old-growth forests were becoming off-limits, while the price paid for gold in the Nizina River creeks had gone up—from $39 an ounce to nearly $200 in the early 1970s. The loggers came north despite talk of a national park in the Wrangells, which seemed likely to bring at least as much environmental scrutiny as efforts to protect endangered owls in the Pacific Northwest.

A package of thirty patented Dan Creek claims, extending almost three miles along the creek bottom, had been purchased in 1975. Ray Trotochau, dying of brain cancer, owned a share and helped broker the purchase, telling new owner Jim Tallman he was pretty sure he'd identified the hard-rock source of gold on the mountain above. (Any such gold vein, on unpatented federal land, was never found.) The Dan Creek owners said they had the oldest placer mine in Alaska; some of the claims once belonged to Stephen Birch. The land had been blasted by hydraulic hoses and dredges, then mostly abandoned since World War II. Spruce trees in the steep, narrow valley were growing back.

The new owners hired Green and Nash and a third local friend, Fred Denner, to help move and wash gravel, looking for gold missed by the old dredges. They also paid Green to fly supplies in his Piper Cub, which he had bought with gold nuggets. Though he was not yet thirty, Gary Green had spent the last few years learning mountain skills—mining, hunting, guiding, flying—from an older generation in the Wrangells. By the time of the mail-day murders, seven years later, he would be the town's principal bush pilot, and everything would likely have turned out much worse that morning if he had not been at the airstrip sweeping snow off his Cessna. The Cub was his first plane, though, and this was his first professional job, shuttling fuel drums and supplies to Dan Creek because the bridge across the Nizina had finally washed away.

The loggers set about that summer carving an access road to their diggings from the airstrip. Because the route followed an old riverbed, Gary, Tim, and Fred walked along behind the bulldozer, watching for any place the blade scraped bedrock. They found a twenty-foot stretch where an ancient stream, passing over bedrock creases, had left thin cracks gleaming with wealth. On hands and knees for the next three days, the young men followed narrow pay grooves across the rock in every direction, prying and scraping with spoons and screwdrivers, as the earthmoving equipment passed by and the loggers waved. The trio pocketed a film cannister's worth, more than a half pound of gold.

⟵——⟶

Gary Green had come to McCarthy in the late winter of 1973, a twenty-year-old kid from Anchorage excited that President Nixon had removed gold price controls. He drove a snowmachine all the way from Chitina, following the rough new road along the abandoned railbed. He had to speed up crossing the steel bridge above the vertiginous Kuskulana Gorge to jump the gaps between railroad ties. He passed through McCarthy and continued south across the last traces of the Nizina River bridge, whose approaches were about to be clawed away by roving river channels.

His destination was the old placer mining country, where rusting picks and shovels in the underbrush indicated likely places to dig. Green was drawn to the Chititu camp because he needed a roof over his head. The mining operation there in the 1920s had been especially well capitalized, with dozens of buildings and sheds still standing, including a horse barn, a blacksmith shop, and a sawmill. In 1926 the mining camp had saved itself by turning the nozzles of its hydraulic "giants" on a forest fire. Chititu was allowed to continue scaled-down production through the war, getting a special exemption from Congress pushed through by the territorial delegate, Tony Dimond, who had once staked claims on nearby Young Creek. The mine didn't close until 1951, so the buildings were not only numerous and well-made, they had been kept up more recently.

The young squatter's intentions were plain enough to Howard Knutson, the veteran pilot, wolf hunter, and owner of Consolidated Wrangell. Knutson was running an air service and hunting guide operation out of Chitina and getting paid to keep a distant eye on Chititu. Green expected to get run off, but instead Knutson said he could stay in any cabin he chose, draw a watchman's salary of $200 a month, and was welcome to all the gold he could find. It was the start of a lifelong friendship between the wily Wrangell Mountain veteran and the young man starting down a similar path.

The best winterized log cabin at Chititu had been home to the previous watchman. Charley Jacobsen had been gone for two years, but his paperbacks and cooking pots awaited his return, and his flannel shirts hung from nails. Green picked a draftier cabin rather than move in on Jacobsen's ghost. The only person drifting around that side of the Nizina at the time was Mark Goodman, with his loyal dog, Copper—a prospector type, as Green put it, "without a place of his own."

Green had one other neighbor couple. Al and Fran Gagnon lived several miles down the valley at May Creek, by the big airstrip where Mudhole Smith once landed passengers to see the ghost town. A rough road from their place led up to Chititu. Gary Green soon realized he'd been placed in Chititu to keep Al Gagnon out.

Al Gagnon had built a fortress of a cabin and stocked it with enough supplies to get by for a full year after civilization collapsed. His wife, Fran, an Athabaskan born on the Yukon River and raised by St. Anne nuns at the Holy Cross mission school, was a well-known bead artist. The land in the Wrangells was her individual Native allotment, claimed and awarded through the Bureau of Indian Affairs. "Man is but temporary here, and the land will still be here long after man has vanished," Fran once wrote of her home at May Creek, "and how he treats his lands, will determine the length of his stay."

Gary Green gathering firewood near the Kotsina River in 1973, his first year in the valley.

Al Gagnon, who left the worn-out Berkshires in Massachusetts at sixteen, was not happy when the newcomer put up a gate across the road to Chititu. One day when Gary was shoveling gravel in the creek, Al appeared on the bank dandling a shotgun and said Gary was in his spot. Gary moved upstream, inside the gate.

Over the next three years, their relations thawed. Fran liked the kid. So did Howard Knutson, who took Gary on as an assistant hunting guide. The seasonal job was a good one for that country, but it had risks—in his first autumn of guiding, Green was charged by a grizzly while descending a ridge looking and smelling like a caribou, with a hundred-pound load of game meat and antlers lashed atop his pack. All he had in his hand was an ice axe. It happened that the previous year another assistant guide working for Knutson in the Wrangells, Guy George, had survived a similar bear attack by swinging his ice axe like a baseball bat. The story was told again and again, all the previous winter, and eventually in books about famous bear attacks—how Guy George pierced the grizzly's heavy skull with his first swing, and then, when the blade popped free as the lucky guide struggled to shed his backpack, how he met a second charge with one powerful swing that sliced opened the bear's windpipe. Emboldened by the memory, Green counterattacked, waving his axe and screaming. The grizzly pulled up short, studied the caribou antlers coming at him, and fled.

Howard Knutson taught Green to fly. He learned how cool wind flows down the glaciers by day as the valleys warm, and how the air grows still by night. He liked the way an airplane gave one mastery of a big country with so many dangerous rivers. Knutson bought Green his first airplane, a 1941 J-4 Piper Cub, and Green paid him back over time as he continued to pull gold from the local creeks. Together they moved hunting clients all over the Wrangells and the Brooks Range.

By 1977 Green was becoming McCarthy's unofficial air taxi. He built a cabin in town, then prevailed on Laurence Barrett to sell him land just outside the townsite on a ridge of terminal moraine looking across at the glacier. Counting tree rings, he judged the spot had been under ice two hundred years earlier. Green planned to salvage and reuse local materials to build his new cabin. Thus was he drawn into a feud with the man known as the town bully.

⟵—⟶

The ruins in dispute this time did not date from mining days. The feud was over the washed-out remains of the state's effort, a few years earlier, to build a new bridge across the Kennicott River. Gary Green had been one of the very first to cross that bridge in October 1973, his first year in the Wrangells. Workers moved their tools so he could get past, after jouncing his Chevy truck full of supplies all the way from Chitina. There had to be two bridges, of course, one for each channel, and they looked sturdy: spans of heavy eight-by-eighteen timber stringers, suspended above spruce tree pilings that had been driven deep into the boulders of the riverbed.

Like most of his town neighbors, Gary Green was happy enough to see peace restored by the bridges' collapse. As an added bonus, in 1977 the last timbers from the east fork span broke loose and settled on a gravel bar downstream. They seemed just right for a cabin foundation.

Gary contacted the state and was told the heavy timbers were no longer considered state property. Working with Loy Green (no relation), and with Gordon Burdick's bulldozer, Gary spent several days dismantling the bolts and plates, and stacking the salvaged steel I-beams and timbers. They figured the steel would greatly improve the rudimentary bridges on Burdick's road up McCarthy Creek, where Loy lived. Crossings at the time required careful steering across parallel timber beams.

But when Gary Green returned to the gravel bar a week later to retrieve the beams, they were gone. Ron Andersen had taken them.

Nearly everyone in McCarthy had a story about a tussle with Ron Andersen. He was a big, strong, eager, red-faced man with small eyes set back in his head. He was born in Nome and had followed the dictates of his heart when he moved from Valdez to McCarthy: his doctor had told him he would have another heart attack if he didn't slow down. In Valdez, he had worked at the boat harbor, run garbage and school bus routes, owned a laundromat, and had undergone triple-bypass surgery. A heart attack followed, and then Andersen, still in his thirties, made a permanent move to McCarthy in 1974. He brought along his two school-age kids and their stepmom, Cora.

"He was trying to get away from it all," recalled his daughter, Kathy Andersen Hemphill. "Not realizing it was probably ten times harder."

That first summer, the bridge was open, and the road was dusty with traffic. This kept Ron Andersen busy, as he now owned most of the town's heavy road equipment and had bought out the McCarthy Fuel Co. He was hardworking, confident, pushy, and palled around with state transportation officials, who wrote him maintenance contracts for grading the airport, clearing culverts, and fixing washouts on the McCarthy road. In winter, at a seeping spring in a bluff, he maintained an oil-drip "firepot" to keep an ice glacier from building across the road.

Andersen set about remaking the town. Neighbors complained he acted like he owned it, as if one thing the hermit kingdom lacked was a king. He dragged the streets with his grader, turning ruts into bare gravel and leaving berms you had to step over. He put up a modern metal building, in the midst of the old structures, inside which a noisy generator ran day and night. He helped himself to old trucks and antiques. Others, to be sure, had done the same—but the practice was becoming more controversial with tourists now walking around town. Neighbors said he unbolted the globe-topped gas pump at J. B. O'Neill's store and sold it to a dealer.

O'Neill's belonged to the new lodge owner, Jerry Miller, along with the Golden Saloon next to it. Miller had made his own impacts on McCarthy since buying the lodge from Winnie Darkow. He had moved the Golden's wood bar into the lodge, hosted John Denver, and reported the pipeline hookers scam to the troopers. He did not get along with Andersen, nor with Andersen's wolf-sized dog named Dog. He noticed Dog glaring ravenously at the lodge's laying hens and moved the coop up to the second floor of the Golden Saloon. Dog got into the chickens anyway, and when Dog climbed the stairs a second time, the lodge owner shot him, as he had threatened to, tracking the wounded predator to finish him off on Andersen's front step. A neighbor recalled hiding in her house that day, watching from the window as Andersen walked the street pounding his fist in his palm.

Andersen set about subdividing one of the old homesteads across the river, in Jim Edwards's neighborhood. In the summer of 1975, he scraped the topsoil off the old farm roads along the river, replacing the wildflower-strewn lanes with perpendicular thoroughfares of polished river rock. "You used to be able to ride bikes on the roads," said Eric Wasserman, who lived nearby. "Suddenly it was hard even to walk."

Jim Edwards became Andersen's most determined adversary. Edwards went all the way to the Alaska Supreme Court to fight what he deemed excessive bulldozing, tree-cutting, and related crimes against the valley inflicted in the name of the "Wrangell Mountain Estates" subdivision. Cutting his access road past Edwards's Swift Creek homestead, Andersen measured out the one-hundred-foot-wide section line easement and felled all the trees inside the easement, though the road itself was only twenty-five feet wide. The parsimonious Edwards hired a lawyer, despite his well-known aversion to the way white-collar professionals keep the meter running when you are trying to have a simple conversation. The court found that Andersen had assured Edwards he would only clear what he needed for his road, and "do as little damage to the area as possible." Edwards won a jury judgment for triple damages. But the judgment got tied up in appeals, and it was six years before the Supreme Court cited jury-instruction errors and remanded the case for retrial. At that point, Edwards gave up paying his lawyer and settled for less than his legal costs. He was sore about the fight with Andersen to the end of his life.

"He was nice enough if you happened to play pinochle with him," Edwards said of his nemesis, years later. "But he was so sharp that he'd take advantage of people who were trusting. Then he'd cut people short—put them in a bad position and say it was their own fault."

Gary Green wasn't surprised to find himself in conflict with Andersen. He had worked for the man and had seen him in action. "He didn't mind stepping on toes," Green said.

It appeared Andersen had made his own arrangements, as the state's contractor, to remove the bridge beams after the washout. The beams were to be Andersen's payment for seeing that the beams were disposed of safely. Gary Green had saved him a lot of work. Andersen had already trucked the steel beams off to Chitina to be sold.

Green complained to Andersen's bosses. Valdez backed Andersen, but the regional bosses in Anchorage realized they'd given out conflicting information and had no written policy covering scavengers. Green filed a formal complaint with the Alaska attorney general. The state Ombudsman's Office opened an investigation.

The state took another year figuring out how to dispose of jökulhlaup damage. Finally, in 1979, Green received a $974 check for his salvage work on the bridge. "The current situation tends to place the director in a position of appearing to exercise favoritism," the ombudsman had written, noting that the state transportation department was already controversial enough in McCarthy for its efforts to build a highway into the Wrangells. Even after its death, the short-lived bridge into McCarthy had been a huge headache for state transportation officials.

The steel beams were long gone, but several of the remaining timbers ended up in the foundation under Gary Green's cabin on the glacial moraine.

Ron Andersen's daughter, Kathy, and her older brother, Jack, knew a different sort of man. They were aware of the tension in town and the ire directed at their father. But they felt largely exempted as children. Kathy, in sixth grade when they moved from Valdez,

McCarthy residents gather for a drink, early 1970s. (From right) Cora Andersen, Ron Andersen, Barbara Darkow, Winnie Darkow, Adrian Darkow, Butch West, RoxAnn Knutson, and Archie Poulin behind the bar.

said it took a while to get used to the outhouse and woodstove. The only other kids in the vicinity were Steve and Shelly Edwards. Their fathers were at war, but Kathy and Jack were always welcome to play with Steve and Shelly, and they remained lifelong friends. They hiked together to the glacier and rode Honda mopeds up the old mining roads to Kennecott. At Christmas, the Andersen kids helped their stepmother, Cora, deliver baked goods to neighbors in balsa-wood mandarin orange boxes, even riding a snowmachine up the tram line into the alpine to reach Tim Mischel's cabin at the angle station.

A determined, stubborn streak ran through the family. Ron Andersen's mother refused to open any letter with the address misspelled as "Anderson," Kathy recalled. Ron had an army six-by-six with a fording kit that sealed the engine so he could drive across the Kennicott River most of the year without worrying about the footbridge or the tram. He had a heavy fuel truck that he sometimes drove to Chitina, pounding the primitive road he was paid to maintain. Kathy recalled a trip in the truck's cab that took eight hours, crossing mudholes where they cut logs for traction and pull the truck through with a power winch.

"My dad was a very hard worker providing for his family. I had a great childhood living there," Kathy said. After a year of homeschooling, the siblings were sent to Glennallen, boarding with local families to attend public school.

The year Dog was shot, the town had rival Christmas parties. Jim and Maxine Edwards and friends joined Jerry Miller's family, while the Heglands and a few others were at the Andersens'. Mike McCann, a horse-packer who wore his hair in braids and had a winter trapline on the upper Chitina, was enterprising enough to attend both gatherings. Ron Andersen seemed quiet that night, McCann recalled, perhaps a little more scarlet-faced than usual, and generally not partaking in the spirit of the season, while Andersen's wife, Cora, was an especially enthusiastic hostess.

A year later, Cora Andersen moved to Anchorage and filed for divorce. Cora found a waitress job at first in Anchorage and stayed with a friend. The next summer, she moved part way back to Copper River country. Mike McCann, the plaited horse-packer, said he was surprised to find Cora pouring coffee at the Eureka Roadhouse, near Gunsight Mountain along the highway to Anchorage. McCann was working that summer in Nabesna, on the north side of the Wrangells, for an old cowboy named Lee Hancock, who had a 1923 newspaper clipping of himself winning Anchorage's first rodeo. McCann told her they were headed to Anchorage for some errands when they stopped for lunch. Cora replied that she would be driving to Anchorage herself, in a few hours, as soon as she got off work. She was due in divorce court the next day to make her final demands. She presented McCann with a necklace made from porcupine quills he'd once given her.

McCann and the old cowboy continued to Anchorage, where McCann recalled conducting most of his business at the Chilkoot Charlie's bar. The pair stopped again at the Eureka Roadhouse on the way home and asked where Cora was. A waitress informed him that Cora had never made it to Anchorage, never showed up in divorce court. Her pickup truck, with a camper shell on back, had been found by state troopers parked back in the tall cottonwoods at the Moose Creek wayside, along the highway to Palmer.

Cora Andersen was never seen again.

State trooper investigators descended on McCarthy, interviewing locals about Cora Andersen's relationship with her husband. Ron Andersen had been in McCarthy the whole time with his teenaged kids, but the general sentiment in town, as recalled by multiple residents from that time, was that he could have somehow been behind her disappearance.

"Police questioned me and made it clear that they thought he did it, or at least hired it done. Couldn't prove it," Jim Edwards said a few years later. "Andersen always played up to the law."

A few years later, Howard Knutson and his wife, Adina, decided to divorce. Howard, busy in summers fishing salmon in Bristol Bay and annoyed by the new park rules, prepared to move to Anchorage. Adina would remain in Chitina and continue serving as postmaster. Howard drew up an alimony agreement, but he said Adina wouldn't sign. "She told me, 'If I sign this, I'll end up like Cora Andersen.'"

Did the troopers ever manage to sort rumor from fact, or come up with any hard evidence? Was it true, as people in McCarthy said, that Cora was planning to raise her demand in divorce court, from $10,000 to $50,000, the day she disappeared? Did the troopers find evidence that exonerated Ron Andersen of any involvement? Did they blow the investigation?

It is impossible to say. Forty years after her abandoned pickup truck was discovered in 1979, the state trooper investigative file in Cora Andersen's case remained a guarded secret. The Alaska Department of Public Safety turned down a formal public records request during work on this book, and also an appeal to the commissioner's office, citing a regulation that blocks release of information that could compromise an open investigation. The commissioner's office refused to answer a single question about the case.

Kathy Andersen Hemphill was surprised to hear the state considered her stepmother's disappearance an open case. After seven years, she recalled, she and her brother were told the case was closed. A death certificate was issued. That would have been in 1986, because Kathy remembered that Cora attended her brother's high school graduation, in the spring of 1979, and not hers, in 1980.

A state trooper investigator told them in 1986 no reason had turned up as to why Cora might want to disappear. Her identification and money and jewelry were found in the pickup truck. There was no sign of a struggle. It was possible, he told them, their stepmother had fallen into the river or had been eaten by a bear.

"My opinion is that my dad had nothing to do with her disappearance," Kathy said.

Ron Andersen sold his commercial interests in the Wrangells after his wife disappeared and left Alaska to be near his mother. A year later, in March 1981, he died in Seattle of a heart attack.

# 10

# Museum Pieces

A s MCCARTHY BEGAN to crack open to more visitors in the 1970s, an unfortunate deficit hampered the growth of its reputation as a ghost town: an absence of individual, discernible ghosts whose personalities could be guessed at and fussed over. Maybe it was because the historical trauma in the valley had been more broadly social and economic, a general failure of life (and death) to take root on this glacial outwash plain. One exception might have been the Rose Silberg affair in 1918. The *McCarthy Weekly News* reported how that sordid chapter began:

> *On going his rounds for orders this noon, Mr. Marshall discovered*
> *suspicious circumstances which disclosed that a brutal murder*
> *had been committed in our midst. He immediately reported to the*
> *marshal, who proceeded to investigate, in company with the com-*
> *missioner, and found the body of Rose Silberg, a Jewish woman,*
> *lying in a rear room of a house in the restricted district, known*

*as Chili Con Carne parlor. The body was in a nude condition but
for the shoes and stockings. One gash in the neck had severed the
jugular vein, and extended back to the vertebrae. Another from
under the left ear, extended to behind the right ear. Many stabs
and gashes had been inflicted on breasts and arms.*

Silberg was a prostitute in the private district by the creek, and
suspicion fell on her ex-boyfriend, the drug store owner Gustave
Priesner, with whom she had recently argued over money. The owner
of the Golden Saloon reported seeing Priesner leaving Silberg's place
shortly after the murder. Soon the saloon owner himself was found
dead, fully clothed, on a bed in the Golden Hotel above the bar—
poisoned. Priesner skipped town and was never charged with either
murder.

That would seem anguish enough to sustain a ghost or two—
yet as life in McCarthy started coming back, the only apparition
sighted seemed unconnected to those unsolved murders. Reports
of a spectral presence among the period antiques on the second
floor of Ma Johnson's Hotel were inconsistent—a child in the hall,
an old woman glimpsed in the corner of a bedroom mirror. That,
anyway, was a description you might hear from the lodge owners,
who were haunted mainly, like the rest of the town, by the ghost of
Lost Prosperity.

Is absence of haunting unresolved trauma really a problem?
Flames had consumed Ma Johnson's first hotel in the 1921 fire, it
was true, but what bitterness could linger in a community that
responded by passing the hat for the innkeeper everyone knew as
"Ma," and her husband Pete?

"They are our oldest and most respected business people," wrote
the *McCarthy Weekly News* in May of 1921. "An appeal is here made to
all old timers all over the Copper River valley to help." Contributions

came pouring in, including $135 from the Mother Lode Mine, with a note to Ma:

*The Mother Lode boys were deeply grieved to hear of your recent misfortune and desiring to be of some material help in apprecia- tion of your many kindnesses, prompted from the goodness of your heart, have most graciously contributed for the amounts shown opposite their names, for which I am enclosing check and currency. Trusting that it will meet some urgent want.*

The newspaper printed the name of each donor and whipped up competition among the outer mining camps. Contributions of ten dollars came from, among many others, John Barrett, Archie Poulin, Blanche Smith, and Kate Kennedy. Ernie Gercken and Al Doze gave five dollars each. The storekeeper J. B. O'Neill gave twenty-five, and his wife another ten. Well over a thousand dollars was raised to help with rebuilding, which Ma Johnson acknowledged in a letter thankful for "the wonderful outpouring of material aid which has been given us in the dark hour of distress which has come."

Ma Johnson's Hotel, now part of the McCarthy Lodge, had been on the market for a few months in December 1973 when Jerry Miller toured the snow-bound town. The bridge across the Kennicott River, finished that fall, would mean an open road next summer. Miller later said it took him several years to sort out who actually owned various properties that Winnie Darkow had given him to understand, during their walk in the midwinter twilight, belonged to the lodge.

Jerry Miller bought the lodge in McCarthy because he saw inn- keeping as a lifestyle more than a moneymaker. He planned to keep the lodge open year-round. Miller, who had dark curly hair and a moustache, was by trade a master airplane turbine mechanic. For

The McCarthy Lodge was open year-round, February 1977.

Wien Air Alaska, the airline that pioneered jet service to gravel strips in the bush, Miller had been the troubleshooter sent out to retrieve broken-down jets. When Wien tried to transfer him from Fairbanks to Anchorage, however, he split instead for rural Alaska. Settled in McCarthy, Jerry and his wife, Joanne, with their two small children, kept the lodge warm all winter. If visitors arrived, they lit more kerosene lamps. The handsome wood bar and decorative wainscoting from the Golden Saloon became a social center in the lodge. He was the last owner to display the sign, "Please Check Guns At Bar," not as something cute for tourists. A journalist who passed through said Miller had "an air of controlled wariness, like a tame wolf." His attitude toward "progress" was that he wanted McCarthy to stay open to opportunity—he did not want a national park, he did not want an end to sheep hunting and mineral exploration, nor, after suffering through the brief tourist boom of 1974, did he want a crush of tourists. He wanted the town to stay like it was.

After the bridge washed out, the Millers managed to supplement the geologist-and-hunter trade with a selective breed of tourist. Some tourists never got beyond the steel rail bridge across the Kuskulana Gorge, which had been improved with planks across the railroad ties but still had no guardrails between a traveler's tires and a 238-foot drop to the river. Others backed away at the plank leading to the half-washed-out footbridge into town. For those who made it across, the Millers secured rights from Consolidated Wrangell to visit Kennecott. It had been twenty years since Mudhole Smith's Sourdough Tours.

In John Denver's Alaska movie, filmed in the fall of 1975, the camera pans around the lodge and lights on Joanne Miller, who exclaims, "I am alive because I learned to live in the mountains!" Change was coming, she warned, and her kind of freedom, America's heritage, was going to disappear. It would be "extinct just like the seals and the bears and the eagles." A few months later, as Jerry was driving a rock truck in Valdez to make money for a balloon payment, it was Joanne who disappeared, with their children, moving to the Lower 48. Jerry returned to find the lodge in the hands of a caretaker who was using a hatchet to split kindling on the new linoleum floor.

Even when he was feeling low, Jerry Miller had a habit of whistling while he worked. If he was working outside, you could hear him a block or two away. His whistling provided a kind of downtown soundtrack for a few years, along with the bass rumble of Ron Andersen's generator and Loy Green practicing his trumpet.

Things changed for Jerry the summer after Joanne left with the arrival of a good-looking Santa Cruz undergrad named Judy Richter. She was nineteen, a hardy and opinionated backpacker from the San Francisco Bay area. She had lined up an internship, through the

Santa Cruz college program, to work in Anchorage on national park planning. She visited McCarthy over the Fourth of July with two Santa Cruz alums and fell into an extended argument at the bar with Jerry and a few other obsolete Americans about national parks and the straitjacket of "lifestyle by permit."

On her way back to Anchorage, Judy stopped for a few days in Chitina to dipnet for salmon. Jerry kept a distant eye on her, and when she was ready to hitch a ride back to the city he happened to show up. The two of them argued conservation politics all the way. By the time they got to Anchorage, Jerry had offered Judy a job. She went to see Santa Cruz professor Dick Cooley in Anchorage to talk about her study grant. She told the leader of the Alaska studies program she had to give up her internship because she felt it was more important to learn about the people leading real lives who would be affected by these faraway political decisions. Her teacher said to go ahead and spend the grant learning about that.

Judy moved to McCarthy in August. By February, she and Jerry were engaged. As they got ready for a big Memorial Day opening that year, Jerry collapsed. He was diagnosed in Seattle with a rare leukemia and given six months to live. Jerry and Judy got married in August and leased out the lodge and flew in his plane to a remote cabin at Dan Creek, where despite his initially poor prognosis, they had a baby girl and lived happily for the next thirty-six years.

<hr />

Olaf Holtet, the valley's blacksmith, stayed on for a while after the last train left. The 1940 US Census recorded him as a Norwegian citizen, a single man aged forty-seven, living across the river from town, in what might provide the setting for a ghost town opera— his closest neighbor an older man from South Dakota with a forty-five-year-old Norwegian wife. Holtet was long gone by 1973, when

Jim Edwards moved to Swift Creek, but the old Holtet place nearby seemed to be waiting for his return.

In July of that year, Edwards mailed to his neighbors a public notice regarding salvage of certain items, including a bobsled and a buckboard wagon, taken by him from the Holtet place by himself. In the notice, Edwards said he was tired of watching things disappear since the new road went in. The old Norwegian's house and blacksmith shop had been stripped, and he could hold back no more.

*It has been our intent all along, and we state here in a dated letter before the fact, that if and when Mr. Holtet returns to his farm to refurbish it, that we intend to offer return of these articles, herein named.*

Relics of McCarthy and Kennecott had been flowing out of the valley for a long time. The McCarthy Lodge became a refuge for a lot of what stayed behind. The former photo shop was crammed with Miller's haphazard reliquary: captain's chairs and cast iron pans, and glass cases of old photographs, enameled cookpots, gemstones, coins, tokens, small appliances, tools, antique bottles, and cans with old-fashioned labels.

Space wasn't exactly at a premium. Business at the lodge was off since the footbridge washed away. By late 1977, "tramming" on Blazo Bill's hand-pulled tram—helping one another haul materials across the river—was a social activity knitting the community together, but not every tourist was comfortable joining in. Locals improved the crossing with a rope and pulley for retrieving the tram, so that visitors no longer had to fire a rifle for help. For some new arrivals, though, the splintery platform dangling above the loud glacial cataract was too demanding an initiation.

Bernd Hoffmann saw growth possibilities when he took over the lodge in 1978, even working with the restrictions imposed by a tram. His other business was Alaska's biggest truck stop, in Glennallen. Hundreds of miles from any commercial enterprise of remotely comparable vigor, the truck stop called itself the "Hub of Alaska." Road spokes converged from Anchorage, Valdez, Fairbanks, and Canada. The McCarthy Lodge, located far from the hub of anything, became Hoffmann's summer escape.

The McCarthy-Kennicott Historical Museum was born that year when Hoffmann wanted to add a dining room. Hoffmann hired an old college friend, Benjamin Downs, a bearded African American watercolorist with wire-rim glasses, to cook and run the lodge. To clear out accumulated bric-a-brac, Hoffmann dubbed the old McCarthy railroad depot a museum and moved everything two blocks. At the depot, historical objects would be looked after by Loy Green, who was living in the back and occasionally selling a painting to a tourist. In exchange for the bunk that summer, Loy had promised Wesley Jack to give the exterior a fresh coat of Kennecott red.

Bernd Hoffmann would build glass cases for the museum and go on to incorporate a nonprofit board in 1983. The community got behind it, with Wesley Jack donating the depot, which he'd purchased in 1966 from Howard Knutson for $500. The Barrett family donated land. People dropped off things they'd been hiding from tourists. The collection grew. When Hoffmann moved on, and Jerry and Judy Miller resumed operation of the lodge, they were dismayed to discover a lot of their cool old stuff was missing. They chose not to lay claim to any relics that had ended up at the depot. In a transition that Judy's former Santa Cruz professor might have foreseen, those relics, like the people who salvaged them, were becoming museum pieces.

The McCarthy Lodge was not the only business responding to the growth, still slow, in Alaska tourism. By 1977 a first tender green shoot of commerce appeared at Kennecott with the opening of the Kennicott Glacier Lodge. A local air taxi pilot, Bill Bulfer, had purchased a five-plex apartment that once housed the mine's unmarried middle managers. He hired Rich Kirkwood, a carpenter in his late twenties with an engineering degree, to settle the building's foundation and repair the porch. Kirkwood had bought a place in Kennecott two years earlier, after wading into McCarthy wet because that summer's surprise jökulhlaup inundated his campsite. Carpentry at Kennecott seemed a good break from his weeks in the oil pipeline camps.

The early Kennicott Glacier Lodge was almost as hard to find out about as it was to get to. Marketing was minimal. Over on the west side of the river, where the road ended, the two Edwards teenagers, home one summer from high school boarding in Valdez, were given a CB radio to call Bulfer if travelers were uneasy about crossing on the tram. Bulfer would hop over in his plane. Steve and Shelly Edwards got a few dollars for each guest so delivered. Then Liz Geleszinski took over and started paying attention to fashioning a guest experience, unlike the more come-and-go atmosphere at the McCarthy Lodge. She paid Maxine Edwards $100 for a summer's worth of greenhouse cucumbers and tomatoes.

The original Kennicott Glacier Lodge burned to the ground on the day of the 1983 murders. Rich Kirkwood took over after that and rebuilt today's successful lodge in the rustic architectural style of Kennecott Copper.

Thirty miles away, deep in the Wrangell Mountains, a luxury lodge capitalizing on even greater isolation was born around the same time. John Claus was a backcountry adventurer from Washington, where he climbed and skied in the North Cascades. He moved to Alaska for a teaching job in 1957, learned to fly, and was guiding sheep hunters in the Wrangells by the late 1960s. His favorite hunting camp was on a gravel floodplain along the upper Chitina River. Historians said Chief Nicolai had a camp near there, by the mouth of the Kiagna River, probably for the same reason: both camps looked up at a miles-long precipice that was home to herds of Dall sheep. The mountain had recently been given the name MacColl Ridge, after a geologist who drowned in the Kiagna River in 1961 while mapping Cretaceous sedimentary rocks of the McCarthy quadrangle.

John Claus patented a five-acre "trade and manufacturing site" on a braid of the Chitina River just before the federal land-disposal program was shut down by the 1967 land freeze. He built a small log cabin to accommodate hunting clients. In 1979, when the federal government temporarily banned sheep hunting, Claus threw up his hands and turned the operation over to his twenty-year-old son, Paul.

Paul Claus had learned to land airplanes on glaciers as a teenager. He saw the upper Chitina cabin as an ideal jumping-off point for a mountain climbing business. Indeed, one of topographical 15-minute quadrangles mapped by Bob MacColl was said to have a precipitous top-to-bottom relief of twelve thousand feet, unequaled anywhere in the United States except possibly one other quadrangle in Alaska's Fairweather Range.

The younger Claus changed course in 1982 after his business partner, Gunnar Naslund, was killed by a collapsing snow cornice, during an attempted first ascent of Needle Mountain, in the Granite Range south of McCarthy. With his wife, Donna, Paul built a fly-in tourist lodge. Among the wilderness-survival skills useful to this enterprise was his uncommon ability to get along with federal wilderness managers. While other inholders in the new park chafed over access and other issues, Paul Claus would pull off an ambitious 1992 land swap with the National Park Service once the voracious Chitina

River began tearing into his father's trade and manufacturing site. The Claus family's clients included climbers and, after hunting was reopened in the preserve, a few sheep hunters. But increasingly, the one-of-a-kind Ultima Thule Lodge drew a more exclusive clientele. In the modern age, private-equity executives and movie stars would have an adventure destination of their own in the Wrangells, where hot tub pampering would be provided for clients who "aren't afraid to get their hands dirty and their feet wet."

Among backpackers without the means to hire a bush plane or stay at a fancy lodge, word of McCarthy as a destination circulated privately in the late 1970s. Trudging from the tram under heavy loads, they might find themselves invited to a red railroad bunkhouse by the road to Kennecott. This was the summer home of Tony Zak, the town greeter.

Zak was a friendly Pole who came to Alaska in the 1940s from the Pennsylvania coal mines with a trace of black lung and a taste for plum brandy. He had served in the Australian theater for the merchant marine during the war. Once he caught sight of the Wrangells, he put down $10,000 in 1962 for three-hundred-plus acres of an old homestead that had fallen into state hands. The land had been the location of the settlement of Blackburn, which sprouted in the first days of Kennecott, as a boomtown that lacked John Barrett's fussy building restrictions, then died out during the Chisana mining boom because it lacked Barrett's train depot. Buildings worth saving had been skidded to McCarthy.

Zak bought the railroad bunkhouse near town from the Barretts. Visitors found themselves sitting around Tony Zak's living room while he recited Robert Service poems and filled their glasses from a bottle of Slivovitz. Zak was a union phone lineman in Fairbanks, not quite an authentic aging sourdough though he looked the part, straggle-bearded like a Russian priest. He sounded authentic, too, especially to young people hearing "The Ballad of Sam Magee" for the first time. He welcomed newcomers but deplored change—new roads, new park rules. He smoked Pall Mall non-filters and when he died at eighty-three, in 1998, of emphysema and heart disease, he left his land to the Blackburn Heritage Foundation, which donates to local events and has opened the old bunkhouse for community nonprofit efforts.

◄——►

Residential life was returning to the ruins at Kennecott. Larry Hoare, a young jeweler smitten by the local azurite and covellite, was disappointed when he reached Kennecott in the summer of 1978 to find all the habitable and sort-of-habitable structures in the old mill town already in private hands. Houses had gone cheap in the Great Kennicott Land Company's 1976 sale, cottages for $6,000, and with easy terms: $500 down and payments of $100 a month. Some of the bigger buildings ended up back on the market: buyers put 10 percent down and carried way everything loose and valuable they could find, then stopped payments. One group bought the big powerhouse at Kennecott and stripped much of its brass and copper that way. Over the first five years, the Great Kennicott Land Company would clear nearly $1 million, selling just short of a hundred lots (out of six hundred) in the 1,500-acre subdivision covering the lower half of their holdings.

Sales of raw land did not go so well. The company brochure promised "ideal cabin sites for Alaskans who take their nature, hunting or history seriously." But no one was actually building a cabin when Larry Hoare arrived in 1978, nor for that matter moving in permanently to the old mill cottages. Getting materials to Kennecott, across the tram in summer or the river ice in winter, involved more logistics than most people wanted to take on. In the years to come, as raw-land sales trailed away and buyers started asking who was in charge of fixing Kennecott's roads, Howard Knutson and his flying dentist friends would cut off sales and put together a land and historic buildings package, including the concentration mill and powerhouse, hoping to unload the unsold properties on the federal government. (Such a sale was finally completed in 1998.)

Unlike some of the early Kennecott purchasers, Larry Hoare was not investing in a fantasy about the future. He was looking for a home. Kennecott met his three criteria: "Goats, griz, and glaciers." The area also seemed to have a satisfyingly high percentage of interesting characters. The pilot who flew him to McCarthy, for instance, known to everyone as Elevator, was a stuntman given to sudden precipitous turns and descents. The signature Elevator arrival announcement was to buzz the McCarthy Lodge, climb straight up losing momentum, and execute what is known as a hammerhead stall, flopping into a vertical plunge before restoring power and leveling out at the airstrip to land.

Hoare and his artist girlfriend, Rita Pfeninger, would eventually buy two empty lots on the mountainside above Kennecott and build a cabin accessible by footpath. For starters, though, the best he could buy was a share in an old Kennecott warehouse, still packed with wooden spools of heavy steel tram cable.

Larry and Rita returned in January 1981, rolled the spools out the door, and spent the next year fixing up the warehouse as a home and getting to know their few neighbors. Close by was Mike Monroe, an occasional presence that first winter. People called him "Tanker Mike" because his lot included the two-story steel tank where Kennecott once stored oil for its powerhouse. Monroe was planning to

Early residents at Kennecott could climb at will through the fourteen-story concentration mill.

develop a hikers' hostel. He had cut hinged windows in the tank's curved and rusting metal but did not yet have a plan for the three feet of bunker crude in the bottom of the tank. He lived nearby in a tiny super-insulated cabin that he kept warm in winter with a single kerosene Aladdin lamp. An avid backcountry skier, he once invited Larry and Rita on a ski-camping trip for which he packed super-light—mostly homemade peanut butter protein bars—but carried a heavy vise grip in his pack, in case he found himself caught in a wolf trap.

Another recent settler, Tim Nash, became Larry's best friend around Kennecott. Tim and his wife, Irene, lived a short distance down the mountain, their tiny hand-crafted hut set in the bed of a Mack truck with Minnesota plates. The couple had lived that way for several years, while Tim meticulously assembled a log cabin.

They canned a year's supply of moose and salmon and cabbage. "We expect the economy to collapse any day," Irene told an interviewer the year before, "and I hope it happens soon so they don't put that road in."

Tim was quiet and earnest, dark-bearded, and known for feats of superhuman strength. He was not a big man but his arms, Larry observed, were the size of other men's thighs. Tim was building alone by hand, with a cross-cut saw and no power tools, digging his foundation out of the mountain slope with a shovel, saving level space for their garden. Tim had mined gold at Chititu with Gary Green, and he worked alongside Larry as a carpenter. He told Larry he'd grown up on a farm in Minnesota and in some ways had a tough childhood but came through it with a gentle philosophy around the idea of karma. He had resolved to shrug off any wrong done to him. But something about the slow pace of building and the tight living quarters got to be too much and Irene left. After that, Tim stopped by the warehouse more often, looking for company.

Aside from Tim Nash, the only person full-time at Kennecott in 1981 was Chris Richards. Thin and cantankerous, with a broomstraw beard and wire-rim glasses, twenty-eight-year-old Chris lived at the other end of the mill town from Larry and Rita, near the recreation hall. He had a hundred-pound husky mix named Hawkins, and Larry and Rita had a black lab. Kennecott was split by the ravine of National Creek, and though the dog owners got along fine, neither dog would cross the railroad bridge.

Chris Richards, originally from Toledo, Ohio, had lived in a tee-pee when he first came to Alaska. He moved to Kennecott in 1978 from Homer after the breakup of his marriage. He told people he was looking for a place "in the middle of nowhere." He found a sagging millworker's cabin perched on a bulldozed bench of mine tailings above the glacier's moraine, where the copper conglomerate's empty oil drums were rusting picturesquely.

Chris had been living in the cabin a year when he received a visit from the last person to live there, forty years earlier. Nell McCann had walked out of this same small red-with-white-trim millworker's cottage, taking the last train out with her husband and baby and leaving her washing machine behind. She was now in her seventies and accompanied on her return by her daughter, Sharon, the last baby born at Kennecott. Nell, recalling a nicely painted living room with steam heat and electricity, found a shack with a canvas tarp covering one leaky wall. She was not surprised to find her Maytag and Victrola missing, but she was faintly horrified, according to her daughter's later account, by the generator dripping oil on the living room floor. Sharon noted that her mother was gratified, at least, to see the domestic touch of potted houseplants, not recognizing the pointy five-leaf specimens Chris was preparing for harvest.

At the end of 1981, after their year at Kennecott, Larry and Rita got married in California. Tim Nash flew down at Christmas for the ceremony. One year later, the lonely bachelor would fly out at Christmas for his own wedding, a surprising twist Larry and Rita couldn't have imagined. Meanwhile they found winter jobs away in Tenakee Springs, a tiny hamlet south of Juneau that was big enough to have both a school, where Rita taught, and a municipal government, which hired Larry "because everyone else who could type had already been city clerk." Returning in summer to work on their dream home became their pattern, as it was for others around McCarthy and Kennecott, reversing the classic summer-jobs-away lifestyle of Alaska homesteaders in Jim Edwards's time.

With Larry and Rita absent the rest of that winter, Chris Richards took to calling himself the mayor of Kennecott. He lived alone in Nell's red cottage, although in the summer of 1982 a new neighbor showed up: a reclusive bearded computer programmer named Lou Hastings, whose dream home was a small weather-pounded house at the back edge the ruins—as far from the hub of the world as a person could possibly get.

# 11

# Back to Nature

O N DECEMBER 1, 1978, President Jimmy Carter signed an executive order, under the federal Antiquities Act, creating fifty-six million acres of new national monuments in Alaska. Overnight, the mountains and valleys around McCarthy were swept into a new Wrangell-St. Elias National Monument.

Rick Kenyon was cutting firewood that week. Building the new cabin on his Kennicott River land had pushed other fall preparations into the snow season. Once the wood was stacked, he set out to find what the reports on the Glennallen radio station meant for his new community. His neighbor, Joan Wasserman, wondered if they would be forced to sell out to the government and move away? Indeed, to judge from the indignation of certain Alaska politicians, one might have imagined local settlers were about to be frog-marched out the McCarthy road with their hands up. Carter's proclamation was denounced as an outrageous land grab. The Antiquities Act, critics said, with some historical accuracy, was written in Teddy

Roosevelt's day to protect sites of archeological and scientific interest, not continental-scale ecosystems.

President Carter's order was not unexpected, however, nor would its immediate impacts be felt so much in Alaska as in Washington, DC, where it was seen as a bold move in a longer game. Congress had been working since 1974 on d-2 lands legislation to create new parks and wildlife refuges in Alaska. A compromise was in hand by the end of 1978, but Alaska senator Mike Gravel, a Democrat, blew up the deal with last-minute demands and a threat of filibuster. He wanted more loopholes for development. The bill died. A statewide land freeze, imposed by the 1971 Alaska Native Claims Settlement Act, was about to expire. The State of Alaska filed claim to forty-one million acres of federal land, under the guarantee made twenty years earlier at statehood. A quarter of those lands were inside conservation units proposed by the Interior Department.

Carter blocked the state with his Antiquities Act declaration. He would preserve the status quo until Congress could complete its work. In Washington, it was seen as a chess move; in the Chitina River valley, by some, as the act of a tyrant.

The Wrangell Mountains, considered an Alaska crown jewel since Ernest Gruening's day, had been the subject of much discussion all decade—the region's potential for mining and settlement measured against its spectacular wilderness values. Ben Shaine, who helped launch the Santa Cruz summer program, flew back and forth to Washington DC, working with environmental groups in the Alaska Coalition to draw lines on the map. Shaine had moved to McCarthy full-time with his wife, Marci Thurston, a former Santa Cruz student. He brought his carefully reasoned teaching style to the table with national conservationists, arguing for special rules that would preserve Alaska's bush lifestyles along with its mountain scenery and ecosystem-wide habitats.

The summer after Carter's proclamation, as Congress prepared for yet another run at the Alaska legislation, the National Park Service, charged with managing the new monuments, tiptoed forth. The first rangers sent to Alaska were told to keep a low profile, get to know the country, and try to make friends. They were met with suspicion and hostility.

Rick Kenyon was paying close attention by February 1979 when McCarthy got a barnstorming visit from a bearded orator named Chuck Cushman, head of a new national association of park inholders. Cushman got his start in western states amid the Sagebrush Rebellion protests against federal policies on public lands. Alaska seemed a perfect place to make his case. He warned that McCarthy would rue the day when green shirts started enforcing the law. The National Park Service, despite promises to the contrary, could never abide for long a population of independent landowners inside park boundaries, he said: "It won't happen all at once. It'll happen a little bit at a time."

Kenyon would later describe this visit as his moment of political awakening. It would drive him, within a few years, to launch his crusading McCarthy newspaper. Cushman had shameful stories to tell about the expulsion of rural residents from national parks in the Lower 48. When the Shenandoah and Great Smoky Mountain National Parks were created during the Depression, hill families were bought out, their land condemned, their lives insulted in a back-to-nature effort that even the Park Service today concedes was shortsighted and cruel. But the historical analogy was slightly off-target: in Virginia and Tennessee, local chambers of commerce and state politicians had dreamed up the new parks as a way to attract tourists and then pressed the federal government to push out the hillbillies. By contrast, in the Alaska debate in the 1970s, the local power structures were lined up against the big new national parks, seeing no future in tourism that could compete with the untold wealth of undiscovered minerals.

In the Copper River basin, the business and political center was now Glennallen, a spread-out crossroads settlement of three hundred people on a lake-spotted plateau, with gas stations and a grocery store, snowed-in cabins and mobile homes set in scooped-out gravel cuts, and a pump station for the new Trans-Alaska Pipeline, which pierced the town's heart like Cupid's arrow. With its highway straight to Anchorage, built during the war, Glennallen had replaced Cordova and Chitina as the take-off point for McCarthy's weekly mail plane. The airfield was a few miles north of town, at Gulkana, built by the army in 1943 on an Ahtna village site expropriated without compensation for the war effort.

That first year of the new monument, the three park rangers assigned to the Wrangells never ventured far from Glennallen. They were refused service at the town's restaurants and stores. Their office lease was terminated, and they ended up at a desk in the public library. Alaska congressman Don Young proposed shutting off utilities to all federal buildings in Alaska: "We've got to do something and you can call it civil disobedience." The Glennallen rangers had rooms at the Heartbreak Motel but were forced to leave after a bomb threat. They moved down the highway to the Tazlina Glacier Lodge, where an unknown arsonist burned a local Cessna 180 plane leased to the park.

Hunters were angry that the mountains were closed to taking sheep. The compromise bill in Congress would have left some areas open for sport-hunting, but Carter's emergency proclamation did not. Hunters responded with press releases announcing plans to hunt inside closed areas anyway. A Fairbanks taxidermist promised a free mount for any hunter who succeeded in getting arrested. The park rangers held back, allowing the state to continue managing the hunt.

Even a few mountain climbers, from what one might expect to be a reliable pro-park constituency, were protesting. A self-declared "outlaw faction" of the state alpine club accused the Park Service of wanting to create "a plastic zoo for Winnebago drivers." In 1980 these Fairbanks climbers made a winter "desecration" climb of 12,000-foot Mount Drum in the Wrangells. They were protesting a proposal that would have required climbers to get permits and pay fees. They carried an extra load to the summit—posts, anchors, and a sign that read: "In memory of the Freedom of the Mountains destroyed in Alaska by the President of the United States Jimmy Carter and his Secretary of the Interior Cecil Andrus."

⊂—⊃

The sudden monument declaration collided with a last frantic hunt for mineral wealth that was underway in the Wrangells. Actual mining efforts remained small-scale. Deregulation of gold in the early 1970s had stirred a little activity in the Dan Creek and Chititu areas. Jim Tallman, who brought his logging crew from the Pacific Northwest to work the Dan Creek claims, reported recovering three to four hundred ounces of gold per year. But that production, and the nuggets Gary Green and Tim Nash spooned from nearby bedrock, were exceptions: miners in the Wrangells were more likely to be spending gold than finding it.

The prospectors were now exploration geologists drawing salaries from heavily capitalized multinational corporations using the latest aerial survey tools, their haste driven by negotiations in Congress, their exploration budgets swollen by a recent spike in copper prices, though economics still argued against capitalizing a remote mine in Alaska. One memorable summer night, locals counted six exploration helicopters parked by the Kennicott River. The pilots enjoyed hanging out at the lodge, occasionally slinging heavy loads across the river to save their new friends hours of strenuous tramming.

Field work was being done as well by the US Geological Survey, sent to Alaska to assess mineral potential as Congress argued over the lines on d-2 conservation maps. Kennecott had been a unique surface outcropping, but now teams of geologists had ways of peering into the earth, using drill techniques and chemical tests to analyze streams for nearby minerals. Indeed, the very science of geology had changed radically since the days of Stephen Birch, with a new understanding of ore deposit formation in the context of plate tectonics. Who among Kennecott's engineers would have imagined the chalcocite had originated in eruptions of basalt in the tropics?

In Washington, DC, development interests floated ideas for "national recreation areas" where the usual park restrictions on resource extraction could be relaxed. The State of Alaska made similar proposals. Politicians described mining as a soulful part of Alaska's history. Two visions of mining were in conflict: George Smock's grizzled sourdough visage, bathed in the honeyed light of history's setting sun, versus the plundering plutocrats of Wall Street, the "rape, ruin, and run boys" denounced by Interior Secretary Cecil Andrus. Defenders of Kennecott Copper disputed accusations of rape and ruin—the acid-neutralizing limestone of the Wrangells deposits, and the high grade of the ore had saved the company from the sulfuric tailings lakes that haunt abandoned porphyry copper mines elsewhere in the world. But the "run" part was hard to contradict in a ghost town.

President Carter's interior secretary was the tall ex-governor of Idaho, a proud westerner who kept in his office a poster proclaiming "Idaho is what America was." Andrus said the Alaska lands bill would test the maturity of American civilization—it was time to recognize a limit to the frontier of resource extraction. Carter's election in 1976 had shifted the national political balance in favor of conservation, just as Teddy Roosevelt's election did in the days of the Alaska Syndicate. An unprecedented grassroots campaign by environmentalists in the Lower 48 to "save Alaska" was resonating more powerfully than anyone expected.

The National Park Service, contemplating what to say about mines in a 1976 internal strategies memo, noted there was no shortage of copper in the world. The strategy memo inverted the miners' arguments against "locking up" resources, contending that a park would be the conservative choice, "since restrictive laws are reversible but developmental actions create irreversible impacts."

Even so, the place-holding national monument designation in 1978 did not ban mining outright. The first federal field personnel seemed eager to reassure existing claim holders that mining was part of the history that future park visitors would want to see. They traveled to McCarthy to meet with the few small operators, including Gordon Burdick at Green Butte, and farther up McCarthy Creek, Walt Wigger of Fairbanks, who was intermittently trying to reopen the Motherlode Mine.

Probably the most energetic and ambitious effort in the valley was by the three Barry brothers, from the Palmer-Wasilla area, who had bulldozed forty-one miles of roads to reach the upper Kotsina River, cutting switchbacks through the high country west of Mount Blackburn. The Barry brothers had been working for six years to develop the Silver Star and Pandora Mines, silver discoveries first staked by Neil Finnesand when he was in his eighties. (At his ninety-eighth birthday party, at his home in Chitina, someone pointed to a guitar in the corner and asked Finnesand if he could play the instrument. Finnesand replied, "No, not yet.")

In August 1979 a National Park Service environmental specialist named Al Stumpf flew with bush pilot Jack Wilson into the upper Kotsina strip to talk to the Barrys about their mining. Stumpf reported he found the miners to be apprehensive at first, but after working to dispel "rumors and fears" he had a very friendly visit. The mine and camp were neatly ordered and located on a historic mining townsite, so it was hard to tell who had done what—the earlier inhabitants, Stumpf noted with delicacy, had left the area "set back into an earlier stage of plant succession," while the nearby glaciers had dumped moraine deposits nearly indistinguishable from mine tailings. He said the substantial mountainside scars left by road-building would have to be addressed, but went on to caution future park administrators:

> Care should be exercised in future contacts to prepare NPS personnel with the knowledge of the laudable position that miners, and many members of the public, perceived the miners to be in, as developers opening up the wilderness for the good of all. Any approaches to miners in the new monuments which reveal the bias or stance of regarding these people as criminal despoilers of the environment will be counterproductive and may create schisms that could block communication and cooperation for a long time to come.

That summer, Stumpf visited with miners at Dan Creek, with Jim Edwards on the west side of the Kennicott River, and with Harley King at Long Lake. Jim Edwards offered to sell his Dan Creek holdings cheaply but was turned down and complained the government had limitless money to fly out and monitor his environmental compliance but none to buy him out. Harley King told Stumpf if he wanted to talk about their Dan Creek claims, he should come back when his wife, Jo, was present. In Glennallen and Chitina, Stumpf reported signs on business doors that said, "Due To Personal Feelings We Do Not Desire To Do Business With Employees Of The National Park Service."

Regarding the Barry brothers, Stumpf's toughest recommendation was that they conform to the joined-corner style of older log cabins when building a cabin from trees knocked down for their road. Future bureaucrats, prompted by environmentalist lawsuits and federal court orders, would not be so accommodating. For several years, the Pandora and the Silver Star continued to produce small volumes of silver ore under national park supervision, but they were unable to establish a mill site, repair their road, or continue storing materials on adjacent parklands. The mounting pressures of permitting—deficiencies found in their operating plans, posted bonds, environmental plans, assessment work, access permits, validation reports, and expansion proposals—eventually shut them down.

Another miner working out of McCarthy in those final years was the legendary Phil Holdsworth, now nearly seventy and hiring locals, including Gary Green, to work on core drilling projects at various McCarthy Creek properties. Holdsworth was respected in Alaska as the mining boss who made an unlikely Depression-era success of the Nabesna gold mine, on the north side of the Wrangells. Later he was in charge of a big mine in the Philippines when the Japanese invaded; after joining a guerilla force, he and his wife were captured and held prisoner for three years. Holdsworth eventually served as Alaska's first commissioner of natural resources and played an important role selecting state land at Prudhoe Bay, where oil finds would make the state rich. Now he was spending the summer in a trailer in McCarthy. The former state resources commissioner had a gift for searching out water sources with a divining rod and freely helped his neighbors with his water-witching skills. Some people claimed he could also witch for copper deposits with welding rods. But Holdsworth was in McCarthy as part of the new trend in big-money mining, investigating the

Mother Lode and Green Butte deposits for a substantial Denver mining company, Inexco.

The corporate transformation of mining was plainest to see at Martin Radovan's Binocular Prospect. After decades on the Chitistone, Radovan had been bought out in the late 1960s by Florida investors, who paid him to keep working and sent a crew to help. Radovan objected that the Fairbanks laborers who showed up were "just a bunch of hoodlums never been off the sidewalk before." After several unsuccessful summers, the investors sold the claims to the Geneva Pacific Corporation, an Illinois-based exploration company that sent in a helicopter in 1975. Radovan died that June, at ninety-three, convinced the assay results would at last prove he'd found "the greatest bonanza of all times." Geneva Pacific set up a camp in the Peavine Bar area near Glacier Creek. Instead of climbing the mountain every day, like Radovan, they ascended in the helicopter. Access to one especially steep prospect required setting the chopper's tubular strut on a five-centimeter-wide ledge marked by yellow tape, with the second strut hovering in space. But the further studies, in 1977 and 1978, failed to find the legendary "next Kennecott." In the end, Radovan's lifelong dream of a pure-copper mountain blinked off the screen in a corporate tax write-off.

There would be an epilogue, however—one that captured something of the phantasmagorical nature of mining ambition in the post-Kennecott era.

In 1983 an Illinois company called Cooper Industries, which had gobbled Geneva Pacific, donated ten thousand acres of mining claims in the Wrangells to the National Park Service. Interior Secretary James Watt praised the company for making the largest commercial donation to a park in US history. But 247 acres of the company's claims, including the Binocular Group, had first been pried away, sold by Cooper for $30,000 to Theodore Van Zelst, a former Geneva Pacific president, who had known Radovan and visited his camp. Two years later, Van Zelst donated these claims to the government as well—claiming a personal tax write-off of $2.75 million.

Was that a fair value to put on Radovan's dream? The Internal Revenue Service disallowed the deduction, extensive litigation ensued, and in 1996 a panel of the Seventh Circuit US Court of Appeals ruled against Van Zelst. The opinion was written by Judge Frank Easterbrook, a conservative who specialized in economic analysis of the law. Easterbrook (who often wrote opinions from his second home, in Girdwood, Alaska) curtly dismissed Van Zelst's proposition that the north-facing property in the Wrangells would have made a valuable site for a lodge, providing tourists a unique opportunity to visit a working mine in the wilderness:

*These days the back-country devotees who make pilgrimages to Alaska are more likely to be repulsed by equipment gouging 100 tons of rock daily from the mountain than they are to be attracted by the smell of diesel exhaust and the thunder of explosions that blast the rocks loose and overwhelm the sounds of nature.*

As to whether a working mine could ever have made a profit on Radovan's Glacier Creek claims, Easterbrook agreed with earlier rulings that concluded it would be too costly to ship copper ore via winter Cat-trains down the Nizina River canyon. Previous owners had given up on the idea even when copper prices were 50 percent higher than in 1985, the judge wrote. He said the optimistic mineral appraisal by the Hawley Group was so unreasonable that Van Zelst owed the IRS penalties and interest: "He had to have known that the Hawley Group's estimate was hooey, the sort of number ginned up to put one over on the revenooers."

While the rest of Alaska was arguing in 1979 about the national monument proclamation, the eyes of McCarthy were focused on a more immediate threat to the common weal: renewed efforts by the state to widen and upgrade the road from Chitina. Local opposition to improved access appeared to be hardening. If isolation was indeed their last nonrenewable resource, mass tourism threatened to become the last extractive industry.

The rough pioneer road and tram access had kept the place relatively cut off. Residents had tried propping up the last footbridge, and experimented with ways to improve the tram, including lighter polypropylene return ropes, larger pulleys, and use of a buried length of railroad track to tighten the cable. But the pair of cable crossings, and the five-minute walk across the island between the two channels, made moving supplies an all-day task. Even so, ever since the collapse of the road bridge in 1974, few McCarthyites wanted a replacement. One year a politician running for state house stepped off the mail plane promising to get money for a replacement bridge, only to be told that his usual prodevelopment stump speech was going to lose votes here.

By 1979 the road-and-bridge issue was heating up again. As earlier in the decade, a big push for the road came from Anchorage residents who had purchased or inherited land in McCarthy. They spoke of building summer places or retirement homes, or selling for a good price. A group of urbanites petitioned the state for road improvements under the name "The Prospectors Club," derided in McCarthy as "The Sightseers Club."

Behind those property owners was a wider populist clamor for recreational land. Government agencies and interest groups were fighting over the map, and the average Alaskan wanted in. A state initiative

The Hardware Store before work on the foundation and roof began in 1977.

had passed in 1978 allowing any three-year resident to go out and claim forty acres of state land. That law was struck down by the state Supreme Court, which ruled the state's constitution barred appropriation by voter initiative. "In Alaska, land is a primary asset of the state treasury," the court said. But the legislature followed up with a law requiring the state to sell or give away one hundred thousand acres every year. Remote subdivisions were being drawn on maps almost willy-nilly. There were no state employees to go out and look at how much swampland was being offered. The state owned seventeen thousand acres in the Chitina valley, and in 1980 officials were considering an initial land offering there of twenty-two hundred acres.

The general clamor for sales of state land and road access was resisted in local hearings around the state, especially in McCarthy.

Resources for rural subsistence living were limited, people argued, especially under hunting and off-road restrictions imposed by a national monument. The National Park Service agreed, citing congressional intent language that called for undeveloped private lands in the Alaska parks to be bought up from willing sellers: "We do not want to see repeated in Alaska the land speculation and inappropriate development that mars the inholding areas and the entry-ways in some of our lower-48 parks," Congress said. The land-fever program eventually collapsed under the weight of its own grandiosity, given the many practical difficulties. The state land disposal in the Wrangells would be postponed several years, then shrink to 235 acres.

Meanwhile state voters had approved a bond issue including $377,000, as a match to $3.5 million in federal funds, for construction of new bridges across the Kennicott and Lakina Rivers. It was an essential step toward improving the sixty-mile railbed route to federal secondary-road standards.

In June 1979 the Department of Transportation held a hearing at the McCarthy Lodge about the bridges. Conversation ran quickly to the general question of opening McCarthy to the outside world.

"There are plenty of cities that you can drive to. The United States and Alaska is full of them," Gary Green testified that day. "Everyone's got their rights to choose, as I see it, between living in a city with its highway systems or trying to live in the bush, and I prefer to live in the bush."

"We don't want to deny anyone to come in here, but if you do put a road in here you will take away what we came here to get and it will no longer exist," said Jim Edwards.

Crowded into the lodge, speaker after speaker, longtime residents and newcomers, told the state officials they didn't want the life they'd fled to follow them. The motorhomes of 1974 were invoked frequently. A transcript of the hearing, running to more than one hundred pages, offers multiple variations on the theme that the local "primitive" way of life was worth protecting. Tough access was the practical solution. The tooth-jarring pioneer road, infamous for dust and flying rocks and railroad spikes that punctured tires, a road that forced cars to splash across beaver ponds and to brake and squeeze past pickups coming the other direction, might be the only thing holding back the tour-bus operators and land speculators and casual day-trippers.

"When there's a bridge across the river and people are driving through," said Judy Miller, "they walk through your back yard and they'll pick up an axe you bought a year ago and go, 'Isn't this a neat antique axe? I think I'll take it home.' People have a whole different attitude when they come out here with a car around them."

Some improvements would be nice, McCarthy residents conceded. The Lakina Bridge approaches kept washing out. Bernd Hoffmann, who was running the lodge that summer, said he had seen five or six visitors show up with fingers mangled in the primitive hand-pulled tram. The cable crossing needed work. Bonnie Morris, who had split up with Kelly Bay and moved into a cabin purchased from Gary Green, mentioned potholes.

"I just spent ten hours driving from Chitina to here and it wouldn't break my heart if they did fill a few of those bumps in and fix a few of the culverts. But I would like to reaffirm that it's important that any human being have an option in life to choose different paths, leading off in the forest from the masses, and that this is a basic freedom of the human spirit that should be encouraged, cultivated, and nourished, and not discouraged by any government."

Just about the only person to speak up for a bridge into town was Jack Wilson, who had moved his flying service from Chitina to Glennallen. He said he was speaking on behalf of the "general public" who paid gasoline taxes and had a right to see the country and not have it blocked by McCarthy residents "so they can live their little backpacker's lifestyle and keep it all to themselves."

Loy Green respectfully rebutted him: "When the bridges went in, we denied the people of America to have the experience of McCarthy."

"We do have access in the spring and in the fall when the river is low or when there's ice on the river," Maxine Edwards pointed out.

McCarthy residents had a hard time understanding why the state would build a bridge if the local people didn't want it. Did they hold hearings in McCarthy to ask about bridges in Anchorage?

According to the transcript, a flustered state transportation planner tried to explain the logic of bridges and progress: "You have to remember that this is a secondary highway. You have a secondary highway that ends, that provides no logical access to a community. Whether or not you want the access is a moot point, if you understand what I'm saying."

They didn't understand. And the road planners, in turn, didn't understand those who testified. Resistance confused and unsettled the Department of Transportation. So did the passive opposition of the National Park Service, which had started to think that slowing down to avoid railroad spikes could be a distinctive part of an Alaska park visitor's experience.

One month later, the equivalent hearing in Anchorage heard from a different and more conventional public that favored improved transportation, whether to reach undeveloped property or to provide a new road-trip option. Why, they asked, should a handful of bush residents get a personal playground?

But the transportation officials seemed undone by the local opposition. Within a year, bond funds for the McCarthy bridges had been quietly transferred to other state projects, including a bridge in the state capital of Juneau. The "reallocation," once it became known, was the subject of protests by the Great Kennicott Land

Company, angry letters by elected representatives, internal investigations, rumors of heads rolling, and a critical report from the state ombudsman, who had only recently finished sorting out the Gary Green–Ron Andersen dispute over bridge timbers, and may have felt McCarthy was generating an awful lot of controversy for an abandoned ghost town.

Lost in the furor was the fact that one of the state proposals, a new bridge across the Lakina River at Mile 44, had plenty of local support. When a typhoon in the fall of 1980 washed out the crossing altogether, the state had to improvise by recycling a one-lane bridge from the old Richardson Highway near Glennallen. (The bridge had once crossed the Tonsina River, where James McCarthy, the town's namesake, drowned on his horse.) Using road maintenance funds, the state pulled the ancient bridge from storage, unbolted the trusses, and trucked the pieces to the Lakina for reassembly.

And that was where things would remain for years. A determined traveler could drive the rough road all the way from Chitina to the bank of the Kennicott River. From there, the splintery tram from the 1940s was still the only way to enter the town of McCarthy.

⇐——⇒

Around this time, the homesteader making the most of the industrial detritus left behind by Kennecott Copper, Jim Edwards, had a few scolding things to say about the wanton ways of Kennecott's successor, Alyeska Pipeline.

The scion of the Oregon brick family was sitting on fifty-two shares of Exxon stock, worth just over $200. In March 1981 he wrote a shareholder letter to C. C. Garvin Jr., chairman of the Exxon corporation, one of the major partners in the pipeline project, to complain about "deliberate, destructive waste of everything." He passed along stories he'd heard, some from Maxine, of trucks buried in landfills, hundreds of tons of oak timbers burned so they couldn't be salvaged by locals, and inflated wages paid to "unskilled kids right out of high school" who have "little to do but sit on the company bus listening to rock music and smoking pot." He was particularly irked about the impact of these wages on non-union locals who "can not get on this fast-bucks gravy wagon," describing how that makes life expensive for people trying to do for themselves. And all for what? "Is it simply a top-to-bottom scramble for 'more' until our country stands stark naked?"

Two months later, Edwards received a three-page reply signed by L. D. Woody, president of Exxon Pipeline Company. Woody said Exxon had thoroughly investigated all such charges of waste and "found no instances of significance." Woody invited his correspondent to pass along any specific allegations, adding: "We believe that the stories told of waste in the construction of [the pipeline] are not reliable, but emanate from those unacquainted with the enormity and unprecedented nature of the task."

A full accounting of pipeline era extravagance would be left to future historians. It was the profligacy of Kennecott Copper that was currently vexing the community of McCarthy—and the federal land-use planners preparing for a new park. What should be done to preserve the human-built landscape left behind after Alaska's first experience as a remote colony of capitalism?

To tell visitors the story of that time, it seemed essential, as the Yale historian of architecture Elihu Rubin has noted about ghost towns, to preserve the buildings—foundations alone make a mere archeological site, without the "sense of place" that is essential to visitor engagement. The Kennecott buildings, however slow to deteriorate in the cold, dry climate, would eventually turn to dust without intervention. Yet locals were concerned a federal takeover might lead to massive reconstruction, restoring the buildings to 1938 standards (subject to hazardous materials mitigation, etc.). They worried that such "Disney-fication" would erase the ghostly back-to-nature feeling that so entranced Mudhole Smith's tourists in the 1950s and ever since had caused new arrivals to swoon.

Looking for some in-between solution, a group of McCarthy residents settled on a concept they called "arrested decay." Kennecott's structures would be shorn up just enough to keep them from collapsing. The ambition was to preserve the poignant sunset beauty of the ruins. The passing of time itself would be visible in their half-fallen state, and each park visitor would have the opportunity to experience a "sense of discovery" anew.

Advocates for this approach, including Ben Shaine, said they were speaking of architecture, but they might well have been addressing their hopes for the community itself. They struggled to envision an idealized middle way, not heretofore achieved in the American experiment, in which their town would neither be erased by a back-to-nature effort nor bloated by easy access into a commercial center. Arrested decay, arrested development: if only McCarthy could stay somewhere in between, never losing its balance with nature, sustaining this perfectly poised historical moment.

The immense social and civil engineering effort this middle way would require—to hold back "progress" in one direction and collapse in the other—seemed impractical to some of the career National Park Service employees asked to develop a workable plan for preserving the ghost town. Such a project was surely beyond the scope and ambition of the federal park bureaucracy. The self-mythologizing generation that discovered the Wrangells during the lost decades could be exasperating to work with, Park Service historian Logan Hovis said after he retired. "I have always felt if they wanted to enshrine themselves in Kennecott they needed to write a separate national register nomination. The established landmark significance, the legal justification for all that the NPS has done, ends in 1938."

As things turned out, "arrested decay" would prove as difficult to sustain in architecture as it is in tooth enamel (a problem not lost on the flying dentists who co-owned the Kennecott facilities with Howard Knutson, and who remained eager to off-load the remains to the federal government before they rotted away).

And yet—one of the more successful covert acts during the two-year lifespan of the Wrangell-St. Elias National Monument involved just such an effort to evade change and preserve the ephemeral.

In September 1979 several small work crews traveled by bulldozer and Dodge Power Wagon up McCarthy Creek as far as the never-more-than-speculative Green Butte Mine. Among those participating were Ben Shaine, Gary Green, Tim Nash, and people associated with the Santa Cruz college program. It wasn't resistance or civil disobedience, exactly—they just wanted to do things the old way one last time. The trips took all day, as the Allis Chalmers dozer borrowed from Gordon Burdick had to scrape the trail in some places and winch the truck across the creek in others. The poplars were gold and the creek ran low as cool fall weather slowed the glacier melt. Their mission was to tear down the kitchen wing of the Green Butte's two-story bunkhouse, whose roof had collapsed the previous winter, complicating life for Loy and Curtis Green, who still called the bunkhouse home.

The milled bunkhouse logs were salvaged and numbered and hauled by the dozer across the creek to a bench of land where Loy had filed a mining claim. Trumpet-playing, oil-painting Loy had a peculiar sourdough gravitas and a yen for transcendentalist philosophy that made him a favorite old-timer around the college program at the Hardware Store. The logs were reassembled into a cabin for the Green brothers. With the weathered materials and old tin roof-

Work crew crosses McCarthy Creek on their way to Loy Green's cabin project, 1979.

ing, a few small touches achieved the desired effect: the brand-new home looked like a decrepit hermit's cabin that had been falling down for half a century.

Needless to say, tearing down ruins and building new cabins were not encouraged in President Carter's national monument. For the placeholder park, the rules were placeholders, too, but federal mining law was clear enough—a claim actually had to have mineral potential to be valid. Loy Green had thumbed his nose at the entire process, naming his claim the "Copper View." (He had tried, several years earlier, to file for a legitimate cabin site in the valley, just before the deadline for such claims but made the mistake of trusting the envelope with his paperwork to Gordon Burdick, who lost it.) But park rangers, new to the area and depending on townspeople to fill them in, were willing to go along, up to a point, accepting the assertion that the cabin was historic. The Park Service informally granted Loy life occupancy: after he died, the unpatented claim would go back to the government, and the cabin would fade away.

One year after Loy Green's cabin was assembled, a few of the builders returned for a visit, just as a Pacific typhoon slammed into the Wrangells—the same storm that washed away the old Lakina River bridge. A flood of biblical proportions scoured the floor of the McCarthy Creek valley, taking out the Green Butte Road and Burdick's bridges, and burying Loy's panel truck in gravel, three miles downstream from where he'd parked it. Loy's guests were safe in the Copper View cabin, but the mountains above were liquefying, the slurry of rocks off the cliffs so loud that no one could sleep. After five days, the skies cleared and the runoff abated enough for the hikers to creep home over the top of Bonanza Ridge. At their backs, McCarthy Creek was now coursing through a pristine gravel channel. The valley floor had gone back to nature.

Two months after the storm, in November 1980, Congress passed the Alaska National Interest Lands Conservation Act. Wrangell-St. Elias National Park and Preserve became the country's biggest national park, the size of six Yellowstones. The final bill was a Senate compromise that conservationists saw as fissured with weaknesses and openings for future problems. Their champions in Congress folded, however, after Ronald Reagan's presidential victory that month. This was the best deal they were likely to get. The country's political shift to the right would be felt in the Wrangells, as the new law would be interpreted by the incoming administration. "Every land question means new regulations. It's really going to be a monumental—no, I hate that word—a fantastically huge job," a key aide to Representative Don Young told an Alaska reporter on the night the bill passed. Rules for the new parks would be written by a shrewd and outspoken critic of federal power in the West, Reagan's Interior Secretary, James Watt.

President Carter signed the Senate bill into law in December, one of his last acts in office. The law replaced the national monuments and established almost 100 million acres of new and expanded national parks and wildlife refuges in Alaska. The long political battle, reaching in some sense back to Teddy Roosevelt's era, had resulted in a hybrid piece of legislation—"a grand bargain" the US Supreme Court would call it, forty years later—that declared its intent to safeguard "natural, scenic, historic, recreational and wild-life values," while at the same time providing for the "economic and social needs" of Alaska and its citizens.

Here was a formula for arrested decay on a grand scale. Unlike parks in the contiguous states, Alaska's parks were encouraged to develop special provisions to help preserve rural subsistence life-styles. Of the thirteen million acres in Wrangell-St. Elias National Park, more than four million would be "national preserve," where trapping and Dall sheep trophy hunts could continue. Rural communities and private cabins and working mines were somehow to be accommodated—perhaps even interpreted as part of the visitor experience. But how to keep the number of people living in those private cabins at a manageable level, or keep McCarthy from turning into a gaudy commercial resort of log-cabin motels and trinket shops like national park gateway towns in the Lower 48? The Wrangells had always been, as the Santa Cruz report once put it, in a "classical and enduring sense," about geological change, about destruction and renewal. That was how history moved too. How were you going to stop change?

The settlers of McCarthy braced for what was to come next.

*Bridge*

# THE HOLTET DECLARATION

TO WHOM IT MAY CONCERN—JULY 27, 1973

This letter is to acknowledge the whereabouts of certain articles taken from the farm-homestead of one Ole Holtet, across the Kennicott River from McCarthy, Alaska.

The purpose of this letter is to give a dated and sealed record of the reasons and intents for these articles as removed by me, James H. Edwards, of McCarthy.

When I first moved to McCarthy in 1955, the Holtet Farm buildings were still largely intact and equipped, as were other places in the area. Many of the owners of these places were known or presumed dead, and in most cases, never came around or looked after their property.

In the very early 1960s, others in McCarthy began taking equipment and parts of buildings from the Holtet properties. This practice had been going on for some time and most of the people engaged in it, as indeed many buildings were in fact abandoned, and falling to ruin.

There were at the Holtet farm, two or more bob-sleds, disassembled and in a shed. Since the place was in good condition then, I was reluctant to bother, but when the first sled went to others I took the smaller one as I had work for it then, and it was obvious that it would be taken anyway by someone.

My intent then and all along, was that if Mr. Holtet ever showed up, that I would return his sled parts.

At this time I also took three or four small hand brush hooks, with the same intent.

A few years later, my wife and I found out that Mr. Holtet was alive and living near Palmer, and we undertook to make his acquaintance. Mr. Holtet proved (for us) to be extremely difficult to talk to, and we were not able to discuss these problems with him.

In the late 1960s, various outfits began bringing trucks and equipment in and out of McCarthy, and articles began to go fast from the Holtet property. The blacksmith shop was stripped, and the house became a shell.

There was one article still of value, a small buckboard or wagon, in the barn. With the State then drilling for a bridge at the Copper River, it was obvious that this wagon would soon leave the country. So my wife and I took it. We have it in our warehouse. We wanted these things to remain in the area for historical value, and possible use.

We state here, that we have these articles some bob-sled parts, some brush hooks, and the buckboard. We recognize that these rightfully belong to Mr. Ole Holtet. We cannot return them to the farm because there is traffic now frequently since the bridge is finished, and the articles would certainly leave the country in someone's car or truck, never to be accounted for.

It has been our intent all along, and we state here in a dated letter before the fact, that if and when Mr. Holtet returns to his farm to refurbish it, that we intend to offer return of these articles, herein named.

We of course neither offer nor bear any responsibility for articles taken or destroyed by others.

JAMES EDWARDS

# PART THREE

Men ask the way to Cold Mountain
Cold Mountain: there's no through trail.
In summer, ice doesn't melt
The rising sun blurs in swirling fog.
How did I make it?
My heart's not the same as yours.
If your heart was like mine
You'd get it and be right here.

GARY SNYDER, COLD MOUNTAIN POEMS

# 12

# The Way to Cold Mountain

THREE RIDERS ON snowmachines approached McCarthy
through the last of the mountain dusk. It was the middle
of February 1983. The afternoon had been wet and heavy with falling snow. But now the sky opened and cold poured down from the
stars. The three riders followed their headlights along the unstable
freezing trail. They had tried all afternoon to cross the Nizina River
ice, pushing and pulling their heavy machines through deep wet
snow on top of the ice until they realized they stood in overflow, a
second river prowling atop the first. They turned back. They were
cold-soaked, tired, groggily vigilant for signs of hypothermia. The
silhouette of the town brought no relief. The riders knew they were
not welcome.

In the two years since the creation of Wrangell-St. Elias National
Park, government officials had done all they could to avoid McCarthy. They had never spent a night in the town. The three riders,

all Park Service employees, had not stopped that morning as they passed through. Their objective had been to deliver a sled to Al and Fran Gagnon's cabin at May Creek, on the far side of the Nizina. The new park was now responsible for search-and-rescue covering thousands of square miles of mountains all the way to Canada, and the Gagnon cabin at May Creek was as close to town as they were comfortable basing their remote ranger station.

Al Gagnon had been an outspoken opponent of messing up the wilderness by making it a national park. Now he was selling out to the government. At his cabin, he left behind a short frontiersman's treatise on homestead life, recommending that the rangers ring straight-grained trees in close stands east of the runway for firewood. Let the trees dry four years before cutting and burning. "Wood is *very* important out here. Just as important as meat." Fires were the biggest enemy, accidents second. "You folks that come after us, the first thing to remember to do is, leave the town behind you. . . . Pay close attention to nature, for the more you learn about it and from it, the more joy and pleasure you'll derive from your life out here."

That day the rangers learned from nature how to get their butts kicked. They demonstrated that they faced the same logistical challenges as everyone else in the valley. Except, of course, the park didn't have to take nature's no as a final answer: having failed to cross the Nizina River, the rangers would now fly the sled to May Creek. But in the meantime they were wet and cold and their trucks were still two hours away, parked where the plows stopped partway out the McCarthy road.

The park ranger responsible for the Chitina River valley led the patrol. Trailing behind were the park superintendent, who was older and starting to look frail in the cold, and a park resource specialist apparently succumbing to the flu. The resident park ranger was originally from Indiana but lived now in Chitina, where his job was to enforce the "grand bargain" of Alaska's d-2 parks bill. It was not clear to him how the old way of life could survive in a national park. His stressful job was to inform the people of McCarthy that the pioneer moment in American history had ended. It was a message to be dosed out gradually, he understood, and in hours like this the message did not seem to be altogether true.

He saw a kerosene lamp burning in the window of a small cabin by the creek. The park ranger stopped and knocked on the cabin door.

◄──►

Sally Gibert, short and friendly, with bushels of red hair and freckles, was a former Santa Cruz student. She knew a lot about the Park Service in Alaska, as a graduate of Richard Cooley's Santa Cruz program—a star pupil, in fact, who had done her thesis on Alaska Native land claims and had been hired by the Joint Federal-State Land Use Planning Commission. Yet she worked in Anchorage for three years and never visited McCarthy until 1976, when, to mark the Bicentennial Fourth of July, she went looking for someplace suitably historic, someplace that predated the pipeline boom. She drove out the McCarthy road with a couple of visiting Santa Cruz undergraduates, one of whom, Judy Richter, returned and married Jerry Miller and took over running the lodge. It was an earth-shifting visit for Sally Gibert as well, for soon she was scraping together $15,000 to buy the Hardware Store. The false-front two-story edifice of kindling, built in 1911, with a sinking foundation and a swayback roof, had been home through the years to Raven and Loy Green and Gordon Burdick and Blazo Bill Berry. Sally dreamed of turning it into a youth hostel.

She had an environmentalist's heart and a mind that refracted many angles. In Anchorage Sally's job had been to analyze legislative land-use options for her political bosses. In McCarthy, where she came for three months' leave every year to work on her place, the option that most interested her was one in which community and wilderness found a way to coexist. She reassured several neighbors in 1978 that they weren't being moved out by the government. But she carried her neighbors' concerns back to Anchorage. She registered the Hardware Store as a historic structure and lodged Ben Shaine's college program during summers. Her enthusiasm attracted many admirers. For five summers, friends from Anchorage and students from down south joined locals helping to shore up the store's underpinnings in exchange for sourdough pancakes and bean stew.

"You would have thought we were raising the Taj Mahal, not a sagging old hardware store," Curtis Green wrote in his memoir. "But, of course, it was more than that. A symbol, and certainly a focus for the youthful aspirations of those boys and girls of affluence who saw McCarthy, in particular, and Alaska, in general, as a hope for a better future, a chance to get it right, and not go down that beaten path of exploitation and over-development."

The Hardware Store became the scene of a kerosene-lit party every Labor Day weekend, drawing fiddlers and contra dancers from Fairbanks and Anchorage. The first year, the syncopated spinning and thumping so worried Loy Green that he crawled under the building with a flashlight to monitor the foundation. Sally Gibert filled five-gallon buckets with Tang, rum, and Everclear, and musicians ladled it out with a Sierra cup. With enough Everclear, a person might stand outside in the middle of empty Kennicott Avenue, watching through the windows as dancers leaped in the golden lamplight, and feel the town's ghosts all around.

By February 1983 Sally Gibert had been living full-time in the Wrangells for two years. She had given up her government job: working remote was hardly an option over the Heglands' single-sideband radio, the town's only link to the outside world. She purchased a little

McCarthy in the
winter of 1983, weeks
before the mail day
murders.

cabin near the Hardware Store from a pioneer's widow who, never
having been to McCarthy herself, turned down all previous offers,
thinking those long-distance suitors were vastly undervaluing the
fine mansion her late husband had described. Sally sent actual photos and mentioned her Hardware Store restoration efforts. The little
cabin needed work—crudely built, in the opinion of Jim Edwards—
"patches on it, crooked boards, big gaps, awful." The ceiling sagged,
and the only insulation in the walls consisted of newspapers from
the 1920s. She had turned it into a cozy little home.

Sally Gibert was surprised to find the visitors at her cabin door
that night. She invited the park rangers in and glanced habitually at
the thermometer, already well below zero. She knew, perhaps better
than anyone, given her previous employment, that park rangers had

never spent a night in town. Even as she hung their wet gear by the stove, she wondered if she was doing something that might upset her neighbors. Would her loyalty seem compromised? Sally knew everyone in town, often from multiple perspectives. Al Gagnon, for instance, whose cabin they'd been trying to reach. As a bureaucrat, she had watched Gagnon plat a subdivision on paper to push his May Creek property to the top of the national park's priority-buy list. As Hardware Store host, she had flown to May Creek to buy the departing survivalist's buckets of powdered milk, molasses, and beans.

She made tea now for the travelers, scooping creek water from the pail in her kitchen—McCarthy Creek was silty with glacial melt in summer but clear and delicious when ladled through winter ice.

She knew the park ranger, Jim Hannah, and they got along well enough. His burly swagger put her off, but she recognized that those qualities, not the uniform, gave him credibility in a frontier-macho area with no law enforcement backup. She was on friendly terms with the superintendent, Chuck Budge, from meetings in Anchorage. Budge was conscientious about crossing the social line. He said they should keep going to their trucks at Strelna. He didn't want to get Sally in trouble. She waved him off. Winter safety is no joke, she said. The ailing third member of the party was already nose-down in his steaming mug.

Jim Hannah went to the snowmachines to retrieve their sleeping bags.

◄——►

Official visits to McCarthy were limited to a couple each year, usually on a day when people gathered to meet the mail plane. Sally Gibert remembered one such visit, during the park's first summer, which caused a particular outbreak of consternation.

Larry Hoare and Rita Pfeninger had been walking down to mail from their place at Kennecott that morning when they heard a rifle shot. Upon reaching Tim Nash's cabin, they found their friend hunched over a dead moose in the road. The cow moose had been ravaging his vegetable garden for several nights, and it returned that morning just as Tim was heading to work. He had a job on the Lakina Bridge replacement project, which meant commuting across the tram. Larry offered to take over the butchering so Tim could get to work.

Rita went on alone to the airfield, where she was aghast to find park rangers. Even worse, they asked if they could visit her at Kennecott that afternoon. She felt obliged to say yes, then excused herself, saying she had to gather shaggy mane mushrooms for dinner. Jumping on a borrowed bike, she pedaled up the gravel road to find her husband elbow-deep in an illegal moose kill. "I felt like Paul Revere—'The Park Service is coming!'" Rita said later. "I was so ashamed of how devious we could be. Now I know what they mean when they say caught red-handed." With help from another neighbor, they hastily quartered and moved the carcass and cleaned the road where the rangers would soon pass. Larry shot a spruce grouse out of a nearby tree and spread its feathers across the last blood in the gravel.

In her kitchen, Sally Gibert made a mental inventory—who was living in the valley that winter, who was away during this last spell of dark cold before spring, who might be worried about letting rangers through the door.

Gary Green might not be happy to hear it. He was now the town's licensed commercial bush pilot. Flying in and out of the park, he had been the first to grapple with new rules and regulations. He complained that the country didn't seem as wild any more. Too many helicopters with rangers. Gary had reason, though, to get along with

Maxine and Jim Edwards with his Piper PA-16 Clipper, October 1980.

Sally: he was planning to marry her sister. Nancy Gibert had come to Alaska for a visit and stayed. Nancy was away now, seeing about a job, but would be back soon on the mail plane.

Sally's friend Loy Green would understand. The beatnik philosopher was wintering at his Copper View cabin up McCarthy Creek. Jerry and Judy Miller, across the Nizina at Dan Creek, were zealous guardians of local prerogative. They still owned the McCarthy Lodge, closed now for the winter, as was the area's other lodge, up at Kennecott. Judy had actually put on a ranger uniform for a while, one of the park's first local hires, thinking she could teach government officials important lessons about the place. It turned out all they wanted was for her to represent their ideas to her neighbors, so she quit. But not before warning Eric and Joan Wasserman that rangers were tracking rumors of a poached moose. Fortunately, when Jim Hannah showed up to question the Wassermans, he did not seem to notice the moose roast crackling in the oven.

The Wassermans were not around—Sally had visited with them last month on their way out of the valley for work. Larry and Rita were gone for winter as well. Jim and Maxine Edwards were home at Swift Creek, across the Kennicott. Maxine had gone away for a short while that winter, working in Anchorage in the kitchen at Chuck E. Cheese to make money for Christmas gifts, things Jim would think extravagant—clothing for her daughter, a leather jacket for her son. Now she was back. Sally figured Jim and Maxine would not object to her housing the rangers. Jim groused about their wasteful ways and the way they hassled his little gold mine at Dan Creek, but he recognized they were here to stay.

Besides, Jim and Maxine were letting Ben Shaine and Marci Thurston stay in a small log cabin beside their Swift Creek airstrip, and if anyone in town had a reputation for being park-friendly, it was Ben and Marci. They were gone at the moment, traveling down south to drum up college students for the hardware store program, but they had made themselves into locals—toughing out winter in a remote Spruce Point cabin, building an addition for Jim and Maxine, looking for land. Ben's political views had deepened since writing a coexistence plan for his Berkeley master's thesis, in which he had described how urban Americans might come north to find "re-creation." Now he was thinking about how this could be a different kind of national park, cautioning, in a speech to students, against the "fundamentally exploitationist perspective" of trivializing the Wrangells as pretty scenery or a romantic mining-day relic. At times he could be maddeningly gnomic about the region's importance to the modern world. He spoke of a "presence" that awaited its time, lying deep beyond city-bound definitions of wilderness. In 1980, when two Santa Cruz students interviewed residents at the airstrip on mail day, Ben told them the significance of McCarthy was not easy to see: "It's like Lao Tzu says: 'The secret waits for the insight of eyes unclouded by longing.'" Marci told them of working outdoors and getting to know her own daily rhythms, her own true self.

Jim Edwards had been at the airstrip that same day in 1980, and he provided the students a more straightforward account than Ben. Life was not about disappearing into the woods, in his view, it was about making a home.

> *This is my home in every sense of the word. I have roots here, a life,*
> *a feeling for the place, a sense of belonging. We've built a house*
> *that's comfortable to our standards. We didn't build it to sell but*
> *to live in, and we plan to live here the whole of our lives. And we've*
> *done our outhouse apprenticeship; we've got flush toilets now and*
> *we're trying to shift over from kerosene to hydropower, and I'd like*
> *to figure some way to charge our batteries from wood heat in the*
> *winter.*

"It's an art form to be living out here," he told them. Jim Edwards's biggest worry about the park was that government jobs and facilities would make life in the valley too easy. The challenge of living kept the place from being overrun. He said he refused government hand-outs, though that meant scrimping and leaving in summer to find work. When he flew his family to Anchorage, they pitched a tent in the bushes behind the other private planes at Merrill Field. He was annoyed by the way city drivers raced from traffic light to traffic light: it was such a terrible waste of energy, he told the Santa Cruz students, who noted that Edwards had just flown himself across the river to pick up incoming airplane parts.

Chris Richards was also at the mail plane gathering that day, down from Kennecott wearing a holster and pistol. He told the students he'd had to shoot a porcupine in his kitchen that very morning.

⟵——➢

Counting down the list, subtracting those away on trips, Sally Gibert could hardly come up with a dozen people in the valley that month.

Rick and Bonnie Kenyon were at home, across the river near Jim and Maxine. They would resent the rangers' presence but not an act of charity.

Bonnie Morris lived a few city blocks back in the woods from Sally's cabin with her new boyfriend, Malcolm Vance, a young man she'd first hired as a carpenter. They would be wary. A few years ago, the community had pitched in to fly Bonnie to Fairbanks, to testify in front of a congressional committee about the importance of allowing subsistence living to continue in a park.

Les and Flo Hegland wouldn't like it, but at least they didn't live right in town any more. The old Aiken house, not far from Sally's, was now Flo's "gift shop," with her paintings and antiques and samples of copper ore. They had grown tired of the noise and the "downtown politics." Ron Andersen's generator, running day and night across the street from the Aiken house, had interfered with their weather radio. Since 1976 they had been in their new house, the one with an indoor toilet, by the airfield.

The Heglands weren't reclusive. Far from it—they served tea on mail day, waiting for the plane from Glennallen. Flo was warm and effusive, her practical homemaking balanced by artistic energies that projected her paintings onto all manner of evocative media including cast iron frying pans and moose antlers. She had her midwestern judgmental side, but Rita Pfeninger, who dropped by for artistic advice and inspiration, said she had a green heart. She once advised

Rita, "If you're feeling blue, hug a tree. After a while, you'll feel better." Les Hegland, on the other hand, would stew quietly, in an upper Great Plains way. He ran a trapline in winter, and in summer fished at Long Lake with his friend, Harley King. This country would never be the same with the federal government moving in. After sixteen years in McCarthy, and edging into their sixties, the Heglands were about done—they were talking about a move to Wrangell, a small fishing town in Southeast Alaska.

◄——►

Farther up the mountain toward Kennecott, the bearded mountain man Tim Nash had just returned from his honeymoon. Tim was strong enough to drive a nail with a choked-up sledgehammer, and he once told the park superintendent he would defend his cabin with a gun. But he was a gentle soul, everyone said.

Friends knew he had had a rough year—alone, depressed—when his wife left. And then the previous summer, a short apple-cheeked twenty-five-year-old backpacker named Amy Ashenden climbed off the mail plane. She was auburn-haired and strong-shouldered and uncommonly well-read. She wore plain work clothes and had an air of quiet curiosity. She made friends and hiked across the glacier to explore a drained lakebed filled with ice cubes. Then she settled in as a cabin-sitter and started writing in her journal.

Amy had grown up in western Massachusetts, on a former dairy farm outside the small town of Shelburne Falls. She excelled at private school and graduated from Harvard with a degree in comparative religion. Yet she puzzled her family, who considered her clever but excessively critical—moody and discontented, burdened by the so-called conveniences of the material world. Her college honors thesis, exploring Buddhist asceticism, was titled "Climbing up the

Cold Mountain Path." The title came from the poetry of Han Shan, an eighth-century Tang Dynasty hermit who used landscape imagery to describe a state of mind.

> Cold Mountain has many hidden wonders,
> People who climb here are always getting scared.
> When the moon shines, water sparkles clear . . .
> At the wrong season you can't ford the creeks.

For a long time, Amy had been trying to impose greater spiritual discipline in her own life. The opportunity to follow this path to Alaska came along by chance. She had found seasonal work in national parks during college, then a job at a mountain hut in New Hampshire run by the Harvard Mountaineering Club. A climber boyfriend from the hut took her to Alaska. In Fairbanks she worked in a bookstore and lived in a house of skiers and climbers. After two winters, she broke up with her boyfriend and, impatient with the urban climber-grunge of Fairbanks and her own lack of perseverance, resolved to spend one whole summer in real wilderness before giving up. She caught a ride to Glennallen and flew to McCarthy on the mail plane. Immediately she recognized the landscape of her thesis. What surprised her, she wrote in her journal, was finding a community of "kindred spirits."

> Ever since I bought that pair of snowshoes in seventh grade, I think one of the best dreams has been to be living simply in a place like this. I really feel this is the lifestyle I most want to explore right now, and I feel good about doing it alone. . . . Good people and neighbors to learn from, and the heightened energy and motivation which comes to me from living close to the mountains makes me feel a great potential.

Tim Nash and Amy Ashenden visit Amy's family in Massachusetts, Christmas 1982.

The ghost town landscape offered abundant lessons in Buddhist impermanence. "The history of the area is basically recorded only in the memory of old-timers, so it is hard to learn about, but the feeling of history is rich," Amy wrote her parents.

David and Jo Ashenden flew up from Massachusetts to check on the welfare of their daughter. Amy walked them excitedly around McCarthy and described her plans to stay. The visit went well at first, until her mother took a walk around Kennecott, alone in a misty mountain rain, observing how "all the old buildings of this once bustling community had deteriorated just enough to give the area a sort of charm that inspires certain minds to reclamation." On the porch of a small red house she saw a man, tall and balding, polishing a rifle. He glared at her, as if impatient for her to get out of his sight. She turned away. It rained heavily all the next day as Jo Ashenden tried to talk Amy out of spending the winter in such a "dark and dismal" place.

But soon it was September, the most beautiful month in the Wrangells. The mountainsides of aspen, birch, and poplar blazed gold in low-angle sunlight. After a summer of camping in high valleys, Amy had lined up a small place of her own near Kennecott and started preparing for winter. From Al Gagnon, she bought insulated "mouse boots" and a shotgun. She received many offers of help. "A single woman really awakens the protective male instinct in an environment like this," she wrote to reassure her parents.

Tim Nash had black ringlets and a body carved of marble. He was twelve years older than Amy and emotionally reticent. She was impressed that he hunted all his meat and grew his own vegetables and built with local materials whenever possible. He was a person who thought about how best to spend each day. "A lot of people talk about these things, but it's so refreshing to meet someone who really lives by his principles," she wrote in her journal. "He's also very much attuned to physical health and is in amazing shape. When I watch him literally shoulder a tree and walk to his woodpile with it, I really can't quite believe what I'm seeing."

Like other McCarthy bachelors before him—Jim Edwards, Jerry Miller, Gary Green—Tim Nash wasted no time. Amy settled into Tim's cabin and a neo-neolithic lifestyle. In November she wrote her parents that they were engaged. The couple flew back east to Shelburne Falls at Christmas. Her parents said they'd never seen Amy more radiant. Tim split firewood for Amy's father and built a bookcase for her mother. They borrowed a car and drove to Tim's boyhood home in Floodwood, Minnesota, where, Amy marveled in a letter, they were married by his mother's parish priest—"I, who haven't been baptized, and Tim, an atheist!"

After two months away, Tim and Amy had only just returned to Tim's cabin, up the path toward Kennecott. On Valentine's Day, Bonnie Morris and Malcolm brought them a quarter of a moose for a welcome-home and a mincemeat pie with a heart carved on top. The sunlight had come back, Amy would write her parents in late February. The dark days were over. "We've got this winter licked! BOY IS IT GOOD TO BE HOME! AND IT ALSO IS PRETTY WON-DERFUL TO BE MRS. NASH."

A few days later, Amy would write a more intimate letter to a female hiking friend, in which she said she finally felt on the right path. "It seems like ages since I've sitten (is that really a word? I honestly can't remember) down to write," the Harvard graduate began.

> I guess ever since I studied Asian ways of thought and value sys-tems in school, I have realized that the real work of my life is not to have fun, entertain myself or just get by—it is a pretty deep com-mitment to the attempt to develop a 'spiritual' understanding of life—to plug into something bigger than just me and my ego-desire. I feel I have stumbled on the catalyst to actually make a trembling start in this greatest goal—for the first time in my life—instead of paying it lip service and getting DRUNK AGAIN.
>
> But enough of the heavies. I wonder what I'll be saying next year?!?

The friend, who had been to McCarthy, had been surprised by the quick wedding. She didn't quite get the intellectual match. She remembered Tim as the guy who ate the beavers he trapped. But she trusted Amy's judgment. The friend had asked Amy for a reading list. Amy recommended Han Shan's *Cold Mountain Poems* translated by Gary Snyder, Peter Matthiessen's *The Snow Leopard*, and introduc-tory books on Zen Buddhism and the Tao Te Ching. And she thanked her friend for providing a ready ear.

*Men never understand women the way other women do, I think,
and I guess we'd all like to be understood and spoken to on all
levels possible. . . . I've been going through so many changes and
realizations of late that I almost hesitate to say much—I'm on new
ground, good ground and promising ground, but I need to watch
my step a bit—trust is such a delicate thing. We have a good, basic
and deeply seated common goal in each of our individual selves,
dictating a simple, peasant's lifestyle, and that lifestyle almost
necessitates a partnership for it to endure. There is too much
drudgery and quietness for one to go it alone in a place like this for
a lifetime; the life is good but the novelty wears off quickly.*

The letter ended: "I'd better close here if I'm to get it on this
week's mail plane. I think I could go on forever!" The date at the top
was February 28, 1983. The envelope, addressed and stamped, was on
the table in their cabin the next morning. It was not mailed until
four months later.

⇐――⇒

As the park rangers settled in for the night at her cabin, Sally Gibert's
mental inventory concluded with the three guys in Kennecott.

Nick Olmsted was a good friend of Sally's. They planned to ski
together up the Chitistone Canyon soon for some snow camping.
Nick was quietly pro-park and wouldn't resent the rangers staying
over. Querulous Chris Richards would complain no matter what
Sally did. He had worked away all summer as a flagger on a remote
highway project, brandishing his stop sign with a glint of pleasure as
he impeded the progress of Winnebagos lumbering across the wilderness. Now Chris was back in Nell McCann's little red cottage for
winter, looking after a friend's dog team.

The third guy, she couldn't tell. Lou Hastings lived in a small, unkempt millworker's house by the upper trail to the glaciers. McCarthy was sociable to a degree that surprised outsiders, but Hastings could be unpleasant, and people kept their distance. He was tall, with a bushy beard and a bald head and wire-rim glasses. Lou had come to Alaska and Kennecott the first time on his honeymoon, in 1979, and returned with his wife two years later for a second stay at the Kennicott Glacier Lodge. He belonged to conservation groups and seemed to appreciate the history of the ruins, but the lodge remembered the way he broke the rules about using his camp stove in the tinder-dry bunkhouse, even after being warned. His wife was a librarian, and Lou worked in the new field of computer software development. They bought a cabin in Kennecott and went back and forth to Anchorage. Then pretty soon it was just Lou coming out alone.

Nick and Chris and Lou, alone in their little Kennecott cabins through the long dark winter. Les Hegland, worrying about the new guy, snowmachined up to the dilapidated millworker's house, and left food and firewood by the door.

Sally Gibert loaded one last log in her stove for the night. That was everyone she could think of around the valley. In the winter of 1983, the changes people feared still lay in the future. The pioneer moment was not yet over. Park rangers, like everyone else, depended on their neighbors for survival. You could go to the creek for water and know, from the snowy bootprint in the path, which of your neighbors had passed by.

# 13

# Destruction at Noonday

O N HER WAY to mail that morning, Maxine Edwards walked
from the Swift Creek homestead to the Kenyons' log cabin.
She carried an orange plastic sled to glide her packages home. Her
husband stayed behind to work on some projects. In two weeks it
would be their twenty-fifth wedding anniversary.

The sky was blue, the morning cold but windless, the snow deep.
Snowmachines had cut a perfect hard-packed trail to town. Maxine and Bonnie Kenyon discussed the beauty of the winter's day. In
such weather, there would be no uncertainty about the mail plane
getting in.

The two women often walked together to mail. But on this day
Bonnie declined to go. She kept the reason to herself, the strange
pressure from an invisible hand that she felt the moment she opened
her Bible that morning and read from Psalm 91: "Thou shalt not be
afraid for the terror by night; nor for the arrow that flieth by day; nor

for the pestilence that walketh in darkness; nor for the destruction that wasteth at noonday."

Maxine Edwards walked on alone and crossed the frozen river.

◄———►

Investigators determined that Maxine Edwards reached the town of McCarthy at approximately 10:25 a.m. on March 1, 1983. At that time, she encountered another friend, Bonnie Morris, who offered a ride on her dogsled the last half mile up to the airfield. The dogs were snapping—one was in heat—so Edwards hopped off at the snowy path to the Hegland household. Morris handed over letters for Edwards to deliver and asked her to stop by later for cookies. Edwards agreed, and proceeded on foot down the path to the brown house where she would wait for the mail plane.

After Bonnie Morris returned to her cabin, she told Alaska State Troopers, she heard gunshots in the distance and thought nothing of it.

◄———►

That morning up at Kennecott, in the little red cottage where Nell McCann once lived, Chris Richards was awakened by barking dogs. He'd been up late the previous night playing Risk, the board game of world domination, by the light of a Coleman lamp. His neighbor, Lou Hastings, came by often to play Risk or chess, ever since running out of Blazo for his own lantern.

Chris didn't care much for Lou's company but felt kind of sorry for him. He seemed out of place here—surely the only person in a hundred miles who could look at a snowshoe hare's tracks in the snow and not tell which way it was going. Chris had let him take over the world last night so he would go home.

Now Chris stumbled onto the cold morning floor in his sock feet, wondering if the dogs, staked outside, were barking at a moose. He pulled on his pants. Then he remembered it was mail day.

The window by his door filled with Lou Hastings's wire-rim spectacles and bushy beard. Chris called out to come in. As he turned to his kitchen shelf, he saw Lou set down a heavy pack and take a deep breath.

Chris reached for the coffee pot as Lou entered. Chris turned and felt his head fly backward as a bullet smashed through his glasses and into his cheek. A second explosion hit the back of his head. Lou was holding a pistol wrapped in fur, and Chris reached for it. As they struggled, Lou said, "You should see yourself. You're already dead. Just quit fighting and I'll make it easy for you."

The pistol jammed. Chris picked up a butcher knife and pushed it into Lou's thigh and ran for the door. He grabbed at a .22 rifle hanging from a nail, but it snagged and he let go and ran into the snow in his sock feet. Lou stepped onto the porch, shooting again. Chris stumbled up a snowy ravine past the deserted Kennicott Glacier Lodge to Nick Olmsted's cabin. Nick had gone camping. Chris found a pair of boots, circled through some trees, and descended another gulley, snow to his waist, until the boots fell off.

Gary Green arrived at the airstrip early that morning to greet his fiancée, Nancy Gibert, who was inbound on the mail plane. Gary decided to take a few minutes to shovel snow away from his Cessna 180 before walking to the Heglands for tea.

Nancy's sister, Sally, had gone on a ski-camping trip up the Chitistone with Nick Olmsted. There was a chance they would show up at the airstrip that morning, too, if open water or overflow kept them from crossing the Nizina, as it had the park rangers recently. Sally and Nick planned to double back and catch the mail plane to May Creek. Mail pilots still hopped from strip to strip, still carried news and gossip and the occasional local passenger. It took Lynn Ellis, the pilot, less than an hour to fly from Gulkana. Nancy was probably in the air already.

As Gary Green shoveled around his airplane, he looked down the runway and saw Lou Hastings heading toward the Heglands. He was wearing that hooded pea-green parka of his, with a ruff of hand-sewn fur hanging down to his knees. Hastings stopped and stared back. Gary turned away, disappointed—the last thing he wanted to do was sit around the Heglands with a cup of tea on his knee in awkward silence next to Lou. He would wait in the cold at his plane instead.

Fifteen minutes later, he heard the sound of an approaching snowmachine. Tim and Amy Nash pulled up at the plane. On a sled behind the snowmachine sat Chris Richards, his head wrapped with a bloody bandage.

Tim said they'd heard Chris shouting as he approached their cabin. He was wearing only socks and spoke in a rush. Tim told him to calm down. "I'll calm down when you load all your guns," Chris said.

As Chris described what happened, Tim Nash pulled out his Remington twelve-gauge shotgun, loaded with buckshot, and a .44 Magnum handgun. Amy tended his wounds, then squeezed on back of the snowmachine. They towed the sled with Chris slowly to the airstrip. Along the path, they saw drops of blood—Hastings, with a knife wound in his thigh, was moving ahead of them.

Gary told them he'd seen Hastings walking toward the Hegland house. Green later testified that he and Tim decided to see what was going on. Amy stayed with Chris by the plane.

Jim Edwards walks alone to the McCarthy airstrip the morning after the murders.

As they walked, the goldmining buddies discussed the familiar perils of a long winter. This might be extreme cabin fever: irritable Chris and weirdo Lou arguing until Lou pulled out a gun. But shot in the head? Chris was bleeding pretty bad. They decided Gary should get Chris to the hospital in Glennallen. Gary handed the shotgun to Tim and returned to his plane.

Tim went on alone to the Heglands. He called out when he got to the porch. No sound. He smelled gunpowder as he stepped on the porch and dropped low, avoiding the window. He cracked open the front door. The floor inside looked to be smeared with blood, as if someone had tried to clean up with a rag. Lou Hastings stepped around a corner from the kitchen and fired a rifle. Tim squeezed the trigger of the shotgun and slammed the door. He ran. Hastings stayed in the cabin, shooting ten times through the wall. One of the bullets hit Tim in the thigh.

Gary heard shots as he waited at the plane. Tim told everyone what he'd seen. He insisted his leg was fine. The only radio in town was inside Les Hegland's house. Gary should get in the air and try to reach Lynn Ellis, plane to plane, and tell him not to land. Tim would stay to intercept anybody else who might show up, warn them to keep away from the Hegland house.

Amy helped settle Chris inside the Cessna. She climbed out and refused to get back in the plane. She would stay and help Tim. Gary Green taxied off without them. As he lifted off, he realized his 180 was a target and banked away sharply. The last thing he could see was Amy by the side of the runway, and Tim Nash walking toward her.

◄──►

Harley King stopped at the Kenyons' an hour after Maxine Edwards left. The old wolf-hunter was driving his yellow snowmachine from the Long Lake homestead to meet the mail plane. He had a passenger that morning, a young woman, bundled in a puffy down jacket, standing in the metal sled behind his sno-go. Donna Byram had been living with several others in a small squatter's cabin at the east end of Long Lake. It was a one-room log cabin chinked with cement and sections of the *Anchorage Times*, with a loft and a skylight: the area's top-of-the-line squatter's shack. There were several women, several children, and a man named Rocky who ruled the roost. The cabin grew smaller as the winter wore on, and Donna was getting out.

Harley King had been kind to her that winter, sharing paperbacks from his collection of Louis L'Amour westerns to teach her survival tips. He picked her up on his way to the airstrip. They chatted with the Kenyons, then headed on toward McCarthy.

When they reached the airstrip, Donna saw blood on the snow in the distance. She was annoyed that a trapper would leave carcasses out in the open. That was one reason she had to get out of McCarthy, she told a friend: the raw intensity of this place was too much. Just then, chips of ice began exploding out of the runway. She heard buzzing and realized bullets were flying past. Something hit her arm and she cried out. Harley looked back at her and as he accelerated his knee exploded. The snowmachine crashed into the snow berm beside the airstrip and rolled, throwing both riders clear. Harley couldn't move. Donna tried to pull him onto the sled.

A man carrying a rifle was limping down the runway toward them. Donna froze. Harley said, *Both of us don't need to die. Go up and see if Les has a gun. I'll distract him.* Then he grinned up at her, like one of Louis L'Amour's heroes, and she broke for the house.

As she ran up the snowy path, she heard the old hunting guide shout—*Here I am. Over this way.* She heard a gunshot, and then, as she stood in front of the house, two more.

The door to the Heglands' porch stood open. The back door was open, too, and a breeze puckered the plastic windows, *pop-pop-pop*. Donna was afraid to enter, thinking an accomplice of the shooter could be waiting inside. She clutched her elbow against her puffy blue jacket, so the blood would not drip into the snow, and circled to a small greenhouse. She hid behind the greenhouse and burrowed into the snow.

The man with the rifle stopped in front of the house. *Everything is all right,* he said loudly. He seemed to think she was inside, possibly with a gun. *If you come outside, I won't hurt you,* he said. *Your friend is still alive.* Then, after a moment, *If you don't come out now, I'll kill him.*

The man with the rifle stayed outside the house. He walked around back. Donna held still. The gunman looked inside the greenhouse. She

Nancy Gibert talks with Jim Edwards while state troopers work the crime scene.

could hear him talking, possibly to other shooters—*There's still one more. Over here. One not dead.*

Then it was quiet. After a while, she heard a snowmachine start up and fade into the distance.

She stood and dashed into the trees.

Much later, as the afternoon grew colder, she heard new voices by the Heglands' house. She ran out and a man looked up in surprise and pointed a rifle at her. On his fur cap was a state trooper badge.

◄——►

Gary Green reached Lynn Ellis on the radio soon after he took off. By the time Gary landed at Gulkana, an ambulance was waiting along with three state troopers. They had commandeered an Alyeska Pipeline helicopter from the pump station. The pilot was one of many Vietnam vets flying for oil companies in Alaska.

The troopers flew east above the white channel of the Chitina River, preparing to enter a possible hostage situation. They spotted a lone figure on a snowmachine racing toward them on the McCarthy road.

He was a mile from reaching Long Lake, where several families with children were out ice-fishing.

The helicopter circled and the snowmachine driver, bald and bearded and wearing a long green parka, waved. He stopped, and the chopper set down in front of him. Three troopers dropped to the snow, spread yards apart, and trained their guns on the snow-machiner's chest.

"What's the problem?" were the man's first words. Blood clotted his beard and saturated his right pants leg. He told the troopers his name was Chris Richards, and he was going for help because Lou Hastings had "gone crazy" in McCarthy. The troopers put the man in handcuffs. If you're Chris Richards, they said, who's that in the hospital in Glennallen?

"My right hand's cold. Will you hand me my mitten?" the prisoner asked. He had bared his shooting hand.

In the seat compartment beneath Hastings was a folding-stock semi-automatic rifle, a Ruger Mini-14 with a thirty-round clip in place and the safety off. In a pack they found a .22 pistol and ammunition, a police radio scanner, black commando clothing, and several homemade "bombs" of gunpowder and paraffin. The metal on the guns had been sprayed black to reduce sun glare. The serial number on the rifle had been erased. There was also a long computer printout of the names of Alaska politicians and prominent police officials.

They placed the handcuffed prisoner in the helicopter and flew on to McCarthy. They pressed him to say if any accomplices were on the ground or wounded victims left behind. He said something about a woman in a blue parka. The first place they landed was the street by the McCarthy Lodge. The afternoon was clear and cold, perfectly still. One of the troopers stood in the street hollering. When there was no answer, he said later, "It scared the hell out of me."

⸻

The state troopers found Harley King's body when they approached the runway. Tim and Amy Nash lay in the snow not far away. Investigators determined that the suspect, upon hearing Gary Green's plane take off, had crept to the runway behind a plowed-up snow berm and shot the couple from ambush. Tim Nash was hit in the back. Tim and Amy had multiple wounds to their extremities, and, like Harley King, fatal head wounds from close range.

Three bodies were found in the Hegland house. Maxine Edwards and Les and Flo Hegland had been shot multiple times and then once at close range at the base of the skull. Investigators concluded that the Heglands were already dead when Maxine Edwards entered the house. The bodies were stacked on the floor behind the bed, out of sight of the door. On the nightstand, investigators found a silencer wrapped in a bloodstained fur.

Camp robber jays, tamed by the Heglands, had entered the open door and were hopping along the kitchen counter as the troopers looked around. The last readings recorded at the weather station in the house were at 9:41 a.m. A spray of buckshot had hit a plaque that read: "Peace to All Who Enter Here."

The troopers were still gathering evidence at the Hegland cabin when Jim Edwards showed up and demanded to see his wife. They would not allow him to enter the crime scene, and he grew agitated. The trooper sergeant in charge asked him to wait. Jim Edwards stood in the doorway of the house while the trooper went into the bedroom. After a while, he returned and handed over Maxine's wedding ring. Jim gazed down at it. The trooper waited. Then Jim closed his fist and walked away.

◄——►

Lou Hastings's public defenders considered several explanations for the events of March 1, 1983. They studied literature on the mood-altering effects of light deprivation and cabin fever. They talked to an expert on hypoglycemia, considering a sugar-overdose "Twinkie defense" because Hastings had eaten so many chocolate bars in his cabin that winter. They even looked at copper, the noble metal of Kennecott: taking samples of his beard and pubic hair, searching for mineral traces sufficient to account for aberrant behavior. He had drawn drinking water from a creek that flowed through Kennecott mine tailings and used copper paint, a preservative, on his foundation.

The proposition that this had been an act of political terrorism, that the shootings were, in the mind of the thirty-nine-year-old defendant, a blow struck in defense of the environment and Alaska wilderness, emerged only later, when psychiatrists testified at a hearing called to determine if he was insane.

Hastings decided in December to plead no contest to the murder charges against him and hope for a ruling of guilty but mentally ill. There would be no trial. The written reports of the psychiatrists therefore provide the sole record of Hastings's own words and thoughts.

Lou Hastings had a fierce ego, the doctors testified. His neighbors might not have guessed it from how quiet and withdrawn he could be. The doctors described the defendant as having a superior intellect despite a lifetime of failed relationships and low achievement.

They found him to be devious, a secret-keeper. He'd been lonely and depressed as a boy, developing guilt-ridden hostility in response to the "frustrating, demeaning, stunting influence of an immature, ungiving, and even openly rejecting father." He sought solace alone in untrammeled nature and the mountains of Colorado, where he found it annoying to encounter other hikers. He found similar solace in solitary work with computers, a skill learned in the air force. Living in California's Bay Area, he got a job in data processing at the Stanford University library and talked a librarian into marriage—an unsuccessful pregnancy played a part—and after a honeymoon in Kennecott, Alaska, they decided to move north.

But the marriage deteriorated, and Hastings spent more and more time in the Wrangells, alone, in the small red cottage they had purchased at the mill site. His wife told authorities that he rejected suggestions to seek help for his mental health. She had hoped he would "get his shit together" out there, living in nature, in the shadow of the concentration mill. His work on the cabin roof was desultory, though, and he put himself on strange diets. For a while he ate only peanut butter sandwiches. That last winter, when it got really cold, he huddled in one disheveled room beside his woodstove as he ran out of Blazo for his lamps.

Hastings's grandiose notion that he could make himself into a purposeful environmental terrorist—John Muir reimagined as John Brown—developed during his time in the Kennecott ruins. He told the psychiatrists he had been thinking about suicide for two years. But he said he wanted to achieve something meaningful when he made his exit. His plans might seem bizarre, one doctor testified, but it was the same kind of pretentious thinking seen in someone out to hijack an airplane or assassinate a target for political purposes.

Hastings told the psychiatrists he was angry and depressed about what he saw happening to Alaska. Shortly before the murders, he wrote a letter to his wife expressing outrage that the governor, a Democrat, had sought help from oil companies to retire his campaign debts. The oil boom was bringing money and population and tourists and corruption. Every time he flew out on the mail plane and picked up his van in Glennallen, he saw the source of all he had come north to escape. He was hardly the only person to talk about blowing up the pipeline in those early days—before joking about terrorist acts became so unfunny, and before Big Oil became so embedded in the identity of modern Alaska. For Hastings, though, it was no barroom joke.

He told his interviewers that he planned to ignite an explosion at Pump Station Twelve in Glennallen. In winter, he reasoned, eight hundred miles of oil between Prudhoe Bay and Valdez would cool and congeal, putting the Trans-Alaska Pipeline out of commission, possibly forever. He described a plan to hijack a fuel truck and crash it through security. At one point that winter, he said, he tried hitchhiking from Palmer, hoping to carjack a vehicle that could get him to Glennallen so he could put his plan into action. But no suitable car would pick him up. He decided instead to use an airplane. He would hijack the mail plane in McCarthy. He had once taken a few flying lessons. Though he had never flown solo, the McCarthy airstrip was a long one, built to handle planes heavy with copper ore, and he was confident he could at least take off.

The psychiatrists felt these vainglorious plans, which he never came close to accomplishing, grew out the petty resentments he expressed toward the people around him. His cold contempt was born of envy for their perceived happiness, the doctors said. He "couldn't deal well with these emotions because he considered himself above them . . . so instead tended to think in lofty terms about doing some great favor for humanity."

And so nature and history met and turned, and turned again. The settlers of McCarthy would be the first to go. "As a result of his isolation and inability to tolerate the ideas of others, he raises the value of his ideas above those of others and the value of his life above others." He recounted making plans for the disappearance of the population in the tone of someone reaching for a lofty goal. Hastings saw his neighbors as the first settlers of a new era, not the last hold-outs of an old one. They did not belong there because they were not part of nature. He would wait for the day they all gathered. After he dumped the bodies from the hijacked mail plane, they would never be found in these mountains. When the plane crashed in flames at the Glennallen pump station, Lou Hastings would be just a name on the list of the vanished. No one would know who was responsible for blowing up the pipeline. Kennecott had found its avenging angel. Back to nature.

"Ahh! A birding triumph!" he wrote in a letter to his wife, one week before he murdered his neighbors. "I was outdoors a minute ago when a tweeper flew over. I imitated its tweep, and it (a rosy finch female) came down & landed 3 feet from my feet! She pecked around a bit, then decided she'd been misled and flew on."

Meanwhile, he trammed two thousand rounds of ammunition across the river and hauled it up to his cabin. His neighbors helped pull the tram rope and gave him rides in their trucks. Gun periodicals piled up by his mattress on the floor. He bought a popular rifle of the day, a civilian version of the military M-14, scaled down to use .223 cartridges, with a pistol grip and folding stock. He had never been a hunter—in fact, he belonged to several wildlife protection groups—and knew it might therefore be hard to shoot a human being, even though, assessed logically, people were nothing more than group-ings of chemicals. To test himself, he asked Chris Richards how to track a snowshoe hare. Finding a bunny, he took a deep breath and closed off the feeling part of his brain and made the thinking part take control as he touched the trigger.

"Overall," wrote David Coons, one of three forensic psychiatrists who produced similar accounts, "his plan was 'to reduce the population' so that he could make a place where 'people like myself' can live. . . . He very much wanted to carry off one great legendary deed before he died, to make up for all of his past failures."

From another perspective, however, Hastings's "environmentalism" looked like nothing more than a convenient way to justify his resentment toward his fellow human beings. He belonged and they did not. Coons and the other doctors offered caveats to the story he told. Hastings refused to tell the troopers or the doctors anything about the printout of Alaska officials in his duffel—or about the charred remains of the Kennicott Glacier Lodge, discovered the morning after the murders. (Snow, sliding off the roof in the heat, had buried the propane tanks behind Kennecott's first commercial venture, preventing an explosion that could have spread the fire throughout the historic mining camp.) The "plan" had many holes, they noted—not the least being Hastings's lack of flying experience. His scheme for anonymity was blown by Gary Green's escape in the Cessna, but he kept killing. As for his decision to commit suicide, he had evidently reconsidered by the time he hesitated outside the Hegland house, afraid Donna Byram might be inside and armed, or when the troopers landed their helicopter and watched to see if he went for his rifle.

Judge Ralph Moody, the same Superior Court judge who had been tough on the swindlers in the Barrett land case six years earlier, ruled Hastings was not mentally ill. He simply held the view that human life was meaningless.

Alaska has no death penalty. Lou Hastings was sentenced to 638 years and, as of this writing, is serving that time in the state's maximum-security prison in Seward.

←——→

Malcolm Vance, Bonnie Morris, and Jim Edwards on the morning after the murders.

Two months after the mail day murders, the ashes of Amy Nash came home to the family garden in the hills of western Massachusetts. Amy's father, David Ashenden, read to a small gathering from her journals and letters. He also read from the letter of a close friend of Amy's in Alaska, who said she so admired Amy's courage and her "sense of destiny about going to McCarthy . . . wrapped in a very spiritual need to live alone, get to know herself again, and cleanse herself of worldly things." And then, having gone there to let go, the friend wrote, "she found love, peace of mind and a home: more than she ever hoped. In a way I see it as a mystical kind of fulfillment that she was allowed to pass from this world to the next at such a happy time."

David Ashenden said they tried to focus on the positive. But Amy's mother, Jo, was haunted by old premonitions and fell into a depression from which she never fully recovered.

In McCarthy and Kennecott, the question everyone kept asking was, *Why?*

"If the guy hated the rest of the world so much, why take it out on people who had come just as far as he did to get away?" said Chris Richards, bitterly recuperating from his wounds. "And why would you put a silencer on to kill the only other person in a ghost town?"

Jo King finally sat down to write her memoirs after she lost Harley. "The people he killed were the true environmentalists," she wrote. "They loved the expansive country they lived in and tried to blend with the environment in a very special way."

Bonnie Morris finished knitting a hat Amy had started for Tim, and sent it to Amy's father. She could not shake her daze. She thought about the smoke they smelled when they were up the creek cutting house logs, the Kennicott Glacier Lodge burning to the ground.

People asked if they had done enough? Had they somehow made things worse? Everyone, it seemed, had a story of reaching out, offering help, getting spurned. A person was free to live out here the way he wanted. They left him space to dwell alone with his misanthropy.

Now his act would define their community. The airstrip built by Howard Knutson for his ore planes, the town's social center, was a crime scene.

It was hard not to get sucked into that same darkness. Had they misjudged Eden? The survivors searched for some small redeeming thing, some way to keep the mail day murders from exerting a warping gravitational force on the arc of McCarthy's story.

The very evening of the murders, hearing the news over the radio, Bonnie Kenyon had told her husband and son an invisible hand had stopped her from going to mail. She read to them from Psalms, about how those who dwell in the Lord receive the protection of angels against the destruction that wasteth at noonday. The Kenyons fell to their knees, weeping prayers of lamentation and thanksgiving.

But if God spared Bonnie that day, did that mean their friends and neighbors had been consigned to die? Surely not, Bonnie said years later. They were all such good people. It was hard to account for. The role of Satan, of evil itself, had to be considered.

Loy Green, the transcendentalist, rejected the notion that the murders were any kind of judgment. On mail day, he had been painting at his cabin up McCarthy Creek. The next morning he heard a news report on AM radio and jumped on his snowmachine. At the airstrip, he had consoled Bonnie Morris and Jim Edwards and spurned a handshake offered by park ranger Jim Hannah.

"There is a meaning to things that becomes apparent out here," Loy said a few months later. Hastings had resisted learning this. "It was not a negative thing about this place. He brought his evil with him. Evil does not exist outside the mind of man."

The community faced a decision. They were getting ready to build a new tram across the Kennicott River. It would be easier for people to get to McCarthy. Did that make sense any more? Why would they want that?

"For a while in the spring," Sally Gibert said, "everybody just sat around and talked about the shootings, until somebody would say we've got to talk about something else. And then we'd talk about it some more."

No one came up with a satisfactory explanation for how such a thing could happen. No one ever would.

# 14

# Kindred Spirits

THE SUMMER AFTER the murders, I made my second trip to McCarthy—not flying this time, but driving the rough road over the path of the abandoned railway. I parked at the river and pulled myself above the waves in the river on the wooden tram platform. I had come back to write another newspaper story.

A small dozer and tools sat by the riverbank, signs of new construction underway. Work had started in spring, a few weeks after the shootings, before the snow softened too much for travel. Sally Gibert had climbed Porphyry Mountain all the way to where big trees still stood. She helped a friend tramp out a half-mile trail with snowshoes and brush the route with a chainsaw so they could climb up there with their underpowered early-model snowmachines. They picked the best eighteen-inch white spruce, felled and limbed them, and sledded them one at a time to town.

Nature provided the timber, history the steel. Five snowmachiners ascended to the aerial tram angle station, in the bowl below the

Bonanza Mine. Several hacksaw blades later, they had severed two long sections of braided steel cable. The cable was heavy and hard to budge. Gravity, that endlessly renewable Wrangell Mountain resource, offered a solution—once the snowmachines got the cable strands sliding downhill, they did not stop until they reached the river.

The tram project had been in the works long before the murders. People realized they did not have to go on living in the Blazo Bill era. His sagging cables and splintered carts, across the east and west channels, had been the only way into town since the wrecked highway bridges washed out altogether (the last bridge to go, over the west channel, could be crossed on foot via precarious planks until 1981). The cable had grown so slack that two riders with a heavy load risked wet feet. Passengers rolled fast to the middle but it was a hard hoist to the far shore. Waiting lines formed on summer weekends. In this town of do-it-yourselfers, everyone had ideas for how it could be engineered better.

After the murders, people talked seriously about giving up the whole project. But cutting the cable, they agreed, would be what Lou Hastings wanted.

However difficult it had been to settle on an explanation for the murders, they had little trouble agreeing on a theme for their response. Anybody who said they did not belong here was wrong. They would still pursue that idealized middle way—neither cutting their ties nor building a bridge. A safe, well-built, easy-to-use tram would be their bargain with the future. Tramming, their communal ritual of renunciation and connection, would go on. Visitors were welcome if they showed the essential psychological hardiness—like the three guys who pulled their wheelchairs across the old tram that summer and rolled into town on knobby wheels.

"A tram is the perfect self-administering interview system," Sally Gibert told me after I hiked twenty minutes into town and threw my sleeping bag in an upstairs room at the Hardware Store. I'd been told she was the person to start with, as she had tracked down $90,000 in state funds for the project—not from the Department of Transportation, which was still sulking about local opposition to the improved road, but from the community development wing of the Department of Community and Regional Affairs.

"McCarthy rebuilds," Sally said with a smile, dishing up a headline.

⟵——⟶

The August sky was full of light, the valley full of life—such a contrast to my first visit. The next day, Bob Jacobs was clipping a carabiner onto the cable across the river's western channel and testing his weight on a safety sling. The cart had been left tied-off on the far side by some tourist unfamiliar with tram protocol. The nylon return rope couldn't budge it free. Jacobs tugged on work gloves and began to pull himself hand over hand on the steel cable, unable to hear our shouts above the roaring cataract.

As a summer-only resident, Bob Jacobs was a B-lister. Organizers had divided the list of potential workers in two. The paid jobs went mostly to A-listers. Jacobs was an exception for his special skills. He was a mountain climber, lanky and lightweight, with a climber's strength and good-humored doggedness. He had recently moved to McCarthy to start a guiding business—the town's first new business in many years. He'd read a magazine story about backpacking in the Wrangells and decided it would be more fun to pioneer a new area than to continue guiding clients up Denali's busy West Buttress. He'd bought the old Motherlode powerhouse next to McCarthy Creek as a headquarters for his new guiding business. The guiding part had started slow—he spent his first few summers loading rocks into gabions to steer the creek away from his new investment.

On the tram project, he observed, McCarthy's settlers worked hard but not easily in tandem. "One person will be out there to work fast and get the thing up, and the next guy will be just a perfectionist," he told me. "You never notice these differences when you're helping a neighbor move a few boards."

The workers met at the saloon every morning to drink the lodge's coffee and argue about the day's work plan. Someone described the operation as "a commune run by anarchists." The state made them form a nonprofit and they named it "Kennicott Cross Purposes." Their paperwork was being handled for free in Anchorage by Doug Pope, the lawyer and lot owner who had been pulled into court by the Burdick-Barrett-Brown land swindle.

The group hired an engineer, reluctantly, at the state's insistence— and then fired him because his plans were too expensive. They had wasted $20,000 in empty holes and cold-rolled steel. The second project engineer kept a distance from his opinionated clients, proffering suggestions via Caribou Clatters, the nightly radio broadcast from Glennallen. Determined not to bust the budget, they cut their own wages from twenty dollars an hour to fifteen. Foregoing home chores, the crew worked through the good weather at the heart of summer, taking off only for mail day. A few qualified A-listers were away. Bonnie Morris was at her regular summer job, mending salmon nets in Cordova. Gary Green was guiding bear hunters in the Brooks Range.

One of the A-list crew was Judy Miller, the Santa Cruz student who stayed and married the lodge owner. Homestead-strong and poker-faced, she told me she planned to use her earnings to rent a helicopter and sling a piano to her Dan Creek cabin, where Jerry, responding well to leukemia treatment, and their daughter, now three, awaited her return.

She wanted me to understand that the project should be seen as a symbol of resilience, an affirmation of life. "It's not like we're cutting

Rebuilding the Kennicott River tram, August 1983. (From left) Jim Miller, Judy Miller (rear), Jim Edwards, Curtis Green, Nick Olmsted, and Sally Gibert.

the cable, putting up signs saying 'go home,'" she said. "It's just the opposite. We're opening our arms to the world."

✦

One full-time resident avoided the tram project that summer. I found Chris Richards at his disheveled little red cottage at Kennecott, obsessing about the upcoming murder trial, in which he expected to be a star witness. He was still dazed from the gunshot wound to his head, his vision askew. "I feel like I've been violated," he told me. "Like he took a little bit of his insanity and pushed it into my brain."

Janet Hegland had dropped off a box of groceries when she closed up her parents' home. Chris was running low on food again.

His clothes lay in piles. He apologized for the mess: "The troopers came in and cleaned up. I still can't find my pants and my coat." He said they'd looked the other way when they came across his "glaucoma medicine"—the houseplants admired a few years earlier by the visiting Nell McCann.

Chris Richards took me on a tour of the fourteen-story concentration mill. Its many tiers of gabled windows, black and empty, stared out at the glacier with the blank gaze of a haunted skyscraper. Inside, through powerful smells of dust and creosote, Chris led me up ladders and into the structure's many-chambered heart, past the jaw crushers and jigs and apron feeders. He was a masterful tour guide, passionately attacking the ruthlessness of big business while pausing to demonstrate where to step across missing floorboards. At the top, we climbed into daylight. The roof was gone. *Trotochau.*

Chris said he had been coming up here a lot since the murders. He would sit for hours, gaze down on the tarpaper roofs below. Rocks sliding down ice in the moraine made the glacier seem alive. He could hear the beat of a raven's wings a quarter mile away. "This is a place where man went apeshit," he said. "But I look out at it and I think Mother Nature's winning. Another hundred years and it will all be grown back."

◄──►

Everyone else was rebuilding. When they weren't sure what to do next, they turned to Jim Edwards. Edwards considered trams an ingenious tool of the country, even though one time he almost died hanging from the abandoned one across the Copper River. The big tram buckets that once hauled ore from the mountaintops used gravity to generate electricity. Simpler hand-over-hand trams carried prospectors and their freight across deadly glacial rivers. One afternoon beside the Kennicott, he described how the rangy miner

Chris Richards, recuperating from his wounds, surveys Kennecott from atop the mill building.

Martin Radovan built a tram by himself across Glacier Creek—deep, swift, murky, shifting, surging on hot sunny days. Radovan cut four hundred feet of three-quarter-inch steel cable off a spool that had been left on a gravel bar six miles from his claims. Without a dozer, he worked for days, slinkying loops of heavy cable tens of yards at a time, on a hand sled until he got the whole length to his cabin. In winter he crossed on the ice to hang the cable. The hard part always was winching the line tight, Edwards said. Radovan rolled boulders into a hole to lever up a tower on a platform base, tying off the cable each time before removing the boulders and repeating, until the cable was tuned like a guitar string.

Innovation based on privation often yielded elegant solutions. But now Jim Edwards had state funding. In his shop, he welded roomy new tram carts, with seats and railings, and hooks to hang bicycles. He custom-manufactured steel plates and bolts to fit the timbers in the towers. Beside the river, he was consulted on every step.

Jim Edwards remembered me from the runway five months earlier when I flew off with a note for his son. He invited me to dinner, provided I could convince Sally Gibert to come along and cook. We talked that night about Zheng He's voyages of discovery and whether architectural similarities between the pyramids of the Incas and Egyptians meant they had been visited by the same space travelers. He was interested that I worked for one of the Anchorage newspapers, because he was thinking of advertising for a new wife.

His opinion had not changed about building a modern highway into the Wrangell Mountains. "McCarthy has tremendous charm for the casual visitor as well as the person who lives here," he said. "Put a road in, and all that will be gone."

◄——►

There are those who say the 1983 tram project marked the era of McCarthy's greatest togetherness—that for the rest of the decade, before tourism into the park started growing exponentially, the bonds forged in the aftermath of the murders gave the town its most coherent sense of purpose. If so, it would be one more irony of the lost decades—that the sullen newcomer who came down the mountain to erase man from nature should have left the town more sure of its place in the natural world and more than ever the community of "kindred spirits" Amy Nash had been seeking.

The morning after our dinner together, a faint smile of satisfaction painted Jim Edwards's face as he worked his D-7 Caterpillar, backfilling over a concrete deadman to hold tension for one of the new tram towers. The work crew was finishing up on the far west side of the Kennicott River, where the road ended at the water's edge.

The cart with railings and bicycle hooks was suspended from the cable on rollers. The crew threaded the pulley ropes. They had built a deck where people could stand more easily to pull. The beauty of the system was apparent to newcomer and local alike: your turn came sooner if you helped speed others on their way. The close study of tramming etiquette was another thing that drew the McCarthy community together in the summer of 1983.

Finally it was my turn to cross the river. I climbed into the swinging cart, many hands grasped the pull rope, and I flew into the future.

# EPILOGUE

# "Gone with the Wind"

O N A SUNNY weekend in July 2016, I left my cabin in the Wrangells and drove to Swift Creek to attend a memorial for Jim Edwards. After it was over, I drove on to the end of the road for an evening in modern-day McCarthy.

I found a space that evening at a private pay-to-park campground by the Kennicott River. It was a busy weekend. During the afternoon, packrafters had raced over Bonanza Ridge and paddled down McCarthy Creek. The prize, a new packraft donated by a national manufacturer, drew racers from all over the state. That evening a rock concert was getting underway. Revelers milled around a stage erected beside the rushing waters, nearly within reach of a jökulhlaup flood. The crowd wasn't more than a few hundred, but the vibe was bigger: there were wristband tickets, a beer tent, and an aerial gymnast hanging from silks in the pastel glow of the sun beyond Mount Blackburn.

I walked into town across a pair of clanging steel footbridges. The timber cable towers for the old tram stood in silent vigil beside the river, overgrown in willows and skinny poplars—the latest ghost town relics. By 1997 lines at the tram had grown unbearable. The town's traditional contrariness had asserted itself, even then: residents agreed to a state-built footbridge so as to preclude a road bridge. No motorized vehicles would be allowed across the narrow footbridge. The question of whether "motorized" meant four-wheelers had touched off another few innings of McCarthy feuding.

Back in 1997, at the footbridge dedication ceremony, the special guest was a longtime Alaskan who won the bridge construction contract from the state. As a young carpenter new to the north, Al Swalling had the job of shutting down the section houses on the last train out of Kennecott. Now, aged eighty-six, he looked back on a career as one of the state's biggest contractors, the builder of Anchorage's first steel high-rises. In 1998, when he was named Alaskan of the Year, the state legislature cited him for "developing everything from office buildings and a coal mine, to a bank and an airline." One of his last jobs had been to reattach the ghost town he left behind.

Twenty years later, however, the steel footbridge, like most efforts to build connection in the Wrangells, was succumbing to the tumult of erosion and change. The Kennicott Glacier was pulling back from town in fast retreat—a spasm in geological time, and a reminder that the fast-warming industrialized world was making itself felt here in ways far more pervasive than a mere search for new and exploitable travel-and-leisure destinations. The glacier's melt had opened up a lake, which imposed major hydrological changes downstream. The east fork of the outlet was now almost dry. In its wide, boulder-filled channel, where townspeople once fought over washed-out bridge beams, pool toys floated in a sun-warmed swimming hole. Meanwhile the whiplashing west channel thundered past the bandstand at the end of the McCarthy road with enough redoubled fury to raise questions about the survival of the footbridge—not to mention the long-term investment value of the pay-to-park campground.

Downriver from the footbridge, a private span across the main channel of the river now allowed vehicle access into town. A local family of builders had come up with a market solution for keeping recreational vehicles from overrunning the place: a bridge pass cost hundreds of dollars. Weekend visitors parked and used the footbridge, but landowners were happy to pay so they could haul in lumber and Costco supplies.

A cabin-building boom was underway. The Barretts had sold some town lots, and land had been sold by the University of Alaska, which received a state land grant south of McCarthy Creek. National park restoration work at the Kennecott mining camp, through local-hire provisions, was paying wages to a new landed gentry, a local elite with solar panels and no running water. Two mail planes came each mail day that summer, the second packed with boxes from Amazon Prime.

The growth in summer visitors now meant there were two places in town to eat. The McCarthy Lodge offered a choice of a tasting menu on white tablecloths or cheeseburgers and craft beer at the New Golden Saloon. A block away were burritos and curly fries at the Potato, part-owned by Malcolm Vance, Bonnie Morris's long-ago boyfriend. Crowds strolled between the two joints in the easy way they must have moved when the boomtown had a half dozen restaurants and speakeasies.

The surrounding mountains were receiving more visitors too. A pair of air services, run by Gary Green and Kelly Bay, stayed busy carrying backpackers to high drop-offs where pilots once landed sheep hunters. There were also two main backcountry guide services: Kennicott Wilderness Guides, which lived on after the death of its founder, Chris Richards, in a fire that destroyed Nell McCann's little red cottage; and St. Elias Alpine Guides, started by Bob Jacobs, and subsequently owned and managed by Ben Shaine's daughter, Gaia, and her husband.

Indeed, the year 2016 seemed to mark the precise stage in the town's embryonic capitalism where there were two competitors in every field. The exception was the category of corporate robber baron: only one outside company was making money out of the Kennicott River valley. The export product, this time around, was mythology. Discovery Communications, cable television's leading home for "reality programming," was producing a TV series in which a handful of agreeable McCarthy "eccentrics" were paid to improvise dialogue around small-town squabbles dreamed up by scriptwriters in Burbank, California. (They had not yet hit upon the idea of stuffing live ammunition into split firewood.) Final storylines were constructed in an editing room from the best bits—a work process not unlike that of a local historian. With its fist-pumping soundtrack and gritty, clenched-teeth title, *Edge of Alaska* shamelessly stoked fantasies about "the last frontier town in all America." No tourists wandered in front of the cameras, and no mention was made of the national park where the action took place, though a park ranger stood off-camera during certain scenes to make sure nobody got hurt.

Television reality notwithstanding, there was no getting away from the National Park Service in this edgy frontier town. Several decades of back-and-forth disputes, most notably a fight with the smooth-talking newcomer who called himself Papa Pilgrim, had molded relations between park and community. Yet the Park Service was still taking a fairly light touch, apart from all the expensive restoration work underway at Kennecott. It was not the government, but Kelly Bay's wife at Wrangell Mountain Air, Natalie, who knew where camping parties were stashed in the high terrain. Travel into McCarthy was on the rise that summer, to nearly twenty thousand visitors, a disproportionate number of them Europeans, who seemed to enjoy toting their Old World aesthetic off the beaten tourist path to contemplate the ruins of American progress. At Kennecott, a few ranger uniforms were ever-present. But the park's headquarters and visitor center were far away, along the main highway outside Glennallen. Most park "visitors" got no closer.

For all the changes by 2016, McCarthy retained its sense of being a place apart. The road from Chitina was still too narrow and rough for tour buses. The scale of enterprise remained small and locally owned. Young people nailed together cabins and struggled to live out wilderness dreams. A hardy few spent the winters. Residents gathered at the airstrip on mail day. Stories of life before the park, when the persistence of human endeavor was not yet a given, still circulated in living memory. The park's interpretive team was struggling with whether to present stories not only of Kennecott Copper but of those ghost town decades, "the in-between years," as enriching to the visitor experience.

Ghost towns are monuments to impermanence. At Jim Edwards's memorial that afternoon, as dozens of locals, including many longtime summer residents, reminisced good-naturedly on the lawn at the Swift Creek homestead, the guests of honor were absent. That was how things had felt in McCarthy for a long time. Only now, the venerated apparitions were no longer miners and nurses and prostitutes from the park's historical plaques, but the ones who came after, the hold-outs and dreamers who made the abandoned town their home. Stories from those unbridled times were fading, along with memories of departed friends and neighbors—as the memory of those in attendance would someday fade, as the ruins would decay and tumble, and the park itself would one day be gone from these cold, indifferent mountains.

Turnout for the event was good. On hand were Sally Gibert, who turned the Hardware Store over to a local educational nonprofit, the Wrangell Mountains Center, to continue hosting the college program and community events; Eric and Joan Wasserman, who lived in Anchorage now, near their grandchildren; Bonnie Kenyon, on her own since Rick's death from a 2014 heart attack; and Mudhole Smith's son, Kenny, who spent long summers on the family land near Swift Creek since he retired as director of Anchorage's international airport.

Jim Edwards had lived in the valley longer than any of them. He had been here twice as many years as Kennecott Copper. Late in life, after his reputation spread to newcomers who never met him, he'd been invited once a summer to show slides and tell stories to crowds spilling out the doors of the Hardware Store or the lodge's dining room. He was eighty-five when he died that June. At the memorial, friends fondly recalled his single-mindedness, his attentiveness to the natural world, and the bittersweet wit in his stories. They spoke of Maxine but not of the mail day murders, in keeping with customary local reticence on the topic. Instead they invoked her saintly tolerance while they apotheosized Jim's legendary iron pile, his Kennecrap, and the jimmied-together truck named Rigormortis. As so often in the Wrangells, there were stories about the difficulties of getting from one place to another. Friends recalled the epic cross-country bulldozer treks, and the 1962 Christmas shopping trip with the woodstove in the backseat of Maxine's pale green Chevy, and his early and inadvertent float trip down the Copper River, bobbing on his backpack to safety—surely the first packrafting in the Wrangells.

A question posed at the memorial on the lawn but never quite answered: Was Jim Edwards so successful at doing for himself—at perfecting the "art form" of living in the Wrangells—because he was exceptionally inventive? Or because he was exceptionally cheap?

Jim Edwards crossing the Gilahina trestle during his thirty-day journey from Chitina in 1961 to deliver his wife's pale-green Chevy DeLuxe.

People talked about the used teabags and coffee cans of bent nails straightened by the family during quiet winter nights. Jim ran cold creek water through a car radiator in the wall of his house to create a free refrigerator for the hot summer weeks. In his later years, infuriated by the volume of paper piling up in the mail shack by the airstrip, he set to building a storage shed out of junk mail, whose thick walls of double-wide stacks of magazines, phone books, and catalogs were mortared together with leftover latex paint. The project was going well until a grizzly bear tore into it.

Some of Jim's tools and inventions were on display that afternoon, including a dam and waterwheel for generating free electricity and a pressure-fed water line that, in the event of a forest fire, would send sheets of water flooding across his roof. A separate series of switches and levers pumped water to a shield of sprinkler nozzles mounted atop spruce stumps surrounding his clearing. His engineering method, like his approach to backcountry travel and storytelling, often consisted of an inspired plunge, followed by efforts to solve complications as they arose. The result could be an ungainly concatenation, mapped only in his head. He worried about being gone when a wildfire struck. His sprinkler defenses were too complicated for his neighbors to run.

"Jim wrote up a long instruction manual for the water system and tried to get me to read it," recalled Kenny Smith. "Holy smoke, it was like reading *Gone With the Wind*."

After Maxine's death in 1983, Jim took out a singles ad in the *Anchorage Daily News* classifieds. That was how he met his second wife, Pat, a Florida nurse, who lived with him for ten years. When she came down with cancer, he turned a high-speed drill press into a centrifuge to prepare blood samples for shipment so they wouldn't have to go to town.

When Pat died, Jim got back in touch with the newspaper's advertising department. Through another ad, he found Audrey, his surviving third wife. They met for a polite cup of coffee the day before she was scheduled for surgery. When Audrey awoke from anesthesia the next day, Jim was sitting at the foot of her bed. They were married for twenty-one years of scrimping and improvisation.

"I have to admit I threw a lot of good tea bags away," Audrey Edwards told me the afternoon of the memorial.

As Audrey and I sat on folding chairs on the Swift Creek lawn, I thought back to the morning when I first came to the valley. That day may have been the end of the lost decades, but I was not too late, it turned out, to hear the old-timers' stories. Now I was practically an old-timer myself.

We all have ghost towns. My own story in the Wrangells continued the next year, when I met a smiling-eyed environmentalist who happened to be building a cabin above the Nizina River canyon. She had lived in the Wrangell Mountains her first summer in Alaska and talked about leaving the city someday and going back. We finished closing in her cabin the summer after we got married. Her place became my place, as we explored the country and hung out with her friends. She was a kindred spirit with Sally Gibert and Gary Green, with Loy and Curtis and Jim Edwards. She played fiddle for contra dances at the Hardware Store. Dancers leaped to her tunes in the golden lamplight. She died young, and that is another reason I see ghosts when I go to McCarthy.

More than three decades had passed since the day I flew out from the Wrangells carrying a message to Jim Edwards's son, Steve. Now here he was, welcoming friends and neighbors to his father's memorial.

Steve Edwards had recently retired from a career as an airplane mechanic for the state. He lived with his family in a birch forest an hour north of Anchorage. His wife, Lana, had been his girlfriend at the time his mother was killed, and she helped him work through the pain, then helped care for his father in his last years.

Steve told me he planned to keep the eighty acres at Swift Creek for their two sons, who were twenty-four and eighteen. They were interested in flying and had picked up their grandfather's mechanical aptitude and scientific curiosity.

But some of the stories from those lost decades were frankly hard for the boys to believe, he said. He mentioned, for example, the time his dad told him to climb down from the bulldozer and stand on the other side of the canyon and prepare to run ten miles back to McCarthy for help if the Cat fell through the rotting trestle. "I grew up with these stories. I thought a lot of people live that way," he said. "Later, I realized—no, other people don't do that."

# ACKNOWLEDGMENTS

T HIS LOCAL HISTORY could not have been written without the help of many members of the McCarthy-Kennecott community, past and present. Special thanks, for their patient replies to multiple inquiries, to Kenny Smith, Gary Green, Sally Gibert, Howard Knutson, Steve and Lana Edwards, Bonnie Morris Phillips, Paul and Glenda Barrett, and Patsy Barrett Crawford. Other essential pieces of the picture were provided by Ben Shaine, Bonnie Kenyon, Mark Vail, Cynthia Shidner, Corinna Cook, Kathy Andersen Hemphill, Janet Hegland, Bob Leitzell, Sunny Cook, Neil Darish, Eric and Joan Wasserman, Kelly Bay, Barbara and Adrian Darkow, Kathy Drury, Tim Mischel, Danny Rosenkrans, Mike Loso, Ralph Lohse, Gayle Vukson, Doug Pope, Judy Miller, Larry Hoare, Rita Pfeninger, Jim Tallman, Mike McCann, Bernd Hoffmann, Rich Kirkwood, Paul Claus, Dan Talcott, Tom and Catie Bursch, Jim Harrower, Tony Oney, Mary Eckart, and Nick Olmsted.

Valuable help with the history was also rendered from the Copper River basin by Ron Simpson, Bill Simeone, Art Koeninger; and, from farther away, by David Ashenden, Sharon Whytal, Mike Metrokin, Jim Jansen, Kes Woodward, Andrew Goldstein, Mike Swalling, Karen Brewster, and Traeger Machetanz.

I am especially grateful to Jenny Carroll for sharing the transcripts of her 1985 interviews with Jim Edwards, Bonnie Morris Phillips, and Loy Green.

Limited written material exists from this period, and the National Park Service now has much of it. NPS officials were extremely helpful, especially Logan Hovis and Geoff Bleakley (historians both now retired), Carol Harding, and archivist Desiree Ramirez at Wrangell-St. Elias National Park headquarters in Copper Center.

Historians Terrence Cole and Stephen Haycox offered useful suggestions, as did Elihu Rubin at the Yale School of Architecture, who teaches a class on ghost towns. Like so many local historians before me, I bow gratefully to the interlibrary loan staff at my local public library in Homer.

Readers outside McCarthy who offered helpful advice include Nancy Lord, Rich Chiappone, Carol Snow, Blaine Harden, and Chip Brown. I am also thankful for enduring support from Nancy Gordon and Steve Williams.

This book-writing effort got off the ground with a generous artist fellowship from Alaska's Rasmuson Foundation. The project received an early endorsement from the board of the McCarthy-Kennicott Historical Museum. A share of revenue from book sales will go to the museum.

Thanks to the McCarthy area's multi-talented artist Kristin Link for assembling a savvy map of the region.

And thanks to Jeremy Pataky and Porphyry Press, because if you're reading this, it means he managed to tear the manuscript out of my fingers and turn it into a book.

\* \* \*

# PUBLISHER'S AFTERWORD

R EADERS WILL APPRECIATE this book as an emplaced story that bridges McCarthy's local concerns with global ones. The seeds of this book were outtakes from Tom's previous one, a *New York Times* bestseller, as he tells in the introduction. That book, *Pilgrim's Wilderness*, focused on a contemporary saga also set here in McCarthy, decades after this book's time frame.

I remember Tom's presentation of the newly published *Pilgrim's Wilderness* in 2013. He read from the book and also read some cuts—outtakes saved especially for us, a local audience. That surplus material prodded the deep backdrop of braided stories spanning multiple decades of McCarthy's past. In the years since, Tom expanded and refined that content into a much different kind of book, a local history suited for a much wider audience.

Now, with *Cold Mountain Path*, Tom has approached book writing like so many McCarthy characters have approached construction over the years, dismantling relics and expired things, reintegrating old scraps and parts into new structures. The research and craft required to move beyond those few anecdotes left over from a much different project and to create a cohesive, thorough history of a nearly forgotten time evince Tom's mastery as a writer and wisdom as a thinking person. I suppose there's an element of endurance, as well, in publishing one book to rave reviews only to start anew with its castoffs.

In assembling so many disparate stories with scads of major and minor characters and events, Tom found a new form to give shape and sense to the material. Given his own personal ties to and knowledge of the area, he had to stretch the canvas large enough to fit everything while framing it to accommodate the perspectives of nearby locals and distant, removed readers alike. Both in terms of process and form, he brings an originality and vision that ranks him among the great inventors, make-doers, waste-nots, and raconteurs of the Wrangells.

Through my prior work in McCarthy, first as a guide and then as executive director of the Wrangell Mountains Center, I knew well how wide those "lost decade" gaps in McCarthy history were. Having gotten to know old-timers like Jim Edwards over the years, I also knew that the threat of collective amnesia was real, with sad implications for our community—and the larger society that often enough seems like McCarthy's foil.

This book documents local history with uncommon sensitivity and insight, shouldering forward communal foundations of life then and now in this remote place, in this country of resource extraction and commerce, in this time of ongoing great change when ambition ripens to solastalgia. Our pasts and our histories are with us whether or not we know them. There is immense value in that knowing, in cultivating an awareness that helps us understand the contours of the present.

In the end, stories teach us where we are. The glacier ice all around is melting, but Tom has planted a major stay against the loss of our stories. Alaskans, generally speaking, as well as Tom all know better than to lean too hard on the worn romance of old tropes. Alaska is not wilderness but home—both to Indigenous people who've thrived here since time immemorial and to settlers who've come. Our literatures—oral and written alike—have had strong impacts on our cultures and Alaska's role in national and international imaginations. Today's Alaskan writers inhabit a place as its complex self-identity evolves. We live here as the north becomes more visible in national and international eyes, moving from fringy margins to center stage, shifting its weight from a stance of boundlessness to fragility.

I began contemplating the possibility of starting a McCarthy-based book publishing company in the years after grad school. Alaska's art and our network of arts organizations, including literary ones, are changing fast. Alaska literature is no longer only about Alaska, even as we look to many of our writers to inform us about our home. Similarly, Porphyry Press will not restrict its catalog to works by Alaskans and most certainly not to books that "are about" places here, per se.

Author Sherry Simpson, one of our finest and most missed, once said Alaska is "a kind of literary refugium, not necessarily in the books it produces but rather in the conditions that it offers writers. For one thing, it remains a place where people can have lives and experiences they can have nowhere else. The fact that our state's history and social conditions and expectations and physical realities are shifting and lurching, sometimes colliding with those old frontier myths, is both unsettling and enormously exciting—the very ecto-plasm of creativity. We're still a place where we can take old symbols and ideas about what it means to be American, to live in Alaska, to live at this time—and we can hammer at them and hold them up to the light and scuff them up and reshape them."

Sherry's words speak directly to some of my motivations to found Porphyry Press and also to the value of a book like this one. Kennecott-McCarthy, the Kennicott Valley, and the Wrangell-St. Elias inspired my own first book, *Overwinter*. Now the same rocks, glaciers, mountains, and histories inspire me to establish a remote, off-grid small press—probably the most remote publishing house in the country.

Based as we are in remote Alaska, surrounded by glaciers and proximal to the largest non-polar icefield in the world, a circumpolar ethos inflects our reading even as we court, welcome, and seek readers and contributing authors from all over the country and beyond. Our commitment is to an ever-broadening whole community that Alaska is privy to and part of not from the fringes, not from terra incognita, but from the center of many crossing roads and airways that together map home with piles of Xs marking points of interrelation.

Having debuted Porphyry Press with this literary history, we anticipate developing a catalog that also includes poetry, lyric essay collections, novels, hybrids, and more. We'll collaborate with partners as we go to serve readers and audiences with experiences and conversations that broaden the scope of any individual book. And we'll continue to tap into two increasingly precious resources abundant here in the Wrangell Mountains that Sherry also saw as characteristic of Alaska's literary refugium: solitude and community. Both are essential themes in *Cold Mountain Path*, and they also serve as two ends of a spectrum where I see Porphyry Press operating.

Neighborly and even strangerly support is customary in Alaska, still. Because our circumstances require cooperation, we're inherently wired for community-building. It happens naturally here. We still know that survival can be difficult and that cooperation is mandatory. The sense of place and social networks of individual Alaskans often span hundreds and hundreds of miles, not to mention races, ecosystems, generations, and more. Perhaps it's appropriate to do this work in a state as varied as it is large, surrounded by a patchwork of diverse ecologies, cultures, climates, languages, histories, blessings, and problems.

To that end, I'm pleased to donate a percentage of sales of this book to our partner and neighbor, the McCarthy-Kennicott Historical Museum. And I'm grateful for the supporters and those who preordered who helped launch this press, and to Tom Kizzia, for his generosity and trust in opting for a local publisher for this community-inspired project. Thanks to you, too, readers. I hope you'll stay with us on the path into Porphyry Press's publishing future, having started here by helping to protect a phenomenal place from the loss of some of its important stories, which is to say its very self.

JEREMY PATAKY
McCarthy, Alaska
*July 2021*

# NOTES

**ABBREVIATIONS**

WRST        Wrangell-St. Elias National Park
WSEN        *Wrangell St. Elias News* (full set of issues available at M-K
            Museum)
NPS         National Park Service
M-K Museum  McCarthy-Kennicott Historical Museum
UAF         University of Alaska Fairbanks

Cold Mountain Poems: Epigraphs in this book are drawn from the collection of twenty-four short poems by Gary Snyder. They are translations from Chinese of the classical work of Han Shan, a famed hermit poet of the Tang Dynasty whose work has been handed down from sometime between the seventh and ninth century. "The ideas are Taoist, Buddhist, Zen," Snyder wrote. "He and his sidekick Shih-te (Jittoku in Japanese) became great favorites with Zen painters of later days—the scroll, the broom, the wild hair and laughter. They became Immortals and you sometimes run onto them today in the skidrows, orchards, hobo jungles and logging camps of America."

## PROLOGUE

This chapter is based on my reporting from McCarthy for the *Anchorage Daily News* in March 1983.

## 1. THE LAST TRAIN

9   **The steam locomotive pulled:** No single description has turned up of the last train's consist. Eugene McCracken, who interviewed eyewitnesses, said there were ore cars, but the 1938 Kennecott operations report says the last shipment of ore left Kennecott on October 31. Eugene M. McCracken, "The Copper River and Northwestern" (unpublished manuscript, 1963), UAF Rasmuson Library archives, reprinted in *WSEN* November–December 1998. See also *Alaska Mines Annual Report, 1938*

(Kennecott Copper Corporation, W. A. Richelsen, superintendent), 37. M-K Museum.

9 **the steepest grade:** Ron Simpson, "The Copper River Crossing at Chitina," *WSEN*, January–February 1998, 6–8.

10 **Nell McCann, traveling:** Sunny Cook, "Nell & Bertha, Singles Life in the Company Town" (unpublished manuscript, 2017), M-K Museum.

10 **"I fall kerflop":** Ethel LeCount journal, November 7, 1938, NPS, Wrangell-St. Elias National Park and Preserve, Records of WRST 20747.

10 **Ethel LeCount would recall:** Ethel LeCount correspondence, NPS, Wrangell-St. Elias National Park and Preserve, Records of WRST 20747.

11 **William Hermann was given:** Cited in M. J. Kirchhoff, *Historic McCarthy: The Town That Copper Built* (Juneau: Alaska Cedar Press, 1993), 88.

11 **Everyone knew a day like this:** Details of the shutdown procedure are given in *Alaska Mines Annual Report, 1938*. Account of ammonia "syphoned to waste" is on page 39.

11 **In a ritual every spring:** Lone E. Janson, *The Copper Spike* (Anchorage: Alaska Northwest Publishing, 1975), 138; Alfred O. Quinn, *Iron Rails to Alaskan Copper* (Whiteface, NY: D'Aloquin Publishing, 1995), 138–43.

12 **plunged into the river:** Ron Simpson, "The Copper River Crossing at Chitina," *WSEN*, January–February 1998, 6–7.

12 **according to a short history of the railroad:** McCracken, "The Copper River and Northwestern."

13 **The abandonment of McCarthy:** An excellent source for the overall story of Kennecott's rise and fall in Alaska is Melody Webb Grauman, "Big Business in Alaska: The Kennecott Mines, 1898–1938," Occasional Paper #1, National Park Service; an adapted version of her study, "Kennecott: Alaskan Origins of a Copper Empire, 1900–1938," *Western Historical Quarterly* 9, no. 2 (April 1978):197–211. See also Robert A. Stearns, "The Morgan-Guggenheim Syndicate and the Development of Alaska, 1906–1915" (PhD thesis, UC Santa Barbara, 1967).

13 **A Russian expedition:** The Russian explorers were killed by the Ahtna. The official Russian account attributed the murders to trade concerns, while Native accounts said the Russians had abused Ahtna women. William Simeone, *Ahtna: The People and Their History* (Glennallen, AK: Ahtna, Inc., 2018), 150–55.

13 **the popular story went:** See, for instance, Janson, *Copper Spike*; Elizabeth A. Tower, *Icebound Empire: Industry and Politics on the Last Frontier, 1898–1938* (Anchorage: EA Tower, 1996).

14 **the "beyond river":** Simeone, *Ahtna*, 17.

15 **drive the original inhabitants out:** A discussion of how the modern NPS narrative focus on mining excludes the Ahtna relationship to land can be

found in Margot Higgins, "Prospecting for Buried Narratives in Wrangell-St. Elias National Park and Preserve," in *Critical Norths: Space Nature Theory*, ed. Sarah Jaquette Ray and Kevin Maier (Fairbanks: University of Alaska Press, 2017), 287–316.

15 **could not legally stake:** See Thomas Bundtzen, "Ivan John Minook, 1874–1940," Alaska Mining Hall of Fame Foundation (website), updated 2009, http://alaskamininghalloffame.org/inductees/minook.php.

15 **whether Nicolai was duped:** William Simeone, "The Chitina River: An Ethnographic Summary and Description of Sites Related to the Lower Ahtna," Alaska Department of Fish and Game Division of Subsistence, 2005. See also Simeone, *Ahtna: The People and Their History*. The subtitle of Simeone's history, in the Athabascan language of the Ahtna, would be apt, as well, for this account of McCarthy's lost decades: netseh dae' tkughiit'e',– which translates as "before us, it was like this."

15 **one of the most densely valuable copper deposits:** At its peak operation, in 1916, the Alaska mines were producing one-third the ore of the famous Anaconda Mines of Butte, Montana—but with 550 workers, not the 15,000 needed in Montana. William C. Douglass, *A History of the Kennecott Mines*, Anchorage, 1964. Douglass, a mining engineer, worked in Butte and was superintendent at Kennecott.

15 **Stephen Birch wrote:** Stephen Birch, "Pioneering Capital," *Alaska-Yukon Magazine* 9, no. 5 (April 1910).

16 **"We want to go into the territory":** "Mr. Guggenheim Tells Vast Plans for Alaska," *New York Times*, April 3, 1906; cited in Tower, *Icebound Empire*.

16 **political sentiments in the nation:** For more on Alaska and the Progressive era, Stephen Haycox, *Alaska: An American Colony* (Seattle: University of Washington Press, 2002); Thomas Alton, *Alaska in the Progressive Age: A Political History, 1896 to 1916* (Fairbanks: University of Alaska Press, 2019).

17 **shot himself:** Tower, *Icebound Empire*, 173–95.

17 **newspapers all over the country:** Janson, *Copper Spike*, 124–27.

17 **The *Seattle Post-Intelligencer* reached for a phrase:** Editorial, January 18, 1910. Quoted in Alton, *Alaska in the Progressive Age*, 148.

18 **Grauman wrote:** Grauman, "Big Business in Alaska," 54–55.

19 **with most of the high-grade ore:** Charles Caldwell Hawley, *A Kennecott Story: Three Mines, Four Men, and One Hundred Years, 1897–1997* (Salt Lake City: University of Utah Press, 2014), 252–63.

19 **a Hollywood feature:** The only known surviving copy of the seven-reel silent movie is in a Moscow film archive.

20 **"skim the gravy and get out":** "Meeting the Challenge," a speech by E. L. "Bob" Bartlett at the Alaska Constitutional Convention, November 8,

1955. https://www.alaska.edu/creatingalaska/constitutional-convention
/speeches-to-the-conventio/opening-session-speeches/bartlett/. I am
grateful to the historian Terrence Cole for pointing out Bartlett's interest
in Kennecott.

20   **a 1915 fire:** H. J. Lutz, "Ecological Effects of Forest Fires in the Interior of
Alaska," USDA, Technical Bulletin No. 1133 (Juneau: USDA Forest Service,
Alaska Forest Research Center, 1956), cited in *Fire History in the Copper
River Basin*, Alaska NPS Wildland Fire Management Program.

20   **Bad weather delayed:** *Alaska Mines Annual Report, 1938*, 38.

21   **"The Irish are a moody race":** Ethel LeCount journal, NPS, Wrangell-St.
Elias National Park and Preserve, Records of WRST 20747.

21   **two caretakers:** *Alaska Mines Annual Report, 1938*, 40; US Census 1940,
Third Judicial Division Alaska, Kennecott Village.

21   **Alaskan of the Year:** This award was chosen by ballot by a statewide private
membership association, 1967–2002, thereafter by the state Chamber
of Commerce.

21   **described the mournful process:** Al Swalling, *Oh to Be Twenty Again—
and Twins* (Anchorage: A&M Publishing, 1999). Additional biographical
information from "Al Swalling—A Toolbox and A Dream," by Ann Chan-
donnet, a postscript to another collection of his memories, *Big Red, Too
Much Johnson, Others, and Me*, (self-pub., 1993). Swalling died in 2004.

## 2. NO SAFE PLACE TO LIVE

22   **Jim Edwards once told me:** Jim Edwards, interview with author,
2010. Also Jim Edwards interview with Jenny Carroll, July–August 1985
(referred to hereafter as Edwards-Carroll interview, 1985), in author's
possession.

23   **"There was something":** Jim Edwards, interview with author, 2010. Also
Edwards-Carroll interview, 1985.

23   **Edwards was twenty-two:** Jim Edwards was born January 7, 1931.

23   **Newberg, Oregon:** The Oregon Encyclopedia, an online project of the
Oregon Historical Society, says Jesse Edwards, Jim's great-grandfather,
was a leading businessman and Quaker who is sometimes credited as the
founder of the city. https://oregonencyclopedia.org/articles/newberg/#
.XjNGDS3MzrJ. See also "Jesse Edwards (businessman)" Wikipedia, last
edited October 19, 2020, https://en.wikipedia.org/wiki/Jesse_Edwards_(businessman). Other personal history from Steve Edwards is from an interview
with author in 2018 and from interviews with Jenny Carroll in 1985.

23   **The driver of the Model T:** Except where noted, the stories and quotes
about Bill Berry and Ernie Gercken are from the Edwards-Carroll interview, 1985.

23 **known as Blazo Bill:** He owed his nickname to the ubiquitous cans of Chevron white gas shipped into the country for use in lamps and cookstoves.

24 **A few folks teased:** Audrey Edwards, interview with author, 2021

25 **"You don't look at things":** Edwards-Carroll interview, 1985. For more on Jenny Carroll, see chapter 7.

26 **a woman who bought and restored:** Sally Gibert, interview with author, 2018.

26 **Berry fashioned horse snowshoes:** L. Jo King with Lone Janson, *Bird in the Bush* (Anchorage: KiwE Publishing, 2007) 65; see also, Bill Berry obituary, *The Ghost Town Gazette*, August 1958.

27 **Berry noticed his woodpile:** Woodpile story from King and Janson, *Bird in the Bush*, 65. Howard Knutson identified the firewood filcher as Gercken.

27 **Ernie Gercken:** The spelling of Ernie's surname is from his 1942 draft card. The *McCarthy Weekly News* in 1921 spelled it Gerckin, and the 1940 census had Gerckens.

27 **Blanche Smith:** Letters from Margaret Wilhelm, caretaker at Kennecott, to her daughter, translated from German and made available by Ron Simpson.

27 **Blanche boasted:** Kirchhoff, *Historic McCarthy*, 66.

28 **a supply of beckoning graveholes:** E. M. MacKevett, "A Geologist's History of the Kennecott Mines and McCarthy" (unpublished manuscript), courtesy of NPS historian Logan Hovis.

28 **"Brunswick didn't need any more help":** Letter from Margaret Wilhelm, to her daughter. Possibly Peter Brenwick, age fifty-four, from 1940 McCarthy census.

29 **George Flowers:** Biographical info drawn from unpublished "Kennecott Kids" interview with Richard H. Osborne, May 22, 2002, by Vicki Snitzler and Bonnie Houston, NPS, Wrangell-St. Elias National Park and Preserve, Records of WRST 20747.

29 **a typewritten letter:** Letters written by George Flowers, reprinted in *WSEN* July–August 1999, 15–16

30 **John Hazelet:** Hazelet and his brother George C. Hazelet, the founder of Valdez, are profiled in Tower, *Icebound Empire*.

30 **Ku Klux Klan events:** See "The Kennecott Story," NPS flyer for Wrangell-St. Elias National Park and Preserve. Also author interview with NPS historian Geoffrey Bleakley, 2021.

31 **a few farms:** Oscar Anderson and John Fagerberg homesteads at Long Lake. Rolfe Buzzell and J. David McMahan, *McCarthy Road Cultural Resources Reconnaissance Survey*, December 1995, 26.

31 **one-room cabin:** 1940 US Census, Long Lake Farms, "George Flowers." The cabin was later owned by Phil Collins of Cordova/Long Lake. Rolfe Buzzell, *McCarthy Road Cultural Resources Reconnaissance Survey Compendium* (Alaska State Office of History and Archeology Report Number 50, December 1995), 85.

32 **formally abandoned:** Janson, *Copper Spike*, 155–58; Buzzell and McMahan, *McCarthy Road Cultural Resources Reconnaissance Survey*, December 1995, 29.

32 **Fuel drums:** McCracken, "The Copper River and Northwestern."

33 **"skyboy narrative":** Katherine Ringsmuth, *Alaska's Skyboys: Cowboy Pilots and Myth of the Last Frontier* (Seattle: University of Washington Press, 2015).

33 **Mudhole Smith:** Most of the material regarding Merle "Mudhole" Smith is from Lone Janson, *Mudhole Smith, Alaska Flier* (Anchorage: Alaska Northwest Publishing, 1981). Also Kenny Smith interviews and correspondence with author, 2017–20.

34 **Bradford Washburn:** See Katherine Ringsmuth, *At Work in the Wrangells* (Washington, DC: US Department of Interior, 2016), 183–86; Janson, *Mudhole Smith*, 72–73; Beth Day, *Glacier Pilot: The Story of Bob Reeve and the Flyers Who Pushed Back Alaska's Air Frontiers* (New York: Holt, 1957), 155–69.

34 **staged an expedition:** A vivid account of the 1937 climb and journey home is told in David Roberts, *Escape from Lucania* (New York: Simon & Schuster, 2002).

36 **described in his journal:** Quoted in Roberts, *Escape from Lucania*, 20.

36 **called this saga:** Quoted in Ringsmuth, *At Work in the Wrangells*, 184.

36 **Terris Moore:** Ringsmuth, *Alaska's Skyboys*, 146–53.

37 **led by Ernest Gruening:** For background on Gruening's visit, see Ernest Gruening, *Many Battles* (New York: Liveright, 1973), 244–45; Geoffrey Bleakley, *Contested Ground: An Administrative History of Wrangell-St. Elias National Park and Preserve* (Anchorage: National Park Service, 2002), 11; Michael Anthony Lappen, "Whose Promised Land?" (master's thesis, University of California, Santa Barbara, 1984); and Hawley, *A Kennecott Story*, 261–62.

37 **"ineffective busybody":** Claus-M. Naske, *Ernest Gruening: Alaska's Greatest Governor* (Fairbanks: University of Alaska Press, 2004), 24.

37 **On the 1938 trip:** Riding with Gruening in Mudhole's plane were Harry J. Liek, the superintendent of Mount McKinley National Park, and John D. Coffman, chief Alaska forester for the National Park Service.

38 **Things got a little dodgy:** Janson, *Mudhole Smith*, 69–72.

38 **"I have travelled":** Memorandum to Secretary of the Interior from Ernest

Gruening, Division of Territories and Island Possessions, November 7, 1938. NPS, Wrangell-St. Elias National Park and Preserve, Records of WRST 20747.

38 **Panorama National Park:** Bleakley, *Contested Ground*, 12.

38 **Roderick Nash:** Roderick Nash, *Wilderness and the American Mind*, 3rd edition (New Haven: Yale University Press, 1982). This edition included an essay on Alaska.

39 **Tony Dimond:** Dimond mined at Young Creek, south of the Nizina. See William R. Hunt, *Mountain Wilderness* (Anchorage: Alaska Natural History Association, 1996), 67–68.

39 **saw "no urgency":** Lappen, "Whose Promised Land?"; Hawley, *A Kennecott Story*.

40 **For a handful of Japanese:** "Kennecott Kids" interview with Richard Osborne, NPS, May 22, 2002.

40 **On November 6, 1940:** "Ora Jackson Is Thought Killed in Huge Blaze, Fire All But Wipes Out McCarthy, Taking Life of Postmaster's Wife," *Cordova Times*, November 8, 1940.

41 **The delegation's 1942 report:** Memorandum to the regional director, National Park Service, from Mount McKinley National Park Superintendent Frank Been, February 6, 1942, Wrangell-St. Elias National Park and Preserve, Records of WRST 20747.

42 **He wrote about the trip:** Ickes diary quoted in Terrence M. Cole, *Blinded by Riches: The Permanent Funding Problem and the Prudhoe Bay Effect* (University of Alaska Anchorage Institute of Social and Economic Research, 2004), 42–43.

42 **"a hole in the ground":** Cole, *Blinded by Riches*, 45–46.

42 **The post office closed:** Donald Orth, "McCarthy," *Dictionary of Alaska Place Names*, (Washington: US Government Printing Office, 1967).

42 **As a Black man:** "Kennecott Kids" interview with Richard Osborne, NPS, May 22, 2002.

43 **was then abandoned:** Andrew Goldstein (Valdez Historical Museum curator), interview with author, 2018.

43 **the territory provided access:** Ringsmuth, *At Work in the Wrangells*, 63.

43 **sold for scrap:** Kenny Smith, "From Rails to Road," *WSEN* July–August 1999, 1, 17; and interview with author, 2017.

44 **Kenny Smith:** Kenny Smith, interview with author, 2017.

44 **a bitter on-going feud:** The story of the feud between Archie Poulin and Henry Schulze was told by Jim Edwards to Jenny Carroll (1985), with details added from author interviews with Eric Wasserman, Janet Hegland, Adrian Darkow, and Kenny Smith. The story of Schulze and FDR is from E. M. MacKevett Jr., "A Geologist's History of the Kennecott

Mines and McCarthy" (unpublished manuscript), courtesy of Logan Hovis, NPS.

46 **Kenny Smith said years later:** Kenny Smith interviews and correspondence with author, 2017–19.

## 3. THE GHOST MANSION

47 **Sourdough Tours:** Accounts of Mudhole Smith's tourism venture from Janson, *Mudhole Smith*, 115–16, 130–31; Kirchhoff, *Historic McCarthy*, 91–92; Ringsmuth, *At Work in the Wrangells*, 201–10; Edwards-Carroll interview, 1985; Howard Knutson and Kenny Smith interviews with author, 2017–19.

47 **Mudhole had pulled strings:** Kenny Smith, interview with author, 2017.

48 **the President's death:** Harding fell ill a few days after sailing from Alaska and died in San Francisco of a heart attack on August 2, 1923.

48 **Hubrick had advised:** *McCarthy Weekly News*, May 1921, reprinted in *WSEN*, May 1996.

48 **reopened the saloon:** Drew McKillips, "Sourdough Tour Relives the Past," *Anchorage Daily News*, July 22, 1957.

48 **The battle that followed:** The account here is drawn from Howard Knutson and Kenny Smith, interviews with author, 2017–18, and Edwards-Carroll interview, 1985.

49 **Delphia Brown recalled:** Helen Gillette, "Former Alaskan Recalls Days of Roughing It," *Anchorage Times*, June 23, 1978.

51 **"The strange tale":** Brochure quoted in Logan Hovis (NPS), "Kennecott Alaska: An Introduction" (unpublished manuscript, 2004).

51 **Company memos tacked:** "Tourists Relive Old Days of Alaska on Trip to McCarthy, Kennecott," *Anchorage Times*, June 17, 1954.

51 **Homes still had carpets:** "City in Silence—A Sketch of Kennecott," unpublished manuscript by George Herben describing a 1954 visit, NPS, Wrangell-St. Elias National Park and Preserve, Records of WRST 20747.

52 **most of the original machinery:** "Kennecott Mines," National Register of Historic Places Inventory-Nomination Form, US Department of the Interior, 1978, NPS, Wrangell-St. Elias National Park and Preserve, Records of WRST 20747.

52 **honeymoon mansion:** Kenny Smith and Howard Knutson, interviews with author, 2017–19.

52 **wrote Jo King:** King and Janson, *Bird in the Bush*, 66.

52 **Stephen Birch:** Elizabeth Tower, *Ghosts of Kennecott: The Story of Stephen Birch* (Anchorage: Publication Consultants, 2012); Hawley, *A Kennecott Story*, 77–84, 209–15, 257–60; Katherine Wilson, *Copper-Tints: A Book of Cordova Sketches* (Cordova, Alaska: Cordova Daily Times Press, 1923, Facsimile edition 1966), 41–44.

54  **disappeared into a glacier:** Peter Porco, "DC-4 Wreck Still Glowing in Memories," *Anchorage Daily News*, July 31, 1999.

54  **Civil Aeronautics Board:** Accident Investigation Report, Civil Aeronautics Board, File No. 1-0025, adopted July 23, 1948. NPS, Wrangell-St. Elias National Park and Preserve, Records of WRST 20747.

55  **left his windup watch:** Katherine Ringsmuth, *Tunnel Vision: The Life of a Copper Prospector in the Nizina River Country* (Anchorage: National Park Service, 2012), 64.

55  **Jack Wilson:** Jack Wilson, *Glacier Wings and Tales* (Anchorage: Great Northwest Publishing, 1988) 39–42, 143–44. Glaciologist Carl Benson's description of Wilson's use of thermals is from the book's foreword.

57  **She was on her own:** King and Janson, *Bird in the Bush*, 63–71.

57  **"What a bonanza":** Jack Wilson, "The Razing of Kennecott," *WSEN*, May–June 1999.

57  **Jim Edwards, living:** Edwards-Carroll interview, 1985.

57  **No Trespassing signs:** Accounts of the Ray Trotochau era are from author interviews in 2018 with James Harrower, Tony Oney, Kenny Smith, Howard Knutson, Ron Simpson, and NPS historian Logan Hovis; also Edwards-Carroll interview, 1985. See also Grauman, "Big Business in Alaska," 52.

59  **the whole surface estate:** Quit claim deed, February 15, 1957, Kennecott Copper Corporation to Raymond F. Trotochau, sale of three thousand acres for one dollar "and other good and valuable considerations." NPS, Wrangell-St. Elias National Park and Preserve, Records of WRST 20747.

60  **The idea of a government buyout:** Kenny Smith, "The Razing of Kennecott-part two," *WSEN*, July–August 1999.

60  **federal officials said Trotochau:** Ringsmuth, *Alaska's Skyboys*, 134–36.

61  **Gordon Burdick:** Background on Burdick from author interviews with his daughter Kathy Drury (2018) and Kenny Smith (2017–18), and from Edwards-Carroll interview, 1985.

62  **detonate a nuclear bomb:** C. M. Bacigalupi and R. B. Petrie, Inspection Report, Kennecott Mines, Kennecott Alaska, August 5, 1959, University of California, Lawrence Radiation Laboratory. Courtesy of Logan Hovis, NPS.

62  **the Plowshare Program:** For background, see "The Off-Site Plowshare and Vela Uniform Programs: Assessing Potential Environmental Liabilities through an Examination of Proposed Nuclear Projects, High Explosive Experiments, and High Explosive Construction Activities," U.S. Department of Energy, September 2011. See also the fine treatment of the subject in Dan O'Neill, *The Firecracker Boys* (New York: Basic Books, 2007).

64  **wiped out by a 1907 storm:** Janson, *Copper Spike*, 52.

64 **One of the engineers:** Raymond Harbert, interview by Mary Palevsky, UNLV Nevada Test Site Oral History Project, April 3, 2006.

64 **wrote up their reports:** The Kennecott mine doesn't show up in a 2011 government-published history of the Plowshare Program. But one proposal that did make the report was a joint study in 1965 with the Kennecott Copper Corporation "to consider the overall feasibility of using nuclear explosives for fracturing low-grade copper ore bodies for subsequent recovery of copper by conventional in situ leaching methods." Feasibility study in hand, Kennecott offered use of an Arizona copper mine to test the concept, though the idea was eventually dropped.

65 **a ranked middle-weight fighter:** Frank DeCaro's accounts of Joey Lopez and the first ore reaching the Tacoma smelter are from Kenny Smith, interview with author, 2018.

66 **"He didn't have the heart":** Kenny Smith, "The Razing of Kennecott—part two," *WSEN*, July–August 1999.

66 **Kennecott's loveliest ruminative relic:** Kenny Smith and Howard Knutson, interview with author, 2017–19.

## 4. UNACCOMPANIED MINERS

67 **Mineral exploration in Alaska:** Danny Rosenkrans, NPS geologist (retired), interviews with author, 2017–19.

68 **Martin Radovan:** Ringsmuth, *Tunnel Vision*, is a biography of Radovan. I drew much of this Radovan material from the Edwards-Carroll interview, 1985.

68 **Radovan explained:** Jim Edwards, "Martin Radovan" *Alaska Sportsman Magazine*, September 1965.

68 **except for a shot of whiskey:** Adrian and Barbara Darkow, interview with author, 2019.

69 **"whistling like bombs":** Jim Edwards, interview with author, 2010.

69 **"They were in their eighties":** Edwards-Carroll interview, 1985.

71 **Otto A. Nelson:** See Rolfe Buzzell, *Cultural Resource Survey of the Chitina Bicycle/Pedestrian Path* (State Office of History and Archeology Report 103, 2003), 6.

71 **eleven rules for guests:** From "Rules," Spook's Nook, Chitina, Alaska. M-K Museum. Rule no. 3: "Don't use the gas for committing suicide. A rope is provided for that purpose."

71 **Edwards was impressed:** The account of O.A. Nelson is from Edwards-Carroll interview, 1985.

71 **railroad route to the sea:** Steve Edwards and Kenny Smith, interviews with author, 2017 and 2019.

72 **set up a bowling alley:** Edwards-Carroll interview, 1985.

72   **he spotted a pretty young tourist:** This account of meeting Maxine was from Jim Edwards, interviews with the author, 1983 and 2010.

73   **George Smock:** Descriptions of George Smock, the outlaw, are from Howard Knutson and Ralph Lohse, interviews with author, 2018. Also George Smock interview in *Forget Me Not, a Magazine of Alaska Folklore*, Craig Mishler instructor, Anchorage Community College, 1976.

74   **the most famous Alaska painter:** Kesler E. Woodward, *A Northern Adventure: The Art of Fred Machetanz* (Augusta, GA: Morris Communications, 2004).

74   **He told an interviewer:** Joseph Lawton, "Fred and Sara Machetanz," in *Three Artists of Alaska* (Anchorage: Alaska Methodist University, 1965).

74   **the text for his 1971 portrait:** Kes Woodward, correspondence with author, 2018.

75   **Adina, was postmaster:** Adina Knutson was Chitina postmaster for forty-one years. According to Howard Knutson, she got the job through the Republican businessman and politician Walter Hickel, who had hired twenty-three-year-old Howard to build the Traveler's Inn in Anchorage when the couple first arrived in Alaska.

75   **Knutson wrote in a letter:** *Anchorage Daily Times*, February 14, 1968, 4.

76   **The summer Smock met Machetanz:** The account of the 1971 Smock escapade is from Howard Knutson, interview with author, 2018. The tape recording was provided by his daughter, Gayle Vukson.

78   **Ray Trotochau sold:** Buyers were Orville Kiehn and Vernon Conrad. The main source for this account of Consolidated Wrangell was Howard Knutson, Jim Harrower, and Tony Oney, interviews with author, 2018.

78   **wanted to get in on the deal:** After their clash over unpaid air bills, Knutson said, he knew Trotochau would never sell him Kennecott directly.

78   **ballast for its empty backhauls:** Knutson and Jim Jansen, interviews with author, 2018.

79   **a transportation dilemma:** Account of flying the big copper nugget to Anchorage is from Janson, *Mudhole Smith*, 124–26.

80   **the bulldozer hung over thin air:** Edwards-Carroll interview, 1985.

81   **loaded them with ore:** A fully loaded drum weighed eleven hundred pounds.

82   **the new airfield's first crash:** Kenny Smith, "First Crash on the New McCarthy Airstrip," *WSEN*, March–April 2008, 6.

82   **a smaller family venture:** Gayle Knutson Vukson, interview with author, 2020.

83   **they spotted Adina:** Edwards-Carroll interview, 1985.

83   **Edwards recalled with admiration:** Edwards-Carroll interview, 1985.

84   **Full nationalization:** The Chile nationalization story is partially told by

C. C. Hawley in his history of the company's roots, *A Kennecott Story* (Salt Lake City: University of Utah Press, 2014), though he was more interested in the company's early years in Alaska: his book has an index entry for Gifford Pinchot but not Augusto Pinochet.

84  **The company owner's two young sons:** Jim and Vic Jansen, sons of Hank Jansen.

84  **compression brakes could be heard:** Kenny Smith, interview with author, 2018, citing a report by McCarthy resident Tom Gilmore.

85  **getting the ore to Vancouver:** Alaska Department of Highway, Chitina-McCarthy Highway Environmental Impact Statement, 1973, 42.

85  **the Bonanza effort "nearly broke the company":** Lynden's exposure in the Consolidated Wrangell venture is remembered differently by the three principals and by Lynden chairman Jim Jansen. Knutson and his partners say the trucking company was there to haul ore. A 2015 company history said at one point Lynden had a 50 percent interest in the Kennecott properties in return for unpaid shipping bills, possibly from the Trotochau surface mining, and sold the interest back after 1967.

## 5. THE HIPPIE HOLE

87  **Curtis Green noticed:** Curtis Green, "Recollections, Chitina-McCarthy 1963–1987," (unpublished manuscript), M-K Museum. Other Curtis Green observations in this chapter are from the same manuscript.

88  **on a Coca Cola poster:** Gary Green, interview with author, 2018.

88  **pot-smoking Cat skinner:** Kathy Drury, interview with author, 2018. See also Mary Ann Dehlin, "Mining Blooms Again," *Anchorage Times*, May 1, 1967, a breathless front-page account of Burdick's imminent development of the Nicolai prospect.

88  **second-guessing the pillar-retreat:** Doug Pope, interview with author, 2018.

89  **"Basically Gordon made his living.":** Edwards-Carroll interview, 1985.

89  **earlier prospectors:** Among these was Henry Schulze (see chapter 3).

90  **Les and Flo Hegland:** Most of the Hegland story is drawn from their daughter, Janet Hegland, interviews with author, 2018. See also Drex Heikes, "To Get to the Heglands, Turn Right at the Boot and Follow the Path," *Anchorage Times*, October 14, 1979.

91  **air-dropped mailbags:** Kenny Smith, interview with author, 2017.

91  **moved back in 1960:** Kenny Smith, interview with author, 2019.

91  **still talking about how the Kennecott:** Loy Green, interview with Jenny Carroll, August 1986.

91  **"this was better anyhoo":** Maxine Edwards, letter to aunt and uncle, Mr. and Mrs. Albert Prieve, December 13, 1968 (family clipping from local newspaper in Hutchinson, Minnesota, where her letter was reprinted in 1968).

91    **Maxine Krussow:** This portrait of the early years of Jim and Maxine
      Edwards is drawn from their son, Steve Edwards, interview with author,
      2019, and letters written by his parents, which he shared with the author.
      Also from Jim Edwards, interviews with author, 1983 and 2010, and
      Edwards-Carroll interview, 1985.

93    **her mother came to visit:** The story of Maxine's mother's drop-off is
      from Kenny Smith, interview with author, 2018.

93    **In the winter of 1961:** The epic cross-country journey of 1961 was
      recounted by Jim Edwards, interviews with the author, 1983 and 2010.

95    **Two winters later:** James H. Edwards, "A Christmas Shopping Trip,"
      *Alaska Sportsman*, December 1964.

96    **In the summer of 1969:** Accounts of the Darkow family, including their
      ill-fated mining effort, from Barbara and Adrian Darkow, interviews with
      author, 2018. Also see Curtis Green, "Recollections."

97    **a last-minute find:** Kennecott Copper Corporation, *Alaska Mines Annual
      Report, 1938*.

98    **Knutson received a premium:** Howard Knutson, interview with author,
      2018.

98    **back-to-the-land commune:** Curtis Green, "Recollections"; Edwards-
      Carroll interview, 1985; and Gary Green, interview with author, 2018.

99    **Raven wore a feather:** This account of Ron Cole's time in McCarthy is
      drawn from author interviews with Janet Hegland, Ben Shaine, Barbara
      Darkow, Adrian Darkow, Gary Green (2017–19), and Loy Green (1983); plus
      Curtis Green, "Recollections"; Loy Green interview with Jenny Carroll,
      1986; and Edwards-Carroll interview, 1985.

99    **Alaska Supreme Court decision:** Ravin v. State, 537 P.2d 494, No. 2135,
      Supreme Court of Alaska, May 27, 1975.

102   **"Les has lost his head":** Jim Edwards notes, August 17, 1971, courtesy
      Steve Edwards.

102   **the small posse:** Ben Shaine recalled that the posse consisted at one
      point of lodge employees driving the Darkows' blue ambulance and
      shooting at songbirds.

104   **"Alaska Brag Contest":** See ad in *Anchorage Times*, November 13, 1975, 21.

104   **the prize was quietly revoked:** Kenny Smith, interview with author, 2018.
      Smith's father, Mudhole Smith, was on the Alaska Airlines board at the time.

104   ***Alaska Magazine* published:** Ron Cole, "I Was Dying but Not Dead,"
      *Alaska Magazine*, June 1976, 22–24, 58.

104   **Cole charged with shipping:** Steve Hansen, "Couple to Be Questioned in
      Cole Slayings," *Anchorage Times*, October 6, 1981.

104   **"one bad Jose":** Andy Ryan, "Troopers Request Help in Murder," *Anchor-
      age Daily News*, October 7, 1981.

## 6. WRANGELL MOUNTAIN HIGH

113 **wrote Curtis Green:** Curtis Green, "Recollections."

114 **for big shots only:** Curtis Green described the scene in "Recollections," and Ben Shaine identified the big shot as Jack Horton, who went on to play a significant role in Alaska as the first chairman of the Alaska Land Use Planning Commission and supervisor of the environmental impact study for the Trans-Alaska Pipeline.

114 **Sumner Putman:** This account of Sumner Putman is drawn from author interviews with Fate Putman (his brother) in 2010 and Doug Pope in 2018. See also Pete Spivey, "Sumner Putman, His Dreams Had Wings," *Anchorage Daily News*, July 18, 1981.

115 **their only child, Willie:** "McCarthy's First Death Toll Taken," *McCarthy Weekly News*, 1918, reprinted in *WSEN*, noted the death of Willie Jones: "We mourn him and to his sorrowing home folks express our sincere sympathy and admiration of their hero son, now of the army triumphant."

115 **Curtis Green wrote:** Curtis Green, "Recollections."

116 **"national park highway":** Bleakley, *Contested Ground*, 13; Lappen, "Whose Promised Land?," 61; Gruening, *Many Battles,* 217–19.

117 **possibly to "Lost Butte":** Thanks to McCarthy resident Mark Vail for geographical sleuthing.

117 **"About twenty miles east of Chitina":** Russ Riemann, *The Alaskan Paintings of Fred Machetanz* (New York: Peacock Press/Basic Books, 1977).

117 **Machetanz grumbled about the long drive:** Kenny Smith, interview with author, 2018.

117 **camp visit by the politician and the artist:** MacKevett, "A Geologist's History." Walt Holmes lived at May Creek with his wife, Tessa, who ran a roadhouse there in Kennecott Copper days.

118 **Hickel proposed:** Bleakley, *Contested Ground*, 14. Another legislative proposal in the mid-1970s would have turned much of the Chitina valley into a multiple-use national forest.

118 **Wild and Scenic River:** Preliminary draft, Chitina River Wild and Scenic River analysis, Bureau of Outdoor Recreation Task Force, May 15, 1973, https://ecos.fws.gov/ServCat/DownloadFile/49900?Reference=49836.

118 **dam in Wood Canyon:** Final Environmental Impact Statement, Wrangell-St. Elias National Park, December 18, 1973, US Department of Interior Alaska Planning Group.

119 **"gift to the American people":** Lappen, "Whose Promised Land?"

119 **more than six times the number:** Margie Steigerwald (NPS interpretive specialist), interview with author, 2018.

119 **Edgar Wayburn:** Edgar Wayburn with Allison Alsup, *Your Land and Mine: The Evolution of a Conservationist* (San Francisco: Sierra Club

Books, 2004). For Wayburn's trips to the Wrangells, see pp. 198–99, 241.

120 **Alaska environmental studies program:** Ben Shaine, interview with author, 2017, 2019. Ben Shaine et al., *The Wrangell Mountains: Toward an Environmental Plan* (UC Santa Cruz Environmental Studies Office, June 1973), 4. Richard Cooley, *Alaska: A Challenge in Conservation* (Madison: University of Wisconsin Press, 1966).

121 **a Midsummer Night's Dream:** Jenny Carroll, interview with author, 2019.

122 **quarter mile of steel cable:** Rolfe Buzzell and J. David McMahan, *McCarthy Road Cultural Resources Reconnaissance Survey* (Alaska State Office of History and Archeology Report Number 50, December 1995), 29.

122 **He looped a heavy chain:** Story of Jim Edwards crossing the Copper as told to author by Kenny Smith (2016) and Steve Edwards (2020).

123 **the assertive phrasing:** Chitina-McCarthy Highway, Project S-0850(4), Environmental Impact Statement, Alaska Department of Highways Southcentral District, 1973, https://play.google.com/books/reader?id=F -I0AQAAMAAJ&printsec=frontcover&output=reader&hl=en&pg=GBS.PP3.

123 **The Santa Cruz program:** Shaine et al., *The Wrangell Mountains.*

125 **there was a feud:** Skolai Pass dispute over landing rights described by Howard Knutson and Ben Shaine in interviews with author, 2018.

126 **"Whereas the mesas and canyons":** This line from page 14 of the UC Santa Cruz report has been quoted often in the years since it was written by geologist Barry Hecht as a pinpoint description of the significance of the Wrangell Mountains.

127 **Joseph Sax:** Joseph Sax, *Keeping Special Places Special: McCarthy-Kennicott and the Wrangell-St. Elias National Park—A Great Challenge, A Unique Opportunity,* an option paper prepared for Wrangell Mountains Center and McCarthy-Kennicott Historical Museum with state and foundation funding, November 1990. Sax was a prominent environmental law professor at the University of Colorado, University of Michigan, and UC Berkeley and the author of the important book about conservation and public access, *Mountains without Handrails: Reflections on the National Parks* (Ann Arbor: University of Michigan Press, 2018).

129 **knocked on the McCarthy Lodge door:** Barbara Darkow, interview with author, 2018.

129 **McCarthy residents never forgot:** Jim Edwards (1983, 2010), Gary Green (2018), Janet Hegland (2018), interviews with author; Edwards-Carroll interview, 1985; Curtis Green, "Recollections."

130 **McCarthy highway project:** See, for example, transcript of Department of Transportation public meeting, McCarthy, June 14, 1979, 3.

130 **Hidden Creek Lake flood:** The sequence of early bridge and tram projects is spelled out in handwritten memo by Judy Miller, "McCarthy Tram

History," July 1981, NPS, Wrangell-St. Elias National Park and Preserve, Records of WRST 20747.

130 **two German tourists:** The story of the left-behind Mercedes is from Doug Pope, interview with author, 2018.

130 **disgusted by the brief tourist boom:** The story of his 1974 adventures with Neil Finnesand is from Loy Green, "Life in the Wrangell Mountains & Meetings with Remarkable Men and Women" (unpublished manuscript, 1994) in M-K Museum archives.

131 **the documentary they produced:** *Alaska, the American Child*, https://www.youtube.com/watch?v=W2HSBPgK9vg. The occasion of John Denver's visit was commemorated several times at Kennecott in recent years. One month after his McCarthy visit, Denver was named Entertainer of the Year at the Country Music Awards.

132 **"huge 'armchair' clientele":** Roderick Nash, *Wilderness and the American Mind*, 3rd ed. (New Haven, CT: Yale University Press, 1982), 294.

132 **two Alaskans:** Tony Oney, Jim Harrower, and Howard Knutson, interviews with author, September 2018.

132 **Wrangell Mountain Song:** Lyrics at https://genius.com/John-denver-wrangell-mountain-song-lyrics.

133 **One scene that nobody filmed:** Tony Oney, interview with author, 2010.

134 **The movie's star was upset:** John Denver with Arthur Tobier, *Take Me Home: An Autobiography* (New York: Harmony Books/Crown Publishing, 1994), 141–47. Denver died in a plane crash in 1997.

135 **"taking up all the best land":** Hoppy Harrower interview with author, 2018.

135 **warned Denver away:** Denver and Tobier, *Take Me Home*.

136 **paper records blowing out:** Judy Miller, interview with author, 2018.

136 **Deed holders had disappeared:** Paul Barrett, interview with author, 2017.

137 **run off by Les Hegland:** Janet Hegland, interview with author, 2018.

## 7. FAMILY SECRETS

138 **Paul Barrett:** Except where noted, details of the Barrett family story are from Paul Barrett and Patricia Barrett Crawford, interviews with author , 2017–19. General background from Kirchhoff, *Historic McCarthy*.

139 **told the newspaper reporter:** "Tacoma Sourdough Tells of Jack London," *Tacoma Tribune*, May 14, 1944. Unfortunately, none of the many Jack London biographies detailing the author's winter in Dawson mention John Barrett.

139 **his moment of genius:** Kirchhoff, *Historic McCarthy*, 28–29.

141 **He sold land and insurance:** Bud Seltenreich interview by Logan Hovis,

NPS, June 16, 1990, Project Jukebox, University of Alaska Fairbanks Oral History Program, http://jukebox.uaf.edu/site7/p/741.

141 **she named a hanging glacier:** Hunt, *Mountain Wilderness*, 143.

141 **John Barrett "must have suspected":** Kirchhoff, *Historic McCarthy*, 60.

142 **He told a reporter:** "Tacoma Sourdough Tells of Jack London," *Tacoma Tribune*, May 14, 1944.

142 **he sold four railroad buildings:** Howard Knutson, interview with author, 2017.

146 **Uncle Al:** See Alfred Victor Doze death certificate, Rifle, Colorado, age eighty-four, January 14, 1955. Also Statutory Warranty Deed 75-4, McCarthy Recording District, 1975, made out to Copper Valley Investments Corporation, with notarized signature of A. V. Doze, on February 15, 1975. Material shared by Paul Barrett.

146 **Al Doze's sister and heir, sued:** For a summary of the case's settlement and its final resolution outlined here, see Decree Quieting Title and Final Judgment, Estate of Alfred Victor Doze, Deceased v. Copper Valley Trading Company, case 3AN-76-4058 CIV, April 24, 1985.

146 **charges of transporting females:** Background on case H-1988 drawn from Alaska State Trooper investigative records, including interviews with Daniel Lawn (Fluor Corporation), George Hillar (Alyeska Corporation), and Gerald (Jerry) Miller, July 1974. Courtesy of retired AST Sgt. Mike Metrokin. See also September 24, 1974, letter to Carl D. Pool from the state of Nevada Department of Parole and Probation.

147 **Zamarello had already been convicted:** Natalie Phillips, "Grand Jury Indicts Zamarello," *Anchorage Daily News*, August 12, 1995.

147 **convicted of bank fraud:** Ron McGee, "Former Strip Mall Kingpin Escapes Jail, but Not Fine, Probation," *Anchorage Daily News*, April 30, 1997.

147 **a scheme to sell raw land:** Flip Todd, "Zamarello on Buying Spree in Valley," *Anchorage Times*, February 5, 1973.

147 **to satisfy a lien against Brown:** Flip Todd, "Brown Buys Chitina," *Anchorage Times*, June 7, 1974; "Chitina on the Block," *Anchorage Daily News*, May 12, 1976. An associate of Brown's had first bought the Chitina buildings from Mudhole Smith and Howard Knutson.

147 **Ralph Moody:** See Pamela Cravez, *The Biggest Damned Hat: Tales from Alaska's Territorial Lawyers and Judges* (Fairbanks: University of Alaska Press, 2017).

147 **disbarred and convicted:** Kim Rich, *Johnny's Girl: A Daughter's Memoir of Growing Up in Alaska's Underworld* (New York: William Morrow, 1993) 282.

148 **Burdick was the one:** Burdick's daughter, Kathy Drury, interview with author, 2018. She had moved to McCarthy the summer of 1976 at the age of nineteen, to get to know her dad better.

148 **Doug Pope, owner of a disputed lot:** Doug Pope, interviews with author, 2017–18.

150 **subdivision in a Knik River floodplain:** David Hulen, "Homeowners May Be Stuck with Sewer Bill; Windsong Residents in Dispute with Developer over Sewage Plant," *Anchorage Daily News*, February 13, 1987.

## 8. THE GHOST TOWN GAZETTE

152 **sent a memo to park planners:** Melody Webb Grauman, two-page memo to Alaska Task Force, June 6, 1975, NPS, Wrangell–St. Elias National Park and Preserve, Records of WRST 20747.

153 **Ghost towns:** For background on the cultural meanings of ghost towns, see Patricia Limerick, "Haunted by Rhyolite Learning from the Landscape of Failure" *American Art* 6, no. 4 (Autumn 1992):18–39.

153 **body of academic scholarship:** Elihu Rubin (associate professor of urbanism and American studies at Yale University), interviews with author, 2017–18. Rubin teaches a class on ghost towns at Yale's School of Architecture.

153 **Meanwhile philosophers:** See, for example, Sventlana Boym, "Ruinophilia: Appreciation of Ruins," in *Atlas of Transformation*, ed. Zbynek Baladrán and Vit Havránek, (JPR|Ringier, 2011), http://monumentto transformation.org/atlas-of-transformation/index.html.

154 **Alaska's map was pocked:** Mary G. Balcom, *Ghost Towns of Alaska* (Chicago: Adams Press, 1965).

154 **The historian William Cronon:** William Cronon, "Kennecott Journey: The Paths out of Town," in *Under an Open Sky: Rethinking America's Western Past*, ed. William Cronon, George Miles, and Jay Gitlin (New York: Norton, 1992). At the time he wrote about Kennecott, Cronon was president of the American Society for Environmental History.

155 **Of these "neo-pioneers":** See, for example, Chris Allan, "Locked Up!: A History of Resistance to the Creation of National Parks in Alaska" (PhD diss., Washington State University, 2010).

156 **Bonnie Morris, a young seamstress:** Bonnie Morris (Phillips), interview with author, 2020.

157 **The valley had once been home:** Simeone, "The Chitina River."

158 **A Fairbanks pilot:** John Boles, according to Curtis Green, "Recollections."

158 **Slim Lancaster:** Account of Lancaster's arrest is from Kirchhoff, *Historic McCarthy*.

159     **Jim had to get a court order:** Jim Edwards letter to Butch Snyder, December 4, 1970. Courtesy of Steve Edwards.

160     **For the next two years:** Account of homesteading days from Edwards-Carroll interview, 1985; Jim Edwards, interviews with author, 1983, 2010, 2011; Steve Edwards family letters and interviews with author, 2018–19.

160     **red Kennecott-era railroad shack:** Buzzell, *McCarthy Road Cultural Resources Reconnaissance Survey Compendium.*

162     **His eyes lit up like a child's:** Cynthia Shidner, interview with author, 2019.

162     **"One of our neighbors here":** Maxine Edwards letter to aunt and uncle, reprinted in Hutchinson, Minnesota, newspaper.

163     **He told Kenny Smith:** Kenny Smith, interview with author, 2018.

164     **sulfur-smelling creek:** Gary Green, interview with author, 2019.

164     **mail plane pilot saved them:** Eric Wasserman, interview with author, 2019.

164     **Closer at hand were the Wassermans:** Eric and Joan Wasserman, interview with author, 2019.

165     **When she first arrived:** This account is drawn largely from transcribed Bonnie Morris interview with Jenny Carroll, 1985. Also Bonnie Morris (Phillips),interview with author, 2020.

166     **Bay, who would one day found:** Kelly Bay, interview with author, 2018.

167     **a friend's angle-station cabin:** The friend was Tim Mischel, according to Kelly Bay email to author, 2018.

168     **new neighbor family appeared:** This account of the Kenyons' early years is drawn largely from Bonnie Kenyon, interviews with author, 2018; "Alaska Grown," reminiscences by the Kenyons' son, Rick Jr., serialized in *WSEN* 2011–14. Rick Kenyon Sr. died in 2014.

169     **"He's going to plow":** Cynthia Shidner, interview with author, 2019.

169     **They held a fly-in breakfast:** Mike Collins, interview with author, 2020. Earlier owners of the Hoffer and Collins homesteads cited in Buzzell, *McCarthy Road Cultural Resources Reconnaissance Survey Compendium,* 26.

169     **Harley was known for his easy smile:** Eric Wasserman, interview with author, 2019. Also Mike Collins, interview with author, 2020.

170     **Jo King had not slowed down:** Biographical background from King and Janson, *Bird in the Bush.*

171     *The Ghost Town Gazette:* Copies of *The Ghost Town Gazette* are available on microfilm from the Alaska Newspaper Project, Alaska State Library, Juneau.

173     **"You had to have plenty of time":** Edwards-Carroll interview, 1985.

173     **he made headlines in Seattle:** O.A. Nelson, obituary, *Anchorage Times,* June 18, 1962.

174 **The caustic hotel owner had a reputation:** Larry Clarke, *Chitina Past: The Late Forties* (Mansfield, OH: Bookmaster's Inc, 2002); Knutson, interview with author, 2018. See also Karen Brewster, *For the Love of Freedom: Miners, Trappers, Hunting Guides and Homesteaders* (Anchorage: National Park Service, 2018), 225.

174 **"very strict on separation":** Bob Coats, oral history interview with Rolfe Buzzell, Alaska State Office of History and Archeology, November 2015.

## 9. AGGRAVATING CIRCUMSTANCES

176 **northern spotted owls:** The northern spotted owl wasn't given federal status as threatened until 1990, but its declining population in the Pacific Northwest was a concern before that.

177 **extending almost three miles:** Dan Creek claims owner Jim Tallman, correspondence with author, November and December 2018. See also Brewster, *For the Love of Freedom*.

177 **Gary, Tim, and Fred:** This account of gold hunting is from Gary Green, interview with author, 2018.

178 **the mining camp had saved itself:** "Chititu Camp," NPS Cultural Landscape Inventory, 2008. Wrangell-St. Elias National Park and Preserve, Records of WRST 20747.

178 **territorial delegate, Tony Dimond:** Hunt, *Mountain Wilderness*, 67–68.

178 **The mine didn't close until 1951:** However, large-scale company mining at Chititu was discontinued after a major flood in 1944. "Chititu Camp," NPS Cultural Landscape Inventory, Records of WRST 20747.

179 **The young squatter's intentions:** This account of Gary Green's early years in McCarthy from Green and Howard Knutson, interviews with author, 2018.

179 **"Man is but temporary here":** Al and Fran Gagnon, autobiographical essays and instructions for maintaining May Creek cabin, 1982, NPS, Wrangell-St. Elias National Park and Preserve, Records of WRST 20747.

180 **survived a similar bear attack:** Guy George's story was retold in Larry Kaniut, *Alaska Bear Tales* (Anchorage: Alaska Northwest Books, 1983), 25–27.

182 **in 1977, the last timbers:** The timeline of the bridge imbroglio is spelled out in a July 27, 1978, letter from State Ombudsman Frank Flavin to state Commissioner of Transportation and Public Facilities Donald Harris. The bridge washed out in August 1977, and salvage efforts began in October of that year.

182 **Nearly everyone in McCarthy:** Personal disputes with Ron Andersen were described in interviews or written accounts from Jim Edwards, Jerry and Judy Miller, Howard Knutson, Kenny Smith, Gary Green, Kelly Bay, Loy Green, Curtis Green, Mike McCann, Tim Mischel, Kathy Drury.

182 **He was born in Nome:** Biographical background on Ron Andersen provided largely by his daughter, Kathy Andersen Hemphill, in interviews with author, 2018.

183 **moved the coop up to the second floor:** The new owner was Jerry Miller (see chapter 12), and the neighbor was Sally Gibert (see chapter 14).

184 **all the way to the Alaska Supreme Court:** See Ron C. Andersen et al. v. James H. Edwards and Maxine D. Edwards, no. 4586, Supreme Court of Alaska, January 30, 1981, https://law.justia.com/cases/alaska/supreme-court /1981/4586-1.html.

184 **He was nice enough:** Edwards-Carroll interview, 1985.

185 **regional bosses in Anchorage:** See hand-wringing admission in letter to Ron Anderson [sic] from H. W. Lehfeldt, southcentral regional director Department of Transportation, June 8, 1978. Copy provided by Gary Green.

185 **The state took another year:** Final resolution spelled out in letter to State Ombudsman Frank Flavin from Commissioner of Transportation and Public Facilities Robert Ward, March 14, 1979.

185 **they felt largely exempted:** These descriptions of growing up in McCarthy are from Kathy Andersen Hemphill and Steve Edwards, interviews with author, 2018.

187 **Mike McCann, a horse-packer:** Mike McCann, interview with author, 2018.

187 **McCann told her:** A written account of the last meeting with Cora Andersen by McCann from 1979 was shared with author.

188 **the general sentiment in town:** Jim Edwards, Howard Knutson, Kenny Smith, Gary Green, Judy Miller, interviews with author.

189 **The commissioner's office refused:** See Capt. Anthony April, Alaska State Troopers, denial to author of public records request for case 79002213, March 5, 2018; and Allison Hanzawa, special assistant to the Commissioner of Public Safety, denying appeal in email to author, June 11, 2018.

189 **died in Seattle of a heart attack:** Ron Andersen, obituary, *Anchorage Times*, March 11, 1981.

## 10. MUSEUM PIECES

190 **the Rose Silberg affair:** A fuller account of the murders is given in Kirch-hoff, *Historic McCarthy*, 54–56. Michael Hankins, in *Last Frontier Maga-zine*, later traced Priesner after his departure from Alaska to a World War I–era "enemy alien" prison camp in Utah, where he was paroled in return for testimony about a stock swindle. He then disappeared in Mexico.

191 **Reports of a spectral presence:** Neil Darish, interview with author, 2018.

191 **passing the hat:** See stories from *The McCarthy Weekly News*, May and June 1921 issues reprinted in *WSEN*, May–June 1996, 1, 6–8, 18–19.

192 **master airplane turbine mechanic:** Account of Jerry Miller's time at the McCarthy Lodge drawn largely from Judy Miller, interviews with author, 2018.

193 **A journalist who passed through:** Michael Parfit, "Alaska: The Eleventh Hour for America's Wilderness," *New Times Magazine*, September 18, 1978.

194 **His whistling provided:** Kelly Bay, interview with author, 2018.

196 **Edwards mailed to his neighbors:** James H. Edwards, open letter to community, July 27, 1973. Courtesy of Steve Edwards. See interlude after chapter 11, "The Holtet Declaration."

197 **Bernd Hoffmann:** Account of the McCarthy-Kennicott Museum's beginnings drawn from author interviews with Bernd Hoffmann, 2017, as well as interviews with Paul Barrett, Kenny Smith, Sunny Cook, and John Rice, 2018–20.

198 **opening of the Kennicott Glacier Lodge:** Rich Kirkwood, interview with author, 2018.

198 **fashioning a guest experience:** Rick Kirkwood, interview with author, 2018, and Edwards-Carroll interview, 1985.

198 **John Claus was a backcountry:** Account of John Claus and origins of Ultima Thule Lodge from Paul Claus, interview with author, 2019.

199 **given the name MacColl Ridge:** The drowning of USGS geologists Bob MacColl and Don Miller is recounted in MacKevett, "A Geologist's History."

199 **precipitous top-to-bottom relief:** MacKevett, "A Geologist's History." Ed MacKevett worked for the US Geological Survey in the Wrangell Mountains in the 1960s. Regarding the topography, he wrote:

> My main area of fieldwork, the McCarthy quadrangle, contains two peaks greater than 16,000 feet in altitude, and several other peaks that exceed 12,000 feet in altitude. The quadrangle contains rugged, precipitous terrain with a maximum topographic relief of more than 12,000 feet within a 15 minute quadrangle, and with the possible exception of a quadrangle in Alaska's Fairweather Range, probably represents the maximum topographic relief within a 15 minute quadrangle in the United States. Among the impediments to fieldwork in the McCarthy quadrangle are: glacier-fed, at times, roaring rivers and streams; snow and ice fields and glaciers, which in places are strongly crevassed; snow cornices, aretes, avalanches, diverse rock and mud slides, and other characteristics of high-relief, glaciated terrains. During fieldwork in the McCarthy quadrangle I've fallen into a snow-bridged crevasse; partly fallen through a snow cornice; lost my footing while

fording a stream and ended floundering around before getting ashore; been stranded a few times because of helicopter
breakdowns; and had my share of experiences with bears.

199 **Gunnar Naslund was killed:** "Gunnar Naslund, 1950–1982," obituary,
*American Alpine Journal*, 1983.

199 **ambitious 1992 land swap:** Bleakley, *Contested Ground*, 74.

200 **Ultima Thule Lodge:** See, for example, "Top 10 Hideaways," *Outside*, April
2004, or "The Next Frontier: Alaska's Best Luxury Lodges," *Forbes*, June 2015.

200 **Tony Zak:** Biographical information mostly from Dan Talcott (adminis-
trator of Blackburn Heritage Foundation), interview with author, 2018.
Also Tony Zak, conversations with author, 1984.

201 **Larry Hoare:** Account of Kennecott between 1978 and 1981 drawn largely
from Larry Hoare and Rita Pfeninger, interviews with author, 2018,
supplemented where noted.

201 **easy terms:** Rich Kirkwood, Tony Oney, and Jim Harrower, interviews
with author, 2018.

201 **1,500-acre subdivision:** *Kennecott Acquisition: Past, Present and Future*,
report by staff of WRST in cooperation with Friends of Kennicott, January
1997.

201 **The company brochure promised:** The Great Kennicott Land Company
brochure, M-K Museum.

202 **Such a sale was finally completed:** The final transfer to the federal government, through a local nonprofit calling themselves Friends of Kennicott, provided $3 million in federal funds to the landowners. Kennecott
Minerals Company of Salt Lake City donated the subsurface rights, after
investing another $3 million in a cleanup of toxic waste in 1993 and 1994.

202 **known to everyone as Elevator:** Elevator's name was Gary Olson. Hammerhead maneuver description courtesy of Gary Green.

204 **Irene told an interviewer:** Donald Defenderfer and Robert Walkinshaw,
*One Long Summer Day in Alaska: A Documentation of Perspectives in
the Wrangell Mountains* (Santa Cruz: Environmental Field Program,
University of California Publication Number 8, 1981), 47.

204 **He moved to Kennecott in 1978:** Laura Inglima, interview with author,
2018. Also Chris Richards, interview with author, August 1983.

205 **the last person to live there:** Nell McCann's return visit to Chris Richards
is described in Cook, "Nell & Bertha," 2017, M-K Museum.

## 11. BACK TO NATURE

207 **forced to sell out to the government:** Sally Gibert, interview with author,
2017.

208 **A compromise was in hand:** Useful political studies of the passage of ANILCA include Daniel Nelson, *Northern Landscapes: The Struggle for Wilderness Alaska* (Washington, DC: Resources for the Future, 2004); Ken Ross, *Environmental Conflict in Alaska* (Boulder: University of Colorado Press, 2000), 192–228; Stephen Haycox, *Battleground Alaska: Fighting Federal Power in America's Last Wilderness* (Lawrence: University Press of Kansas, 2016), 108–35; Stephen Haycox, *Alaska: An American Colony* (Seattle: University of Washington Press, 2002), 273–318; G. Frank Williss, *"Do Things Right the First Time": Administrative History of NPS and ANILCA,* September 1985, https://www.nps.gov/parkhistory/online_books/williss/INDEX.HTM.

209 **Rick Kenyon:** Rick Kenyon and Chuck Cushman, interviews with author, 2010.

209 **push out the hillbillies:** See, for example, the self-critical NPS history at Shenandoah National Park visitor center in Virginia.

210 **expropriated without compensation:** Simeone, *Ahtna,* 181–82.

210 **That first year of the new monument:** See especially Chris Allan, "Locked Up!"

211 **A self-declared "outlaw faction":** Allan, "Locked Up!" 164–66.

211 **recovering three to four hundred ounces of gold:** Jim Tallman, correspondence with author, 2018.

211 **prospectors were now exploration geologists:** Danny Rosenkrans (retired NPS geologist), interviews with author, 2017–19.

212 **eruptions of basalt in the tropics:** Mike Loso (NPS geologist), interview with author, 2019.

212 **"Idaho is what America was":** Parfit, "Alaska: The Eleventh Hour."

213 **1976 internal strategies memo:** Bleakley, *Contested Ground,* 142.

213 **bulldozed forty-one miles:** Trips to meet with the Barry brothers and see their operation, in August and September 1979, described in memos written by NPS Environmental Specialist Al Stumpf, August 23, 1979, and October 11, 1979, NPS, Wrangell-St. Elias National Park and Preserve, Records of WRST 20747.

213 **At his ninety-eighth birthday:** Loy Green, "Life in the Wrangells" typescript, 1993, M-K Museum.

214 **Stumpf noted with delicacy:** Stumpf memo, August 23, 1979.

214 **unable to establish a mill site:** Bleakley, *Contested Ground,* 230–35.

215 **eventually shut them down:** The paperwork that buried the Barry brothers' mines fills two file boxes at the NPS archives in Copper Center. NPS, Wrangell-St. Elias National Park and Preserve, Records of WRST 20747. In 1992 the Barrys donated mining rights to NPS, saying, "We're tired of fighting the park service."

215 **the legendary Phil Holdsworth:** Charles C. Hawley, "Phillip Ross Holdsworth, 1910–2001," Alaska Mining Hall of Fame Foundation (website), 2007, http://alaskamininghalloffame.org/inductees/holdsworth.php.

215 **hiring locals, including Gary Green:** Phil Holdsworth letter to Alaska Department of Highways, Chitina-McCarthy Highway Project Environmental Impact Statement, November 8, 1972.

215 **his water-witching skills:** Gary Green, interview with author, 2018.

216 **witch for copper deposits:** Doug Pope, interview with author, 2018.

216 **Radovan had been bought out:** Ringsmuth, *Tunnel Vision*, 78–92.

216 **Access to one especially steep:** "Choppers Replace Sweat, Fears, for Geneva Pacific Mineral Explorers," industry newsletter in files, M-K Museum.

216 **donated ten thousand acres:** see Ringsmuth, *Tunnel Vision*, 87–88, and Bleakley, *Contested Ground*, 229.

217 **extensive litigation ensued:** Van Zelst v. Commissioner, US Court of Appeals for the Seventh Circuit, decision November 15, 1996, Supreme Court certiorari denied January 15, 1997.

218 **experimented with ways:** Miller, *McCarthy Tram History*.

218 **a politician running for state house:** Sally Gibert, interview with author, 2017.

218 **A state initiative had passed in 1978:** Allan, "Locked Up!"

219 **struck down by the state Supreme Court:** Thomas v. Bailey, 1979, Supreme Court of Alaska.

219 **a law requiring the state:** Bleakley, *Contested Ground*, 68.

220 **"We do not want to see repeated":** Legislative history, ANILCA, *Congressional Record*, November 12, 1980, cited in May 6, 1985, memo to State Department of Natural Resources by WRST superintendent Richard Martin, Wrangell-St. Elias National Park and Preserve, Records of WRST 20747.

220 **approved a bond issue:** See May 13, 1981, memo from Senate president Jay Kerttula to Robert Ward, commissioner of the Department of Transportation and Public Facilities.

220 **"There are plenty of cities ":** This and following quotes drawn from hearing record, Department of Transportation public meetings, McCarthy, Alaska, June 14, 1979, 104-page transcript plus written submissions.

222 **The "reallocation, once it became":** The funds transfer received indignant coverage in *WSEN* November–December 2000, 35–36. See also December 22, 1980, memo from Jack Morrow, DOT/PF regional director, to Kit Duke DOT/PF director of planning and programming, re: Lakina River Bridge.

223 **he wrote a shareholder letter:** James H. Edwards, letter to C. C. Gavin Jr., chairman, Exxon, March 14, 1981.

224 **a three-page reply:** L. D. Woody, Exxon Pipeline Company, letter to Mr. and Mrs. James Edwards, May 11, 1981.

224 **foundations alone:** Elihu Rubin. "Pilgrimage to Rhyolite: In Search of the American Ghost Town." *SiteLINES: A Journal of Place* 10, no. 2 (2015): 9–12.

224 **might lead to massive reconstruction:** Sax, "Keeping Special Places Special," 1990.

225 **"if they wanted to enshrine themselves":** Logan Hovis, retired NPS historian, interviews with author, 2018, 2019.

226 **In September 1979:** The account of moving and rebuilding Loy Green's cabin is drawn from Ben Shaine, Sally Gibert, Gary Green (2010, 2018), and Loy Green (1983), interviews with author.

228 **told an Alaska reporter:** Bill Horn, quoted in Tom Kizzia, "Next: 'The Biggest Damn Monopoly Game' Ever," *Anchorage Daily News*, November 13, 1980. Footnote to a footnote: it was the author's first-ever *Anchorage Daily News* story.

229 **"a grand bargain":** Sturgeon v. Frost, US Supreme Court case no. 17-949, decided March 26, 2019.

## 12. THE WAY TO COLD MOUNTAIN

235 **The afternoon had been wet:** Account of the park rangers' visit and description of McCarthy in February 1983 from Sally Gibert, interviews with author, 2017–19. See also Chitina Ranger District Monthly Report, February 1983, NPS, Wrangell-St. Elias National Park and Preserve, Records of WRST 20747. The Park Service employees were Jim Hanna, Chuck Budge, and Brad Cella.

236 **the Gagnon cabin:** Al and Fran Gagnon, autobiographical essays and instructions for maintaining May Creek cabin, 1982, NPS, Wrangell-St. Elias National Park and Preserve, Records of WRST 20747.

236 **The park ranger responsible:** Jim Hannah interview with William Schneider, Dave Krupa, Ann Worthington, and Jenna App, June 14, 1993, Project Jukebox, UAF Oral History Program, http://jukebox.uaf.edu/site7/p/697.

238 **raising the Taj Mahal:** Curtis Green, "Recollections."

239 **a pioneer's widow:** The McCarthy pioneer was John Taylor.

239 **crudely built, in the opinion of Jim Edwards:** Edwards-Carroll interview, 1985.

240 **a particular outbreak of consternation:** Account of out-of-season moose from Larry Hoare and Rita Pfeninger, interviews with author, 2018. The Kennecott neighbor who lent a hand was Nick Olmsted.

242 **one of the park's first local hires:** Judy Miller, interview with author, 2018.

243 **tracking rumors of a poached moose:** Eric and Joan Wasserman, interview with author, 2019.

243   **Chuck E. Cheese:** Maxine Edwards letter; Steve Edwards, interview with author, 2019.

243   **come north to find "re-creation":** Benjamin Shaine, "Criteria for Evaluating Alaska National Interest Lands Proposal" (master's thesis, University of California, Berkeley), 1977.

243   **trivializing the Wrangells:** Ben Shaine, speech to San Francisco State University Extended Education Wildlands Research Program, McCarthy, Alaska, 1984.

244   **two Santa Cruz students interviewed:** Donald Defenderfer and Robert Walkinshaw, *One Long Summer Day in Alaska,* 45, 49.

245   **subtracting those away on trips:** Others who were in McCarthy that winter but absent as February ended: Larry Hoare and Rita Pfeninger, assembling a grubstake in Tenakee Springs; Kelly Bay, who was giving up dog mushing for airplanes and was in Seattle learning to fly (he would later found Wrangell Mountain Air); Jim Miller, Jerry Miller's son, and wife, Jeannie, living in the old US commissioner's house in town, who had left their dogs in the care of Chris Richards.

246   **he would defend his cabin with a gun:** Larry Hoare, interview with author, 2018.

246   **started writing in her journal:** Journal entries, letter fragments, and biographical details, courtesy of Amy's father, David Ashenden, 2018, including a seven-page biographical sketch of his daughter, dated October 10, 2018.

248   **observing how "all the old buildings":** Jo Ashenden, "Amy," essay written for biofeedback program, November 4, 1990.

250   **a more intimate letter:** Amy Ashenden to Sharon Whytal, February 28, 1983, courtesy of Whytal.

252   **the way he broke the rules:** Rita Pfeninger, interview with author, 2018.

252   **Les Hegland, worrying about:** Janet Hegland, interview with author, 2018.

## 13. DESTRUCTION AT NOONDAY

253   **On her way to mail that morning:** Except where otherwise noted, this chapter is based on contemporaneous reporting for the *Anchorage Daily News* by the author in 1983; Alaska State Trooper investigative reports; psychiatric reports prepared in 1983 by David J. Coons, Joseph Satten, Irvin Rothrock; and a detailed chronology, based on witness statements and grand jury testimony, in Memorandum of Facts and Law in support of state's motion to dismiss Louis Hastings's appeal based on copper poisoning, by Assistant Attorney General Michael Sean McLaughlin, March 2002.

253   **the area's top-of-the-line squatter's shack:** Tom and Catie Bursch, interview with author, 2018.

259  **this place was too much:** Janet Hegland, interview with author, 2018. Hegland talked to Donna Byram in Glennallen hospital after the shooting.

260  **an ambulance was waiting:** Alaska State Trooper account based on author interviews with troopers Jamie Hall (1983), Mike Metrokin (2018), and official investigative reports.

261  **several families with children:** King and Janson, *Bird in the Bush*, 214.

262  **"It scared the hell out of me":** Jamie Hall (AST), interview with author, 1983.

262  **demanded to see his wife:** Sgt. Mike Metrokin (AST, retired), interview with author, November 2018.

264  **openly rejecting father:** Joseph Satten, MD, preliminary psychiatric report for defense, August 18, 1983.

266  **Gun periodicals piled up:** Eric and Joan Wasserman, interviews with author, 2019.

267  **Snow, sliding off the roof:** Rich Kirkwood, interview with author, 2018.

267  **they tried to focus on the positive:** David Ashenden, remarks at memorial May 22, 1983.

269  **Chris Richards, bitterly recuperating:** Chris Richards, Loy Green, Sally Gibert comments are from interviews with author, August 1983.

269  **"the true environmentalists":** King and Janson, *Bird in the Bush*, 2007.

269  **She could not shake her daze:** Bonnie Morris (Phillips), interview with author, 2020.

269  **Now his act would define their community:** Twenty years later, John Denver would bring up the murders in his autobiography, doubling the death toll and concluding his short, rather dark take on McCarthy's inhabitants with the words: "The slaughter of innocents is probably a fate that is written into the destiny of places were dreams begin to dry up." Denver and Tobier, *Take Me Home*.

269  **told her husband and son:** Bonnie Kenyon, interview with author, 2018.

270  **"He brought his evil with him":** Loy Green, interview with author, August 1983.

270  **"We've got to talk about something else":** Sally Gibert, interview with author, August 1983.

**14. KINDRED SPIRITS**

271  **Work had started in spring:** The account in this chapter is drawn from the author's reporting in August 1983 for stories appearing in the *Anchorage Daily News* and the *Washington Post*.

273  **He'd read a magazine story:** Chip Brown, "August in the Wrangells," *Living Wilderness*, April–June 1978, 26–45.

277  **Radovan rolled boulders into a hole:** Jim Edwards told this story to the author in 1983. It was retold in detail in Ringsmuth, *Tunnel Vision,* 58–60.

## EPILOGUE

281  **Alaskan of the Year:** Al Swalling, *Oh to Be Twenty Again—and Twins* (Anchorage: A&M Publishing, 1999), 260.

282  **A local family of builders:** The Rowland family.

283  **producing a TV series:** *Edge of Alaska*, Discovery Channel, 2014–17.

283  **nearly twenty thousand tourists:** Margie Steigerwald (NPS interpretive specialist, WRST), interview with author, 2018.

284  **The park's interpretive team:** Tom Kizzia, "Amid the Ruins of the Kennecott Mine, New Exhibits Strike a Delicate Balance," *Anchorage Daily News*, June 26, 2018.

# PHOTO CREDITS

# ABOUT THE AUTHOR

Tom Kizzia, in McCarthy, crosses the Kennicott River on the old Blazo Bill–era tram, August 1983.

Tom Kizzia traveled widely in rural Alaska during a 25-year career as a reporter for the *Anchorage Daily News*. He is the author of the bestseller *Pilgrim's Wilderness* and the Alaska village travel narrative *The Wake of the Unseen Object*, recently re-issued by University of Alaska Press in the Classic Reprint Series. His journalism has appeared in *The New Yorker*, the *Los Angeles Times*, *The Washington Post*, the *Columbia Journalism Review*, and in *Best American Science and Nature Writing 2017*. He received a Rasmuson Foundation Individual Artist Award fellowship and was a Knight Journalism Fellow at Stanford University. A graduate of Hampshire College, he lives in Homer, Alaska, and has a place in the Wrangell Mountains near McCarthy.